A HISTORY OF BEL CANTO

A History of Bel Canto

RODOLFO CELLETTI

Translated from the Italian by
Frederick Fuller

CLARENDON PRESS · OXFORD

Oxford University Press, Walton Street, Oxford OX2 6DP

Oxford New York
Athens Auckland Bangkok Bogota Bombay
Buenos Aires Calcutta Cape Town Dar es Salaam
Delhi Florence Hong Kong Istanbul Karachi
Kuala Lumpur Madras Madrid Melbourne
Mexico City Nairobi Paris Singapore
Taipei Tokyo Toronto
and associated companies in
Berlin Ibadan

Oxford is a trade mark of Oxford University Press

Published in the United States by
Oxford University Press Inc., New York

This English edition has been translated from the original Italian
publication Storia del Belcanto © Copyright 1983 by Discanto Edizioni, Fiesole
This English edition © Oxford University Press 1991

First published 1991
New as paperback edition 1996

British Library Cataloguing in Publication Data
Data available

Library of Congress Cataloging in Publication Data
Celletti, Rodolfo.
[Storia del belcanto. English]
A history of bel canto / Rodolfo Celletti ; translated from the
Italian by Frederick Fuller.
p. cm.
Translation of : Storia del belcanto.
Includes bibliographical references and index.
1. Singing—History. 2. Singers. 3. Opera—Italy. I. Fuller,
Frederick, 1908- . II. Title.
ML1460.C413   1996   782.1'0945'09033—dc20   96-28219
ISBN 0-19-816641-9

1 3 5 7 9 10 8 6 4 2

Printed in Great Britain by
Biddles Ltd
Guildford and King's Lynn

Contents

I

The Cult of Bel Canto,
Virtuosity, and Hedonism

To define bel canto and what it stood for, and to clear up the misuse commonly made of terms like 'virtuosity' and 'hedonism', we need to start out from a background of fact. In its most characteristic forms, Italian opera was the product of the taste and sensibility of the age that brought it into being—the age of the Baroque. Baroque art set itself a definite goal—that of creating through the imagination a world more beautiful, more sumptuous than the everyday world, and depicting it in images calculated to appeal not only to man's intellect but to his senses as well. In this respect, no other period has ever so stimulated and fired the human imagination to achieve the twofold purpose first of creating a world of fantasy and then of driving home its message.

Today it is easier for us to venture into the world of the Baroque through the figurative arts, architecture, or music than through the prose and poetry of writers like Marino or Góngora. To describe a scene of fantasy using precise language—the language of words—raises difficulties that sounds and colours can overcome with greater immediacy and comprehensiveness. Also, with the passage of time words lose currency and deteriorate, in terms of poetic meaning, differently and more manifestly than the elements with which a graphic or musical image is expressed. Thus the underlying fascination of Marino's world, that of mythological evocation both as a means of understanding ancient Greek thought and as nostalgia for a legendary Golden Age of mankind, is one from which we are largely cut off.

This does not mean that we can ignore the enormous influence of 'Marinism' in the seventeenth century. 'Marinism' was a phenomenon of history, and such phenomena, whatever assessment we may put upon them centuries later on purely aesthetic grounds, have an impact on the human spirit. They are the expression of an epoch, and they help us to interpret it. Marino, as a parameter for the definition of a society and a culture, was one of the pet aversions—as indeed was the whole world of the Baroque and of Arcadia—of late Romanticism, which also accused both of verbal acrobatics (the cult of virtuosity) and hedonism. But regardless of what we may think today of his artistic achievement, Marino was one of the pillars of an aesthetic outlook which set up as a counterpoise to reality a world of fantasy or, some might say, a stylized and distorted world. But virtuosity, the outcome at once of fantasy and of the search for sophisticated technical progress, is nothing more than the effort to conceive and bring into being something which goes beyond the reality of everyday life and the normal capacities of human beings, and therefore seems 'wondrous, wonderful'.

'Wonder' is precisely the emotion which Baroque art tended to excite and experience. The world of fantasy was set off against the real world, and became identified for that very reason with a whole sheaf of emotions which went under and still goes under the name of 'poetics of wonder'. As I have said, Baroque art aimed at a kind of amalgam of intellectual, abstract emotion and the emotions bound up with the sensibilities of human beings. In its practical manifestations, therefore, it was an art largely based on sensations. But to brand it as hedonistic in the sense of glorifying the senses is mere rationalization. When I read 'Clear, fresh, gently-flowing waters', I would not experience any emotion if the melody of the verse did not call up images and experiences bound up with my sight (clear), my touch (fresh), and my hearing (gentle-flowing—since they flow with a gentle murmur).

Italian opera developed in the direction of hedonism and virtuosity because it was the offspring of the Baroque. But in that it was not an isolated phenomenon. All the music of the period was of a virtuoso and hedonistic nature, inspired by the same emotions and the same sense of amazement as were the aim and object of the poets, the painters, the sculptors, and the architects. This too was the outcome of a particular historical situation—the euphoria which spread across the West following the Battle of Lepanto in 1571. Lepanto was the end of a nightmarish experience which among other things had stifled the pagan outlook on life generated by the Renaissance. Following Lepanto, a Renaissance-inspired neo-paganism began to flower again as a hedonistic view of life. The last thirty years of the sixteenth century were one of the vital periods for music precisely because it was in music that the 'post-Lepanto' eruption of joy found one of its main outlets. This was a climate in which religious music took on board the sumptuousness of the *Sacrae symphoniae* of Giovanni Gabrieli, and which saw the crystallization of cultivated secular music, looking simultaneously towards 'song' (including the 'singing' of instruments in the execution of melody) and towards virtuosity. Divisions, variations, and improvisations, which emerged in the first half of the sixteenth century not as vocal but as contrapuntal displays by the singers of the holy chapels (skilled musicians but wretched vocalists), came within reach of singers better endowed vocally and better trained. It is the starting-point of vocal virtuosity; but it should be pointed out that improvisation by the opera singer was for a long time to bear the imprint of his contrapuntal training.

The development of instrumental virtuosity came about simultaneously. The fascination that the late sixteenth and early seventeenth centuries hold for historical research lies also in the fact that singers and instrumentalists tended to buttress and support one another, each side acting as a spur to the imagination of the other. On the instrumental side, the human voice is declared to be the model to be followed. This is the stated view of the violinists, up to the time of Tartini, Geminiani, and, at the end of the eighteenth century, Galeazzi; of the flautists (it was expressed by Silvestro Ganassi, in *Fontegara*, as early as 1535, and repeated by Quantz more than two centuries later); of the trumpet virtuosi (expressed by Girolami Fantini in a treatise written in 1638); and in general it is the view of the many seventeenth-century writers who stressed the affinity between wind instruments and the human voice. Particular attention was directed towards the cornett, first by Artusi (*L'Artusi, ovvero Delle imperfettioni della moderna musica*), and then by Doni in his *Trattato*: 'Experience with organs and cornetts shows that wind instruments are softer, better able to express pathos, and closer to the human voice than the other instruments.'[1]

---

[1] Earlier still (1584), Girolamo Della Casa (*Il vero modo di diminuir*) observed: 'Among the wind instruments, the finest is the cornett, since it imitates the human voice better than other instruments.' In the late seventeenth century the cornett was used in some English churches specifically to replace the voices of boy choristers.

At all events, the late sixteenth and early seventeenth centuries saw a vast spate of writings concerned with divisions, improvisation, *fioriture*, ornaments generally, and variations (*passaggi*)—vocal, instrumental, or both in combination. These treatises, and their practical application, gave rise in turn to copious interchanges of experience between singers and players, while virtuosity and hedonism (which is really lyricism, in other words smoothness, tenderness, and pathos) developed in both simultaneously. The principle is that instrumental sound should emulate the human voice in colour and expressiveness (for which, as above, read smoothness, tenderness, and pathos), whereas at the outset theorists of singing (including Caccini) advise against the imitation of instruments by the voice, especially in the matter of 'leaps'. To some extent, however, singers feel the need to emulate the daring of certain instrumental figurations, so that in practice the principle crystallizes that the voice has to learn how to play just as the instrument has to learn how to sing. But it is the function of both instrument and voice, as their respective fields of action evolve, to enter into the magic world created by the Baroque imagination and to reproduce it. In either case, whether through expressiveness or through passion, the goal is a fixed and unalterable one: 'poetics of wonder'—amazement translated into intense, overwhelming emotion. Thus the accounts given by the seventeenth-century chroniclers of the sensation awakened in them by the expression, smooth and full of pathos, of famous singers of the time, or by their vocal acrobatics, bear a remarkable similarity to the terms used in notices concerning Arcangelo Corelli: 'It is a joy to watch the dexterity of his fingers and a delight to hear him, for the strings seem to hold a dialogue, passages at the top of the scale discoursing with those lower down, and to chase after one another, now slowly, now at headlong speed; now close together, now far apart.' Similarly, a writer on music of the late seventeenth century described Girolamo Frescobaldi as 'the wonder of the keyboard'.

Imitation of a world of magic, enchanted and superhuman—but created by human imagination—brought both voices and instruments closer to nature, and they were to outdo each other in describing bird-song, tempests, the stream that flows down to the plain, and the echo that dies among the mountain gorges. The reproduction was not to be literal, however, but figurative, stylized, idealized, as in Bernardo Pasquini's *Cuckoo toccata* or Vivaldi's *Goldfinch concerto*; as in 'Mormorate fiumicelli' from Cavalli's *Ercole Amante* and the turtle-dove aria from Alessandro Scarlatti's *Rosmene*; or as in the famous contest between the nightingale (the Baroque symbol of the art of singing) and the lutenist, in canto VI of Marino's *Adone*.

In short, bel canto sprang from a mighty effort of imagination and technical skill in which singers and instrumentalists joined forces, each side goading and spurring the other on in turns. Of the all-pervading impact of bel canto singing on the instrumental music of the seventeenth, eighteenth, and early nineteenth centuries it is positively superfluous to speak. But, in turn, solo song needed the support of a 'thorough-bass' (continuo) in order to take wing; nor would the development of the aria have come about without a simultaneous development of the accompaniment. If we look at an operatic aria from the second half of the seventeenth century, we are led to the conclusion that melodies tended to become more and more expansive, and that vocalises tended to break away from progressions formulated with geometrical rigidity; but at the same time the violins were abandoning the elementary procedure of sustaining the voice part with thirds or sixths in favour of a basically contrapuntal imitation. Or we come upon arias by Steffani in which vocal trills are interwoven with those of flute and oboe in an exquisite interplay of timbres.[2] All this is eminently a bel canto phenomenon, and its concrete results are to be seen later in Handel.

But the paths of the human voice and instruments also cross during the Baroque period in respect of the colour palette and the interplay of intensities. The most lucid definition of what the colour palette meant to bel canto is that given by Reynaldo Hahn in his *Du chant*, which for a book published in 1920 shows an exceptionally acute sense of historical perspective. Bel canto, he explains, required of sound what he called 'infinite variety'. According to the will of the singer the voice should have at its disposal 'non pas trois, quatre ou cinq sonorités, mais bien dix, vingt, trente; il fallait modeler la voix à l'infini, en la faisant passer par toutes les couleurs du prisme sonore' (not three, four, or five sonorities but in fact, ten, twenty, or thirty. The voice had to be

---

[2] The Andante con moto 'Vieni o cara, amata sposa', sung by Teramene, male soprano, in *Briseide* (1696), I. ix.

moulded in an infinite degree, passing through all the colours of the sound prism). But this was not peculiar to vocalism. It linked up with the Baroque taste for variegated imagery, for rare aural sensations, and it applied to instrumental performance as well. The essay by Luigi Rovighi on the subject of Baroque executive practice using bowed instruments (*Prassi esecutiva barocca negli strumenti ad arco*)[3] is an exhaustive review of the 'nuanced dynamics' common both to bowed instruments and to voices. It demonstrates, on the basis of irrefutable documentary evidence, the way in which the bowed instruments, taking as their starting-point *messa di voce*[4] as executed by good singers, sought exactly the ample range of colour referred to by Hahn.

I have already referred to the imitation of nature, viewed as a world of magic, on the part of both vocalists and instrumentalists. But with the advent of Florentine opera, composers found themselves confronted with the problem of imitating human feelings. Clearly, the trend towards expansive melody gradually introduced with the opera of the Roman and Venetian Schools rules out the theory of 'inflected speech' (half-way between speech and song—in other words recitative) favoured by the Florentines, and particularly by Jacopo Peri. Or rather, 'inflected speech' was to serve as a basis for certain types of recitative, while the formal set piece called for singing in the true sense of the word. But at this point, vocalism was to follow two different paths: 'plain, unadorned style (*stile spianato*)—melody without *fioriture* or ornaments, or at any rate with very little of these—and 'florid' style, based on agility passages, vocalizes, and profuse embellishments. Thus virtuosity would not only serve to imitate nature, presenting a stylized, transfigured image of nature; it would also be expected to reproduce certain feelings and passions, here again looking towards stylization and transfiguration.

One of the starting-points for this approach, on which much of Italian and Italian-inspired operatic singing up to Rossini and even beyond was to hinge, is to be found in Monteverdi, and is directly related to the mythological, fairy-tale nature of seventeenth- and eighteenth-century opera. In a letter to Alessandro

---

[3] *Rivista italiana di musicologia*, 8 (1973), n. 1, pp. 38–112.

[4] *Messa di voce* is the singer's ability to attack a sound with minimum intensity, then to swell it gradually and, still gradually and without taking a breath, to return to the initial piano or pianissimo.

Striggio,[5] Monteverdi states that for males and females alike (Orpheus and Ariadne) the appropriate musical language is simple *canto spianato* (plain, unadorned singing), but that divine beings should express themselves in the symbolic language of *tirate* (scale-like runs), *gorgheggi* (shakes), and trills, in other words ornate, allegorical singing. Basically, Monteverdi crystallizes the principle that mythical, legendary characters should be distinguished from ordinary mortals by speaking an idealized language and not the common speech of everyday life. Then when librettists and composers, including Monteverdi, brought on to the stage not only deities but also historical characters from Greek and Roman antiquity, they gave them god-like status likewise, and put allegorical and idealized speech into their mouths.

This did not mean that bel canto opera neglected 'unadorned' (*spianato*) singing. It used it for idyllic, elegiac, and moving expression calling for sweetness of timbre, colour, and utterance later defined as 'lyrical ecstasy' and reaching its pinnacle in the 'laments' of Cavalli, Stradella, Handel, and others. But for both lyrical ecstasy and vocal virtuosity, the art of bel canto needed another stylization device: that of timbre. From this particular point of view, the voice *par excellence* for bel canto opera is that of the castrato. The castrato voice expresses the predilection of the late sixteenth, seventeenth, and eighteenth centuries for unusual timbres, stylized and anti-realistic, a predilection in keeping with an aversion for the more commonplace and 'vulgar' timbres—those of the 'baritone-tenor' (later often identified with the present-day baritone) the mezzo-soprano, and in certain periods the bass, sometimes regarded as a stylized voice (especially the basso profundo) and at other times as a 'commonplace' voice. The combination of colours and resonances in the timbre of the castrato which are typical of the boy's voice, and others which recall the female voice (the castrato male can also have androgynous associations), produces unreal, unworldly sounds somewhat suggestive of that sexual ambiguity which the Baroque took under its wing and which is echoed, faintly perhaps, in the title-role of Marino's *Adone*. But the castrato, for reasons bound up with his physical and psychological condition (abnormal development of the rib-cage and lungs, giving him vocal power and exceptional

[5] Venice, 9 Dec. 1616.

breathing capacity, as well as an unusually sound grounding both
in vocal technique and in musicianship), brought qualities of both
virtuosity and expressiveness to singing that made the castrato the
embodiment of a vocal 'poetics of wonder'. Indeed, it was the
castrato who was given the major roles of mythological and
historical heroes—but it should be noted that in the fairy-tale
climate of bel canto opera such personages are portrayed mostly
as suitors and lovers. Thus quite frequently these roles are played
also by women (sopranos or contraltos indiscriminately), dressed
in men's clothes. This again bring us to the taste for sexual
ambiguity characteristic of the Baroque period. Furthermore,
travesti roles—a woman playing a male part or a man or a castrato
playing a woman's part—were an institution common to the
spoken ('legitimate') theatre and the ballet as well. But both
castrati and women sopranos and contraltos dressed as men, or in
normal roles as women in love, reflect a vocal rule which bel
canto applied fairly strictly until the very beginning of the nineteenth century: lyrical ecstasy, or the delicate, refined, and subtly
sensuous melodies of some arias and some love duets, as well as
the acrobatics of virtuoso passages, rule out male voices (baritone-
tenor or bass) as being too harsh and crude in sound for a type of
singing that called for agility, flexibility, nuance, and a pellucid
and languorous tone. Hence the baritone-tenor (the lyric tenor of
the Romantic type was unknown to bel canto opera) and the bass
were only used in roles such as the rival of the lover, in character
parts, and at some periods in buffo parts. In short, the art of bel
canto, with its extreme sensibility in the face of the heavy,
metallic, crude sounds of male voices, classified roles on the basis
of rarity of timbre and hedonistic, virtuoso qualities and not on
the basis of sex, as was to occur when Romanticism took up the
cudgels for realism. And while operatic trends taken up with
dramatic realism regarded the castrato and women dressed as
men as an absurdity that made the character and the situation
unbelievable, during the bel canto period a baritone-tenor or a
bass pretending to be a lover would be no less implausible and
unbelievable. Their voices do not fit in with the kind of melody a
lover ought to be singing. In short, bel canto singing, even in this
respect a direct emanation of the Baroque, fashioned its own
notions of what was plausible and credible. In this sense, it could
be defined as the historical period which has had the greatest

faith in the expressive potential of singing, a faith so boundless that vocal timbre and vocal melody were all that was needed to create a reality independent of the real world.

By now the goals and the components of bel canto are all known to us and can be itemized. The aim is to evoke a sense of wonder through unusual quality of timbre, variety of colour and delicacy, virtuosic complexity of vocal display, and ecstatic lyrical abandon. To achieve this, bel canto opera dispenses with realism and dramatic truth, which it regards as banal and vulgar, replacing them with a fairy-tale view of human feelings and of nature. Thus a decisive function is performed by: (*a*) so-called hedonism, which actually is the expression of the smoothness, pathos, and tenderness of vocal sound; (*b*) virtuosity, in other words the amazing feats of daring needed to portray the wonders of a world of fantasy; (*c*) symbolic, flowery language which underlines the mythical status of the characters; (*d*) contrapuntal skill and the art of improvisation; (*e*) the abstract nature of the relationship between sex and role, as symbolized by the castrato and the *travesti*; (*f*) the taste for rare, stylized voices and, in contrast, a sort of antipathy towards voices regarded as commonplace and vulgar.

Only when all these elements come together in an opera can we speak of bel canto. Bel canto singing was a historical phenomenon which embraced a specific period. Already in some of Rossini's operas, certain of its basic features show signs of weakening. To apply the term 'bel canto' to later composers is misleading, if not erroneous. It is equally erroneous and arbitrary to claim that bel canto was the private personal property of singers, something they themselves created. In any type of opera, the singing is always the object, never the subject. Schools of singing and types of voice are created, not by singers or by singing teachers, but rather by the most representative opera composers and their librettists, through the writing, the language used, the tessitura, the shape of set pieces and recitatives, the stage situations, and the relationship between singing and orchestra. The art of bel canto was what it was simply and solely because the composers and librettists, even after the Baroque period, were inspired by the aesthetic I have already outlined, and hence built up musical and theatrical structures which enabled the executants to sing and express themselves in that way rather than another. Thus the 'belcantists' are first and foremost the composers, then the librettists, and lastly the singers—assuming, of course, that they are giving artistic performances of the repertory which historically falls within the bel canto period. In any other repertoire, singers are divided simply into those who sing well and those who sing badly.

With Bellini and Donizetti (except for a few operas), the right of the opera historian to speak of bel canto, whether for or against, begins to decline, either positively or in a polemical sense. When the hot-headed fan in the gallery, or the professional hagiographer, refers to a soprano who makes an impeccable job of the runs in *Traviata*, or a tenor who tosses off a top note in *Tosca*, as a bel canto singer, it is simply a misnomer. In fact, the moment opera begins to admit realism and to advocate it in place of abstraction, stylization, and ambivalence of timbre, bel canto is on the wane. The notion of wonder as an absolute emotion, already diluted in the second half of the eighteenth century and later transformed by Rossini into the notion of human feeling expressed 'in a wonderful manner', is replaced by the aim of moving the listener by the portrayal of human feelings laid bare. This naturally had repercussions on all aspects of operatic structure: on the relationship between timbre and role, on vocal language, which began to be influenced by spoken or declaimed language in matters of stress, inflection, and rhythm of breathing; and on the function of the orchestra. The 'love duet' between voice and instrument, or rather, the seventeenth–eighteenth-century instrumental concept of taking the human voice as the point of reference in the search for expressive sound, no longer exists. The final interchange between 'the vocal' and 'the instrumental' takes place with the piano writing of Chopin, Liszt, and Thalberg, the author of *L'Art du chant appliqué au piano*. Symphonic developments open up other paths, which musical theatre was later to tread. Even Rossini's instrumentation caused some perplexity, while Romantic instrumentation was in turn to infuriate Rossini fans because of a certain aggressive competitiveness in relation to the voices (see the polemics on the question of *raddoppi*, or doubling, which was fuelled afresh with the advent of Verdi).

This said, it remains to add that the use of terms like virtuosity and hedonism in a disparaging sense goes back to the anti-opera strictures of the devotees of music-drama, who argue that virtuosity is a mere exhibition of technical prowess, devoid of expressive content. This too is an intellectualist judgement. Virtuosity is the capacity to perform exceptional feats in any field. In music it grew up in the Baroque period, and we have already seen how and why. As a 'wonder-creating' element, it can produce an effect in and of itself. When Chopin heard Slavik, the leader of the Imperial Orchestra, in Vienna in 1813, he was enthusiastic; but what impressed him most was the fact that not since Paganini had he heard playing like it. Incredible as it may seem, Slavik played 96 staccato notes with a single stroke of the bow. But virtuosity is after all a basic element in musical performance. It is characteristic of the great interpreter—orchestra conductor, instrumentalist, or singer. Expression that is apt, telling, moving, is virtuosity combined with the imagination to create an exceptional climate. Indeed, some French critics of the last century used the term 'virtuoso' even for singers whose singing had little or nothing to do with melismata; for true virtuosity is always expressive, whether applied to the melisma or to the *spianato* (unadorned) style.

The revival of bel canto which has taken place over the last thirty years can be traced to the young Callas. When she performed 'Bel raggio lusinghiero' from *Semiramide* or 'D'amore al dolce impero' from *Armida*, she infused into the vocalises and the agility passages a bite, a colour, a rhythm, and an alternating aggressiveness and gentleness which no twentieth-century soprano before her had brought to light. With these performances, Callas not only gave a living demonstration of what was to be understood by true virtuosity, but at a single stroke restored status to a type of melody which writers on music of the late nineteenth century had solemnly dismissed as being 'built up on vocalises'. Callas also demonstrated that Heine was quite right when he charged the intellectuals of his country with stupidity, saying to Rossini:[6] 'Forgive my fellow-countrymen, who fail to perceive profundity in you merely because you cover it with roses, and do not find you sufficiently solemn and serious-minded because you fly through the air on angel's wings.'

Sutherland and Horne were virtuoso artists when, during the

---

[6] *Lutezia. Berichte über Politik, Kunst und Volksleben.*

heyday of their association, they sang the duets in *Semiramide* and *Norma*, revealing note by note all the idealized, angel-like expression that the florid melody brought to feelings such as filial or maternal tenderness or friendship. No less of a virtuoso was the tenor Helge Roswaenge in *Fidelio* in the 1930s. Not only did he sing the Adagio with perfect tone and eloquence, but he attacked and sustained in a tiny thread of voice, desolate and harrowing, the aria 'Und spür' ich nicht linde', preserving the scansion of the verse even at so reduced a level of sonority, maintaining a faultless legato and then swelling the sound in outbursts of desperation, afterwards damping it down with an intensity of expression that never faltered.

Callas's singing was that of a virtuoso artist when she performed 'Alfredo, Alfredo di questo core' with a tiny sublimated wisp of voice which seemed literally to come down from on high. But this effect was made possible not only by the inflections but by an exceptionally well-developed technique. Beniamino Gigli's singing was on the same level in 'Mein lieber Schwan' from *Lohengrin* and in 'Cielo e mare' from *La gioconda.* Gigli not only had a perfect legato at all dynamic levels and could sing his high notes softly with the utmost ease, but in lyrical passages he had a fine sense of inflection, rare use of colour with an exceptional variety of shades, imagination, and, as Fedele D'Amico wrote on one occasion, the singular capacity to seize upon the meaning of the tune from the very first bars. The young Tebaldi was also a virtuoso artist in *La forza del destino*, *Otello*, and *Tosca*, because, in addition to her impeccable vocal line, she expressed unrestraint and transport with a variety, appositeness, sincerity, and nobility of utterance closely allied at all times with an exceptional richness of colouring and nuance. Yet both Gigli and Tebaldi have been accused, especially in Italy, of hedonism. The use of the term here is improper and incorrect. Hedonism was a philosophical system which identified virtue with pleasure, a doctrine which in the light of the total bankruptcy of philosophy is neither more valid nor less valid than any other. When applied to performance, orchestral, vocal, or instrumental, the accusation of hedonism might be levelled at a conductor or a singer or an instrumentalist whose sole or main concern was to produce beauty of sound in order to create a physical sense of pleasure in the listeners. But it is difficult in this context to understand how an art based on sounds can disregard the physical pleasure of the aural sense. Naturally, a singer who sacrifices incisiveness of diction, vigour, and express-iveness to mere beauty of sound could be regarded as hedonistic. But this is pure hypothesis. For a truly great singer, the possession of an excellent technical equipment always ensures that he is able to be expressive without prejudice to the beauty of the sound. If the expressiveness is lacking, the reasons must be sought else-where: either the singer has not understood the character he is portraying or he is performing a work which does not suit his temperament. A singer whose vocal characteristics, temperament, taste, and sensibility point in the direction of lyrical expression will obviously be found wanting in expressiveness in the dramatic field. But this has nothing to do with hedonism. It is simply a question of wrong choice of repertoire.

One final note. Terms like 'bel canto' and 'belcantismo' were unknown in the seventeenth and eighteenth centuries. They spread, in Italy and abroad, between 1820 and 1830, precisely at a time when bel canto opera was on the wane, giving way to other operatic trends and other styles more directly bound up with dramatic expression and at variance with the ancient concept of singing understood as beauty of sound and technical mastery. The term bel canto was thus used in a polemical and nostalgic sense. But nostalgia, it should be stressed, also extended to the express-ive powers of bel canto singers. When Stendhal was in Padua in 1817 visiting the castrato Gaspare Pacchierotti, who was then 73 years of age, he heard him in some recitative and found him 'sublime' (*Rome, Naples et Florence*): 'It is the soul speaking to the soul.' The reaction of Giovanni Pacini was exactly the same when he visited Pacchierotti in 1818. 'His eloquence and expressiveness were such that he moved me to tears. Where today will you find singers who with a *simple recitative* could call forth a cry of general admiration? Where is that eloquence which is heard within the soul?' (*Le mie memorie artistiche*, Florence, 1865); while Rossini, referring to castrati in general, wrote in a letter to Luigi Crisostomo Ferrucci on 23 March 1866: 'Those mutilated crea-tures who could not follow any career but singing were the founders of that "singing which is heard within the soul", and the appalling decline of Italian bel canto began with their suppres-sion.'

II

The Vocal Art in Baroque Opera

FROM RECITING IN SONG TO ROMAN OPERA

The age of polyphony, as may be deduced from treatises of the period, adopted as its vocal ideal that propounded by Hermann Finck in his *Practica Musica* (Wittenberg, 1556): the art of singing smoothly and elegantly (*Ars suaviter et eleganter cantandi*). Elegance implied more than anything else skill in singing 'divisions' and varying the tone. Singing 'divisions' meant transforming the long notes in the text to be performed into a larger number of shorter notes. Adrianus Petit Coclico, in his *Compendium Musices descriptum* (Nuremberg, 1552), gives the example in Ex. 1, with the note: 'Haec est prima clausula quam Josquinus docuit suos.'[1] This, then, is how a theme consisting of three semibreves was varied or 'coloured' by divisions.[2] But this is an extremely simple example; division patterns were as a rule much more complex.

Ex. 1

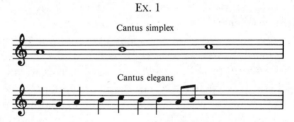

Cantus simplex

Cantus elegans

[1] 'This is the first formula taught by Josquinus to his pupils.' Josquinus is Josquin des Prez.

[2] In 16th-c. notation, the white notes or longer note-values included, in addition to the semibreve and minim, the maxima, the long (lunga), and the breve. The notion of elegant singing according to the theories of des Prez, Finck, Coclico, and other composers, singers, and theorists (including also the Italians Bovicelli and Zacconi) implied that a large proportion of white notes in a melody should be transformed through the division procedure into black notes or smaller note-values. Hence, in the vernacular, people began to use the terms 'blackening' or 'colouring' as synonyms for executing divisions. Hence the term 'coloratura', which even today is used as synonymous with vocal melody hinging on passages of agility, *fioriture*, and ornamentation.

Finck demanded that all voices, including tenors and basses, should practise 'divisions'. He recommended sweetness, and he wanted vocalises to be executed as if the sounds 'tripped lightly off the tongue'. This twofold ideal of sweet singing and elegant singing was undoubtedly observed by singers up to the end of the sixteenth century and even beyond. But the polyphonic style left little or nothing to interpretation. The words sung were frequently indistinguishable because of the superimposition of one voice on another and the exigencies of ensemble performance, which prevented the singer from making the variations of rhythm (rallentando, accelerando, rubato) now beginning to become part and parcel of the interpreter's equipment with the advent of monody and opera. The singers of the late sixteenth century, as Pietro Della Valle noted in a famous letter to Lelio Guidiccioni in 1640 comparing the vocalists of the day with those of the past, were always excellent in agility passages and trills. But they were ignorant of the effects bound up with the interplay of intensity and colour. They were incapable of either swelling or diminishing the tone gracefully, of rendering it bold and ringing or melancholy and full of pathos, or of bringing out the meaning of the words.

The transformation of the vocalist with a polyphonic background into an interpreter was the work of the musicians of the Florentine Camerata. Singing was expected to conform to the expressive capacities of human language (Jacopo Peri) and to eschew the mere acoustic effects of polyphony (Giulio Caccini), the aim being instead to move the listener by imitating the feelings or 'affects' expressed by the poetic text. With such statements the Camerata at times took an extremist position, such as the notion derived from Plato that music was first of all 'speech', then rhythm, and finally sound.[3] But it was to their credit that they championed the value of words and recognized the power of words to arouse 'feelings' or 'affects'. This is the basis of the 'reciting in song' aesthetic identified with the earliest manifestations of Florentine opera.

Caccini, overrated generally as a vocal technician—a field in which other writers had preceded him, and with greater clarity—was nevertheless a noteworthy theorist on the subject of vocal

---

[3] Caccini, Preface to *Le nuove musiche*, 1601.

expression. One of the basic principles propounded by him was that of *sprezzatura*, a term whose meaning is complex. It signifies a kind of singing liberated from the rhythmic inflexibility of polyphonic performance and allowing the interpreter, by slowing down or speeding up the tempo, to 'adjust the value of the note to fit the concept of the words', and hence to make the phrasing more expressive. But to this Caccini added the notion of singing made more varied and more pleasing by means of vocalise passages and ornaments corresponding to the 'rhetorical colouring' of eloquence.[4]

When opera moved on from its Florentine structure to the Baroque structure of the Roman and Venetian schools, some of the principles of Peri and Caccini held their ground. The most important of these is the principle that singing should model itself on the expressive capacity of human speech and 'imitate' the feelings and passions depicted in the poetic text, with the aim of arousing emotion. This, in an imaginative age as thirsty for strong sensations and emotions as the Baroque, was decisive. The other principle which both Roman and Venetian opera inherited from the Florentines was the theory of *sprezzatura*. On the other hand there was a gradual breakdown of the relationship between music and text. The Platonic notion of the superiority of word over sound, crystallized at the outset by Monteverdi himself with the dictum that the 'oration' (i.e. the poetry) should be the master and not the servant of the music, was gradually overturned by the development of vocal melody and the discovery that this could produce emotion even where the poetic text was used exclusively as a pretext for singing. If we take this a step further we arrive at the principle, applicable to the vast majority of Italian operas, that a good libretto is not good because of the literary value of the text, but because of its synthesizing capacity, its diversity of metre, its theatrical effectiveness, and a certain inherent singable quality latent in the verses and capable of acting as a starting-point for the composer in conceiving a melody.

It was natural enough that this escaped the Florentine opera composers, imbued as they were with Platonic ideals, bent on reviving what they thought to be certain structures of Greek tragedy, and concerned with setting to music pastoral fables with

---

[4] Caccini, *Le nuove musiche*, 1614 edn.

extremely simple plots; indeed, it never even entered their heads. It is likewise understandable that at that particular moment in history, the polyphonic spirit had saturated them and inspired in them ideals that ran counter to this: simple, discursive singing calculated to give full value to the words which call up feelings. Yet the recitative style of Florentine opera quickly proved monotonous and arid. This is what happened as soon as the interest aroused by an antiquarian enthusiasm for the alleged parallelism with Greek tragedy and mythology, and by the discovery of the vocal and histrionic expressiveness of the singer-interpreter, had died down. The task of replacing the literary and philosophical ideas of Florentine opera with something less abstract and more imaginative and spectacular fell to Roman opera.

The first operas of the Roman school, works like *Eumelio* by Agostino Agazzari, *La morte d'Orfeo* by Stefano Landi, and *Aretusa* by Filippo Vitali (dated 1606, 1619, and 1620 respectively), hark back to the pastoral-mythological pattern of Florentine opera. The same is true of *La catena d'Adone* by Domenico Mazzocchi, dated 1626. In all these operas, the predominant feature is recitative, as in Florentine opera, but with arioso passages here and there. Arias as such are few and far between, undistinguished, poor in melody, and strophic in form. The melody in general precedes stepwise, ascending and descending, and the intervals are small. Nevertheless, Mazzocchi's *La catena d'Adone* is the first explicit attempt by an opera of the Roman school to break away from the 'tedium' (the word used by the composer himself) of the Florentine recitative, by increasing the number of arioso passages and arias proper, in the sense of set pieces. However, even where there are arias, they are relatively short. With Stefano Landi's *Sant'Alessio* (1634), the aria tends to assume a more definite shape in relation to the recitative, and the vocal ensembles are more fully worked out. This is true of *Erminia sul Giordano* (1637) by Michelangelo Rossi and of *Galatea* (1639) by Loreto Vettori. Then there were *Il palazzo incantato d'Atlante* (1642) and *Orfeo* (1647, produced in Paris) by Luigi Rossi, as well as *Dal male il bene* (1653) by Antonio Maria Abbatini and Marco Marazzoli. By the end of this process of reaction against some of the approaches of Florentine opera, the Roman school had found a formula which, once adopted and developed by successive operatic trends, was to govern the whole of Italian musical theatre until the advent of

Romanticism. Recitative, reduced to the patterns and stereotypes of *recitativo secco*, was to express the dynamic phases of stage action and hence help to keep things moving. On the other hand, the aria—a term that in the seventeenth century also included the duet—was to take advantage of the emotional levels of melody to portray the inner feelings of the characters.

As regards the vocal writing, in recitative here and there we find simple embellishments, in general corresponding to words expressing movement, states of mind, and aspects of nature. In short, the purpose of the melismata is descriptive or imitative. This is a usage derived from the age of polyphony likewise taken over by Florentine opera. Naturally, the procedure is also applied, even more wholeheartedly, to arioso passages. Thus in the prologue to Agazzari's *Eumelio*, sung by Poesia (Poetry), a group of four quavers decorates the word 'sparso' in the phrase 'fronda avvolta in crine sparso', and the same device recurs immediately after, on the word 'lietamente' (see Ex. 2).

Ex. 2

da   cui   son   spes – so   lie – ta–men – te   ac–col –   ta

In the fourth act of Landi's *La morte d'Orfeo*, the aria 'Beva securo l'onda' (sung by Caronte, bass) has slow rising-falling and falling-rising scales on the word 'onda' and shortly afterwards on the word 'inonda'. Here again, the descriptive intention is obvious, as is the tendency to stylize or idealize words of particular significance. In Mazzocchi's *La catena d'Adone*, melismata are used on words like 'fiori', 'contenti', 'amante', 'seren sembiante'. In Vettori's *Galatea*, Neptune (bass) concludes the prologue with a vocalise of five bars on the word 'lucente'. These are just a few examples illustrating the frequency with which formulas of this kind recur. But with *Galatea* and with Rossi's *Orfeo*, the use of melismata increases.

The tessitura for the male alto is extremely low (e.g. the name part in *La catena d'Adone* or the role of Proteo (Proteus) in *Galatea*). At times they go down to the g below the stave, and the compass is hardly more than an octave. Low too is the tessitura of the female sopranos, roughly that of the mezzo-soprano of today. Nor are the parts written for male sopranos unduly high, except in the case of the protagonist in Landi's *Sant'Alessio*, who incidentally reaches a top c.* This is exceptional for the period, but it recurs again in the role of Marfisa (another male soprano) in Luigi Rossi's *Il palazzo incantato d'Atlante*. The bass voice, which even in the age of polyphony was regarded as a stylized, rare voice, has to cope with coloratura passages and to sing down to very deep notes. In Michelangelo Rossi's *Erminia sul Giordano*, Giordano (the River Jordan) reaches D. In Landi's *Sant'Alessio*, the Demon actually sings down to C and up to high f (f″); and in *Galatea*, at the end of the prologue Neptune sings down on a vocalise to C. The tessitura of the tenors is virtually that of baritone: Tancredi in *Erminia sul Giordano*, Acis in *Galatea*.

Roman opera also introduces the so-called buffo roles of serious opera: the pages Marzio and Curzio (male sopranos) and the Demon himself in *Sant'Alessio*; the masked figures Coviello and Zanni (tenors) in *Chi soffre speri* (1639) by Virgilio Mazzocchi and Marco Marazzoli, and even the servants Momo (tenor) and Satiro (bass) or Tobacco (another servant, tenor) from *Dal male il bene* by Abbatini and Marazzoli. In this opera we also find a chambermaid (Marina, soprano). Another vocal type launched by the Roman school is that of the enchantress: Falsirena in *La catena d'Adone* and Armida in *Erminia sul Giordano*.

With *Sant'Alessio*, the Roman school already introduces many features of Baroque opera, but its drama and its structures must be regarded as a phenomenon which is not exclusively musical. Even the evolution of the singing and the emergence of certain vocal types takes on a different look when placed in a setting that embraces the extra-musical components of Baroque opera. Apart from the more or less direct influences of Italian literature, seventeenth-century opera, even as early as the Roman school, was affected by the success of Spanish spoken theatre, and particularly by the tragicomedy of Lope de Vega. Hence the predominance of the fable plot which proceeds by intrigues and stage-tricks; which skims over psychological insight into character,

---

* *Translator's note:* The pitch notation used throughout this translation is the so-called Helmholtz system (middle c = c′):

relying more on types than on character as we understand it today; and which makes no effort to achieve unity of style and tone, lumping together aristocratic elements and others of plebeian origin, comic episodes and tragic episodes. The introduction of buffo roles into serious opera, the bugbear of idealist historians, harks back precisely to the Spanish 'legitimate' theatre, and can be found even in Shakespeare. Its *raison d'être* lies in the taste of the period and not in any misguided notion attributable to the Italian musical theatre alone. Roman opera was likewise to make an attempt to achieve a fusion with the contemporary *commedia dell'arte*, taking over in *Chi soffre speri* the dialectal features and the jokes of the masked figures Zanni and Coviello already mentioned. Baroque opera was also to borrow from Lope de Vega the figure of the confidant, male and female (the *gracioso* and *graciosa*, usually presenting them in the role of servants), as well as the distaste for the tragic dénouement and a predilection for the happy ending. In short, the trend was towards a spectacle somewhat in the nature of a popular entertainment; and this too can be traced back to Lope de Vega.

Baroque opera combined a dramatic approach liberated, unlike Florentine opera, from intellectualism, with a sense of the spectacular perfectly in keeping with the taste for the fantastic and the fabulous characteristic of the period. Even in this, Roman opera was ahead of Venetian opera. The opening of the vast Teatro dei Barberini (not as a public theatre, however, as was to be the case in Venice a short time afterwards) allowed for grandiose scenic effects even as early as Landi's *Sant'Alessio*. This was in the hands of Gian Lorenzo Bernini, with designs that depicted palaces, gardens, forests, infernal regions, together with epoch-making effects such as the flight of an angel through the clouds. There was also great ostentation in Michelangelo Rossi's *Erminia sul Giordano*. Rossi himself appeared in a shining chariot, dressed as Apollo and playing the violin. There were hunting scenes and seascapes; machinery was introduced to simulate wind, rain, hail, and thunder; and a 'dreadful gale' came up when the three Furies, at the instigation of the sorceress Armida, spread their wings and swooped down on the Christian encampment to start the plague. Luigi Rossi's *Il palazzo d'Atlante* likewise lent itself to ostentatious and amazing spectacle and, incidentally, the performance appears to have lasted about seven hours. Out of all this rose the art of the stage set and the effects characteristic of the whole panorama of Baroque opera: scenic perspective 'reaching to infinity'; huge movements of masses such as 'the defeat', depicting troops on the march and armies in combat; magical mechanical 'transformation' devices by which a character could be made to appear or disappear; or the so-called 'apotheosis' scenic effects: lighting effects produced by chandeliers hanging from the proscenium arch and by candles and oil lamps placed in the wings, while ventilation shafts under the stage floorboards carried away the smoke. All this meant making use of the whole of the stage area, installing staircases, fly galleries, and the like. One immediate consequence, as far as the performance of music was concerned, was that the orchestra, which in the earliest operatic performances had been placed on the stage behind the singers, was moved to the front of the proscenium on a level with the stalls. There is no reason to think, given the limited resources of the orchestras of the time and the sparseness of the instrumentation, that there would be a wall of sound between singers and audience. There was, however, a change of internal space relationships in theatres. Beginning with the construction of the Teatro dei Barberini in Rome, capable of holding 3,000 people, and the opening in Venice of the earliest public theatres,[5] the premises were far more vast than the halls in the palaces of the nobility which had housed the earliest operatic performances.

In a word, the advent of the large public theatre had repercussions on Baroque opera in several directions. It accentuated the trend towards drama of the popular entertainment type (which, incidentally, was the type created by Lope de Vega) based on an intricate, legend-inspired plot. It called for splendid, spectacular productions; and it prompted composers and singers alike to seek musical formulas and performance practices in keeping with the new features of operatic spectacle. As far as singing was concerned, presumably the smoothness advocated by Finck as the vocal ideal of the polyphonic period, and vocalises sung 'as if the sounds flowed lightly from the lips', were still a basic element at the time of the pastoral fables put on the stage by the Florentine Camerata, by Monteverdi, and in the earliest operas of the Roman

---

[5] The period 1637 to 1642 saw the inauguration of the theatres San Cassian, San Salvador, San Moisè, Santissimi Giovanni e Paolo, and Nuovissimo.

school; and presumably the advent of the singer-interpreter as envisaged by Peri and Caccini, while introducing a more vibrant attack and an interplay of sonority and colour for expressive purposes, gave rise to a style which today we could define as half-way between the chamber-music style and the stage style. But with the more advanced Roman opera, the singers already had what was eminently a stage style, as attested by the French cellist André Maugars during a sojourn in Rome from 1638 to 1639:[6] 'Il faut avouer avec vérité qu'ils sont incomparables et inimitables en cette Musique Scénique, non seulement pour le chant, mais encore pour l'expression des paroles, des postures et des gestes des personnages qu'ils représentent naturellement bien' ('In truth it must be confessed that they are incomparable and inimitable in this type of stage music, not only in respect of the singing, but in the expression given to the words, and the posture and gestures of the characters they represent in an easy, natural manner'). But even several years earlier, the well-known writer Marin Mersenne had written:[7] 'Quant aux Italiens, ils observent plusieurs choses dans leurs recits, dont les nostres sont privez, parce qu'ils représentent tant qu'ils peuvent les passions et les affections de l'ame et de l'esprit; par exemple, la cholere, la fureur, le dépit, la rage, les defaillances du cœur, et plusieurs autres passions, avec une violence si estrange, que l'on jugerait quasi qu'ils sont touchez des mesmes affections qu'ils représentent en chantant' ('As far as the Italians are concerned, they observe a number of things in their method of reciting which our singers lack, because they do their best to portray the passions and emotions of the soul and the mind—anger, fury, rage, madness, heartache, etc., etc.—with a vehemence so unusual that they almost appear to be actually experiencing the feelings they depict as they sing').

Thus, the vocal style of the earliest Baroque operas had already taken on an emphasis of attack and scansion (I use the word 'emphasis' in a positive sense) which by its very nature also implied a certain level of sonority. We do not know whether 'agility' singing still tended to allow the notes to flow lightly from the lips in the manner of the polyphonists (it is possible); but undoubtedly recitative and certain arioso passages in *stile spianato*

[6] *Responce faite à un curieux sur le sentiment de la musique d'Italie*, n.d.
[7] *Harmonie universelle*, Paris, 1636–7.

were performed with energy. The testimony of Maugars and Fr. Mersenne in any event impugns, as far as the years in question are concerned, a commonplace of the anti-opera controversy to the effect that the Italian singers of the Baroque period were concerned first and foremost with cold displays of virtuosity. We are led to suspect a certain exuberance of interpretation at times expressed in forms we might actually be tempted to define as 'verismo'. One might take as evidence of this the description of the way in which the famous castrato and composer Loreto Vettori[8] interpreted the title-role in the sacred drama *La Maddalena pentita* by Domenico Mazzocchi (1626). The description comes from the Roman chronicler Eritreo (Jani Nicii Erythraei, *Pynacoteca altera*, Rome, 1645). He writes, among other things, that he was moved to tears when Vettori conveyed the moans of the weeping sinner with vocal inflections that reproduced a tone full of compassion and grief.[9] Here we have an early example of that type of more or less realistic imitation of sobbing which became extremely popular at the beginning of the present century among the interpreters of veristic opera. Manfred Bukofzer (*Music in the Baroque Era*, New York, 1947) was not far off the mark in recognizing in the approach to interpretation described by Eritreo something that recalls the blend of devotion and erotic realism to be found in some of Bernini's sculptures.

In addition to heightened expression and actual level of sonority, whether due to the size of the halls or to the more theatrical nature of the plots as compared with Florentine opera, the early Roman Baroque operas bring with them the need for a more and more grandiose and imaginative type of singing, in keeping with the splendour of the scenery and costumes and the magic of the spectacular effects. If it had been otherwise, the frame would have seemed too different from the picture. From this comes an increasing trend towards virtuosity and, in consequence, towards improved technique. About this trend we have little information, nor can we base our views overmuch on the

---

[8] Vettori, born at Spoleto between 1588 and 1604, was one of the greatest male sopranos of his time. Maugars speaks of him with admiration. According to Eritreo, his singing was most expressive and ardent, but at the same time delicate and very sweet and soft.

[9] 'Sensi mihi ubertim lacrimas ab oculis ire, cum ille flentis peccatricis gemitus voce ad miserabilem sonum inflexa repraesentaret.'

composer's score, since the practice of improvisation and variation-singing made the singer's performance very different from the written text. What the composer wrote, even where it included coloratura passages and ornaments, was nearly always a simple basic pattern for the *fioriture* and divisions of the performer—a practice accepted by the opera composer no less than by the singer. The taste of the time would have denounced as arid and monotonous a performance of the text that lacked improvised ornamentation and the rhythm and tempo devices (rubato, lengthening or shortening of time values, swelling and tapering of the sound) which the singer introduced, in this way harking back to Caccini's *sprezzatura*. But it should be borne in mind that the practice of performance not bound by literal adherence to the text is based on circumstances which can easily be explained historically. Meanwhile divisions and improvisation were a legacy from the age of polyphony, deriving from the fact that the sixteenth-century chorister was also a composer, and hence skilled in counterpoint. This twofold status of composer and performer likewise applies to some of the seventeenth-century opera singers. The interpreters of opera of the Roman school all belonged to papal chapels or those of princes or cardinals. This presupposes a thorough musical training and the ability to compose. It is thus easy to understand why the opera composer was willing to hand over to the singer the responsibility for a large part of the coloratura and marks of expression. Most of this—although there were any number of manuals of instruction on how to execute divisions—came into being, or gave the impres-sion of coming into being, on the spur of the moment, or in the glare of the footlights, so to speak, and hence it was regarded as a feature distinct from the creative act of the composer and con-stituting rather a secondary act of creativeness on the part of the singer. Moreover, an age like the Baroque could not fail to assign a considerable importance to improvisation, *fioriture*, and orna-mentation, which it regarded as the fruits of the human imagin-ation. Thus the singer was judged not only for his vocal, technical, and expressive qualities, but also for the refinement and the schooling of his method of executing ornaments.

All this, then, made the performance differ from the text, so that it is impossible for us to follow the evolution of vocalism analytically through the composer's score. Nevertheless, the text does give some indication, since the opera composer's scores gradually became enriched with new formulas which encouraged technical progress, while at the same time they were the outcome of this progress. For example, in Rossi's *Il palazzo d'Atlante*, when Marfisa (soprano) sings the aria 'Si tocchi il tamburo, resuoni la tromba', the voice actually imitates some of the figurations of a trumpet. It is one of the earliest examples of a fact which was to have a noteworthy impact on vocal virtuosity, stimulating the singers to vie with the instruments. This emulation, criticized by Caccini, and before him by some of the theoretical writers on polyphony (for example Bovicelli), actually had positive effects. Not only did it inspire new formulas for virtuosity, but it had repercussions on the shape and variety of the vocal line, moving gradually away from the formula of adjacent note progression and opening up the design to wide intervals.

MONTEVERDI

Orfeo (1607), *Il ballo delle ingrate* (1608), *Il combattimento di Tancredi e Clorinda* (1624), *Il ritorno d'Ulisse in patria* (1641), and *L'incoronazione di Poppea* (1642) contain passages which are basic to an understanding of the vocal art of the first half of the seventeenth century, although *Il ritorno d'Ulisse* and *L'incoronazione di Poppea* should be kept apart from the earlier works as coming within the climate of Baroque opera of the Venetian school.

In *Orfeo*, Monteverdi is close to the concept of Florentine opera. The great discovery of the moment is the expressive value of the spoken word as a factor which arouses emotion by reflecting human feelings. Hence Monteverdi's attention is concentrated on recitative and declamation, and on the unadorned, syllabic singing which springs from them, while both make for an arioso approach. Even in passages which are strophic in structure and could therefore take the shape of an aria, the vocalism is plain and syllabic. Actually, in this matter Monteverdi is more rigorous than Peri and Caccini in their respective versions of *Euridice*, or than Marco da Gagliano, another opera composer of the Florentine school, in *Dafne* (1608). Thus what is lacking in *Orfeo*, apart from particular moments to be considered separately, is the frequent underlining of phrases, courtly words, or descriptive expressions by melismata and imitation.

But the views of Peri, Caccini, and Marco da Gagliano on florid, ornate singing are well known. Challenging the complex polyphonic divisions which made the text performed incomprehensible, they recommended sparing use of florid singing and ornamentation, while admitting the need for it at given moments, either for expressive reasons or to give a sense of 'charm' or 'grace' (Caccini, Marco da Gagliano). Presumably when Monteverdi was composing *Orfeo*, he had views on the vocal art which were in keeping with those of the Florentine composers. This does not mean, however, that he regarded florid song as an element alien to poetry as such and therefore tended to dismiss it or to regard it as a necessary evil that had to be accepted in the nature of things. This is a long-standing prejudice on the part of Italian music historians—long-standing, but bandied about again in recent studies—partly because in Italy a certain supine adoration of German music-drama makes it preferable to regard Monteverdi as a forerunner of Gluck than, for example, as the author of an opera like *L'incoronazione di Poppea*, a work of extraordinary variety, animation, and modernity, but Baroque in structure. It is precisely from this approach that the myth has grown up of Monteverdi as averse to the language of the melisma, with the result that on the one hand bogus executive practices are propounded, and that on the other, people tend to forget a statement by Monteverdi which I mentioned in Chapter I, to the effect that melismatic vocalism has a function which is one of the keys to the language of bel canto: human beings (Orfeo and Arianna) are given simple, unadorned singing ('speaking in song') while deities are given 'elevated-style singing' ('singing in speech'), based on '*tirate* (*passaggi*), *gorche* (*gorgheggi*) and trills' (see p. 7).

The fact is that, in the operas which have come down to us, Monteverdi uses plain, unadorned singing or florid singing in the light of his stage requirements and the 'emotions' to be imitated. And although in *Orfeo* certain vocal formulas seem to be akin to Florentine opera, by the time we reach *Il ritorno d'Ulisse* and *L'incoronazione*, the presence of the set piece is far more widespread, as is also that of florid singing. But the result is different from that paraded by the devotees of music-drama in the German manner. In Monteverdi, actually, both the set piece and florid singing are genuine features of the characterization of the personage and of the stage action and no less effective than recitative and declamation. Being an eminently practical genius, and an opera composer concerned with theatrical effect to an extent unknown to Peri, Caccini, and Marco da Gagliano, Monteverdi even in *Orfeo* has moments in which the use of coloratura rather than plain singing pursues specific ends. When Orpheus asks Charon (Caronte) to allow him to enter the infernal regions, he sings the invocation 'Possente spirto', which as we know is to be found in the score in two versions—one a simple, unadorned arioso recitative, the other highly ornate and florid. The florid version is obviously designed for characterization purposes. At a decisive moment, Orpheus has recourse to his legendary powers as a singer to persuade Charon to give him permission to pass. But the inferences which this passage has inspired in scholars who lean towards German taste are altogether naïve and lacking in common sense. It has been said that the elaborate version, with its accentuated virtuosity, is simply a concession, a sop offered by Monteverdi to the vanity of the singer of the title-role, and that the plain version is the one closer to the spirit of the composer. The truth is that critics of the idealist persuasion have always regarded florid singing as so abhorrent as to prevent them from making the slightest effort to grasp its significance and its values, whether the composer is Monteverdi or Alessandro Scarlatti, Handel or Rossini. But this is not a rational approach. It is a superstition calculated to generate allergies and nervous tics, like all judgements based on 'categories', which automatically favour one genre rather than another. If, on the other hand, we examine the case from an angle which also implies an appreciation of theatrical values and their effects, as well as a certain understanding of the 'operatic climate', it is difficult to deny that the elaborate version is far superior to the other and is calculated to have a disquieting effect on the audience. But all aspects of the matter need to be taken into consideration: in the first place, the effect of the timbre of a male alto castrato voice, almost unreal in its androgynous overtones, dark yet penetrating, on the background of the peculiar colour of the reed organ, the instrument which in the early years of the seventeenth century most vividly suggested an atmosphere of magic. Then the evolution of the voice, to a level of virtuosity noteworthy for the time—'stupefying', in a Baroque sense, but also with a measure of anguish and pain suggested by the dotted rhythms, the constant *ribattute* or 'Tuscan trills', and other melismatic figurations. But all this must be seen in the context of the instrumental parts: the patterns of the two violins which alternate with the voice in the first stanza and anticipate its movements in the ritornello leading to the second stanza; then the sudden entry of the cornetts and their ritornello; next the double harp passage, and its ornamentation and scales, establish a definite rapport between the singing and the solo instruments, making way for an ensemble scene extremely compact in rhythm and hallucinating in atmosphere. It is the first great Italian operatic aria we know of, great in its dimensions, in its design, in its theatrical effectiveness, in its virtuosic boldness (this really is 'elaborate coloratura'), and finally as a sort of distant foretaste of what later was to become the function of concertante instruments in the set piece. The 'plain' version, on the other hand, apart from being far less noteworthy, largely defeats the purpose of the orchestral interventions, which were clearly devised with virtuoso vocalism in mind.

Furthermore, in *Orfeo* Monteverdi coherently applies the principle which ten years later he was to lay down in his correspondence with Striggio. In the finale of the opera, when Orfeo is ascending to Heaven with Apollo, both personages, being divine, sing in florid style. This does not mean, of course, that the Monteverdi who has his characters sing in 'elevated style' is superior to the Monteverdi of plain singing. For example, Charon's solo in the third act, basically built round arioso recitative, expresses in its rugged architecture a saturnine arrogance. The age of polyphony had introduced the vogue, still on the increase in the early seventeenth century, for having the bass singers sing in elevated style. Monteverdi ignores this completely in *Orfeo*. His sense of theatrical effect aims simply at underlining, through the timbre and low tessitura of a bass voice, an inherently satanic quality in the character portrayed. Similarly Pluto, another bass, in the fourth act employs a vocal line which is completely plain; but the same character, transported into *Il ballo delle ingrate* a short time afterwards (1608), is portrayed differently. We find vocalise passages on words with a descriptive or lyrical sense (*strale, lieto*) and figurations which for a long time were typical of the bass voice (the French described them as 'roulements') consisting of passing from a high note to a very low note in a sudden

swoop ('vaulting style') or with wide intervals. The use made by
Monteverdi of this device is simply intended to stress the sense of
divine grandeur and sombre majesty (see Ex. 3) or like 'Oh
dell'infernal corte, fere ministre udite' or 'la condannata schiera',
which takes the voice down to the low D.

Ex. 3

De l'im-mor–tal   to – nan   –   te

    For Venus (soprano) too, there are passages in *Il ballo delle ingrate*
vocalized on phrases of particular significance ('le superbe mura');
but it is a matter of opinion whether in such cases Monteverdi's
writing is merely a rough sketch over the top of which the singer
would superimpose his own *fioriture*, or whether it calls for a
literal reading. The practice of the time would suggest the former
hypothesis; moreover, what has come down to us by way of
divisions and embellishments from the singers who had been in
close contact with the Florentines of the Camerata (Vittoria
Archilei, and the bass Melchiorre Palandrotti) points towards a
more complex type of execution. But all this is part of a broader
problem: in the performance of Monteverdi, whether rich in
melismatic patterns or not, was improvisation on the part of the
singer permitted? Idealist criticism, morbidly obsessed with the
notion of Monteverdi as a precursor of German music-drama, has
long contended that the performance should be, at the express
wish of the composer, literal and textual, citing a 'stage direction'
which appears in *Il combattimento di Tancredi e Clorinda* concerning
the role of Testo (The Narrator), who 'must not sing shakes or
trills anywhere except when singing the stanza which begins
"Notte". The rest should be sung with diction indicative of the
emotions of the speaker.'
    This is of course the very opposite of what has been maintained
up to now. The fact is that (*a*) by pointing out that Testo must not
sing shakes or trills, Monteverdi is implicitly admitting the
existence of the practice, vetoed by him on this specific occasion,
of allowing executants to add *fioriture* and ornaments to what the
composer wrote; (*b*) the veto refers exclusively to Testo and not to

the other characters, who are thus left free to follow the traditional practices; (*c*) the veto does not derive from a general principle (for example, an aversion to melismata and improvisation), but is bound up, like everything in Monteverdi, with a specific expressive purpose. The role of Testo, which is in the main discursive and narrative, does not lend itself to ornate vocalism. Furthermore, it is in this role that Monteverdi launches, together with realistic-dramatic instrumental effects, the *concitato* (excited) recitative likewise based on rapid articulation and a nervous repetition of a single word which was to reappear with noteworthy effects in his late operas; (*d*) in any event, the veto does not apply to the entire role of Testo. The stanza 'Notte che nel profondo oscuro seno' has hardly begun before the singing becomes arioso, the veto is withdrawn, and Monteverdi allows Testo also to sing ornate notes and trills. But he does not write them out himself, as has been incorrectly stated. We need more than the two groups of four semiquavers vocalized in the form of a scale on the phrase 'alla futura età lo spieghi', or the three which recur in connection with the words 'alta memoria', before we can talk of trills! Nor does Monteverdi write any trill sign, having foreseen that in this passage Testo will sing a trill anyway. He leaves the insertion of trills to the discretion of the executant, as was the normal practice.

In essence, to attribute to Monteverdi the mentality and the superstitions of the idealist critics is no less arbitrary than to attribute them, as also has been done, to Rossini or Verdi. Monteverdi does not show a special preference for either ornate singing or plain singing, but uses the one or the other according to the stage action and the particular effects he wishes to obtain. From the notes on performance relating to *Il combattimento* only one precept can be gleaned, and a fairly obvious one at that: textual execution in recitatives and arioso passages in *stile concitato*; insertion of ornaments and trills, even on the initiative of the singer, in arioso phrases of a solemn or lyrical nature and above all in connection with words of evident descriptive or courtly sense, and on long-held notes.

A particular situation arises with *Il ritorno d'Ulisse in patria* (1641), and *L'incoronazione di Poppea* (1642), both of them identifiable with Baroque opera of the Venetian school. Venetian opera began in 1637 with Francesco Manelli's *Andromeda*, which inaugurated the first public theatre, the San Cassian. It is not without significance that Manelli, a native of Tivoli, had begun his activities in Rome, where he had been involved in the beginnings of Baroque opera. His own *Andromeda*, as well as *La maga fulminata* (1638), *Delia* (1639), and *Adone* (1640), transplanted to Venice some of the most typical features of Roman opera: splendour of spectacle, vocalism, and interpretation. Manelli was in fact a singer as well as a composer, and his wife Maddalena was a singer. We know very little about the contacts between Manelli and Monteverdi, but the relations must have been fairly close. In 1638, Francesco Manelli became 'cantor' at the Cappella Marciana, of which Monteverdi was Director from 1613, and shortly afterwards Manelli's wife Maddalena played the part of Minerva in a re-staging in Bologna of *Il ritorno d'Ulisse*. Indeed, she may have given the first performance, since according to some chroniclers the Bologna performances took place in 1614 and hence would have preceded those of Venice, which took place the following year.

The loss of operas composed by Monteverdi in 1627 and 1630 prevents us from determining whether certain changes in outlook suggested by *Il ritorno*, and above all by *L'incoronazione*, were inspired exclusively by the particular climate established in Venice from 1637 onwards or relate to a process which began earlier. At any rate, *Il ritorno* and *L'incoronazione* are representative of a type of vocal art which has gone far beyond the patterns of Florentine opera and shares the Roman school's views on the 'tedium' of recitative. This is illustrated by Monteverdi in various ways: (*a*) in the trend towards the melodic set piece, particularly in duets; (*b*) in the arioso nature of certain passages of old-style 'speaking in song', embellished by an occasional melisma: this occurs in *Il ritorno d'Ulisse* in the course of Penelope's lament 'Di misera regina', on the words 'torna tranquillo il mare' (but likewise arioso in nature is the 'speaking in song' of Ulysses in 'O sonno, o mortal sonno'); (*c*) in the frequent recourse, in other places, to vocalises and ornate singing.

In accordance with the principle that divine beings sing in 'elevated style', Monteverdi assigns florid writing and at times virtuosity to Minerva (soprano), and he also tends towards melismata with Juno (another soprano) and Neptune (bass), who incidentally sings down to low C in the recitative 'Superbo è l'uom' and presents a formula which was to become a ritual: a

rapid descending scale on the word 'fulmine'. But in *Il ritorno
d'Ulisse*, human beings also frequently sing in 'elevated style' like
deities, and hence there is less of the differentiation that
Monteverdi had outlined in 1616 and 1617 in letters to Alessandro
Striggio. Vocalises and *fioriture* acquire a voluptuous significance
in certain passages of the love duet in the first act between
Eurimaco (tenor) and Melanto (soprano); they suggest a cheerful
mood in the solo by Telemachus (tenor), 'Lieto, lieto cammino', or
moments of amazement in the meeting between Telemachus and
Ulysses (tenor) which follows; they express Penelope's simulated
flattery when she intervenes in the trio of the Suitors ('Cari tanto
mi siete'), and they also characterize the gallantry and the rashness
of the three Suitors, particularly Antinoo (bass) who has the most
virtuosic role. Even the comic lament of the hanger-on Iro (tenor)
on the death of the Suitors leads into a vocalise passage and a trill
(the *ribattuta* or Tuscan trill) in preparation of a realistic laugh
('here he bursts into a natural laugh', says Monteverdi). In all these
episodes, the coloratura really has a significance and a function.

But the striking point about Monteverdi's vocalism is a capacity
for characterization of the personages which at times gives a
foretaste of typically modern criteria. Telemachus and Ulysses are
both tenors, but the higher tessitura and the more melismatic
writing denote youth in the case of Telemachus. Penelope is
practically a mezzo-soprano; on the other hand, the young
Melanto, although she has a fairly medium tessitura, is unques-
tionably a soprano. Eurimaco, like Ulisses, is a baritone-tenor, but
he expresses a certain freshness and youth through a voluptuous
lack of restraint and passages of melismatic vocalism. In short, in
Il ritorno d'Ulisse, 'elevated-style' singing becomes not only the
characteristic of divinity (Minerva, Juno, Neptune), but a sign of
youth, gallantry, and sensuous love, whereas 'speaking in song' is
assigned to mature or sorrow-stricken characters.

All this forms part of that sense of stage effect and moulding of
characters which Monteverdi possessed to an exceptional degree
and which led him, even though at a late age, to involve himself in
Baroque opera with great enthusiasm. Since the operas of Manelli
and Francesco Sacrati are lost, it is *Il ritorno d'Ulisse* that demonstrates for us the transition of opera from Rome to Venice and
that underlines the new trends in musical theatre: the more
widespread use of arioso and the set piece; the greater import-

ance given to melismatic vocalism; stage situations involving intrigue, disguise, and recognition; the advent of certain buffo roles which had come to stay (e.g. the hanger-on Iro), or of types like the nurse and confidant Ericlea, Eurimaco (the forerunner of the page-boy), or Melanto, the forerunner of the soprano-soubrette.

All this reappears on a grandiose scale and with more complex and profound patterns in *L'incoronazione di Poppea*. Here, in an atmosphere of intrigue, conspiracy, and princely hysteria, the set piece takes the form of melodies of fascinating lyricism which, even more than in *Il ritorno d'Ulisse*, cope with the dilemma between 'speaking in song' and 'singing in speech'. The melisma actually arises as an integral part of the musical motif. We get the aria 'Apri il balcon, Poppea', sung by Ottone (male alto), which is the first *aubade* in the history of opera and in which the languorous melancholy of certain phrases (for example, 'Sogni portate a volo') derives largely from the coloratura itself. Or we get the first real love duets, those between Nero (male soprano) and Poppaea (soprano), charged with a sensuous quality which is striking even today. The duet between Nero and Lucano (tenor) after the death of Seneca ('Or che Seneca è morto/ cantiam, cantiamo, Lucano'), built up on intricate, rapid passages, is given by the agility singing itself a tone of frenzied gaiety in which the cynicism nevertheless has a lugubrious, hallucinating quality. Certainly, Monteverdi does not renounce recitative and declamation when the stage situation calls for them. For example, he frequently makes use of the *stile concitato*, launched with *Il combattimento di Tancredi e Clorinda*, already broadened in *Il ritorno d'Ulisse*, and here carried to extremes in order to depict perturbation, anger, or disdain. It involves words or short phrases repeated and repeated and uttered with great rapidity, as when Valletto (soprano) utters imprecations against Seneca (bass): 'M'accende, m'accende, m'accende, m'accende, m'accende, m'accende, pur a sdegno, m'accende, m'accende pur a sdegno ...' Then Nero, in the duet with Seneca: 'Tu, tu, tu, mi forzi allo sdegno, allo sdegno, allo sdegno, allo sdegno, allo sdegno'. And again Nero, in the hysterical outburst of anger against Drusilla, who has made an attempt on Poppaea's life: 'Flagelli, flagelli, funi, funi, fochi, fochi ...'. It is typical of Monteverdi's realism that in the famous scene of Ottavia's banishment from Rome he breaks up some of the words to imitate overwhelming emotion or perhaps sobbing: 'A-a-adio Roma, a-a-a-adio patria . . .'. Following the same procedure, but in a slow lingering tempo, Poppaea expresses intense sensual perturbation: 'Son de' tuoi cari, tuoi cari detti i sen-si, sí so-avi, sí so-avi, e sí vivaci . . .'. Nero replies: 'Mertan le mamme tue, le mamme, le mamme tue, più dolci nomi, più dolci . . .' in syllabic, *concitato* style; but immediately afterwards he reverts to the melismatic style, which best expresses sensuality and gives a fairly vivid description of the abandon of the love-making in other scenes between Nero and Poppaea: the quintet in the third act ('Sempre in te perduto mi trovarò') and the final duet of the opera: 'Pur ti miro, pur ti godo'.

The sensuality that comes through in many places in *L'incoronazione di Poppea* is one of the most human and vivifying features of the opera. Monteverdi expresses it as no one else had done in the theatre before him, and as very few did after him. He succeeds in distinguishing through melody and coloratura between the grief and anguish of Ottone in the *aubade* and the insidious suggestiveness of Poppaea and the unbridled carnality of Nero. This gives us some idea of the composer's realistic approach to opera. Conscious that he is writing for the theatre, Monteverdi tends towards the two goals which the true man of the theatre sets himself: the characterization of the personages, and the stage setting. When the nurse Arnalta (contralto) appears first in the guise of a wise counsellor who advises Poppaea to keep clear of kings (I. iv), then as an opportunist who realizes the way the wind is blowing and enjoys in anticipation the advantages which the coronation of her mistress will bring her (III. vii), Monteverdi is delineating, knowingly and realistically, a type of character which Baroque opera was to adopt up to the beginning of the eighteenth century. Thus, when he inserts between the one episode and the other the song of the old servant as she watches over her sleeping mistress ('Oblivion soave', II. xii), we get one of the finest master-strokes in the whole history of opera. It is a moment of purification of a corrupt character expressing her feelings in the grim surroundings of the tragic death of Seneca and the imminent attempt on Poppaea's life. The winged melody of Arnalta, which as it develops relies on slow vocalises, is 'singing in speech', a device at one time reserved by Monteverdi for deities and now put into the mouth of a woman of low rank from whom one might expect 'speaking in song'. The freedom of vocal language attained by Monteverdi in *L'incoronazione*, liberating himself from the formulas he himself had enunciated to Striggio some twenty years earlier, marks the triumph of a man of the theatre over stereotyped patterns, and sets an example of the path he followed in bringing a character to life by giving it to us in an alternating mood of cynicism and tenderness, of ordinary common sense and dream-like effusions, in other words, a figure looked at from different angles, with variation and nuance. Part of this nuance is the light patina of sensuality we gather as a sort of background in the poetic lullaby of Arnalta, now an old hag but at one time, as she confesses, a vivacious and hot-blooded woman.

On another level, Seneca too is treated variably by Monteverdi both in the writing and in the spirit. The philosopher is rightly derided by Valletto as in the sixth scene of the first act he comforts Ottavia. Essentially, his homily consists of nothing more than bombast, in a manner of writing which brings out, through a series of devices (wide intervals, both rising and falling, sudden leaps, vocalise passages, etc.), the double ostentatiousness of his manner and of his basso profundo voice. On the other hand, in the famous scene describing Seneca's farewell to his household (II. iii) the solemnity of the occasion is depicted in simple and broad-ranging declamation.

To sum up, both *Il ritorno d'Ulisse* and *L'incoronazione di Poppea* contain many of the basic elements characteristic of the entire panorama of Baroque musical theatre. They represent, following the earlier manifestation of this trend in the operas of the Roman school, a final thrust in the direction of strophic melody in set-piece form and of arioso recitative. They introduce ornate, melismatic singing performing a function which goes beyond both Caccini's 'rhetorical colours of eloquence' and the underlining of the significance of courtly, lyrical, or descriptive terms, and beyond the division of characters into divine beings and ordinary mortals. In fact the ornaments and florid passages are decidedly part of the characterization of the personages.

At the same time, there is a more widespread application of the *concitato* style which Monteverdi had experimented with in *Il combattimento di Tancredi e Clorinda*. Furthermore, many passages already outline the shape to be given later to the aria as such. Apart from the 'lament', which is to be found in *Orfeo*, *Arianna*, and *Il ballo delle ingrate* even before Penelope's 'Di misera regina' or Ottavia's farewell to Rome, we get the birth of the love duet in its true and proper form (Eurimaco and Melanto in *Il ritorno d'Ulisse*, Nero and Poppaea in *L'incoronazione di Poppea*), and the identification of florid vocalism with gallantry or sensuous melody. We get the first 'laughing aria' (Iro in *Il ritorno d'Ulisse*), the first serenade (Ottone in *L'incoronazione*), the first 'sleep aria' (Arnalta in *L'incoronazione*), the first 'scorn aria' ('Destin, destin se stai lassù' sung by Ottavia), the first 'fury' or 'vengeance' aria ('Flagelli, flagelli, funi, funi' sung by Nero). Simultaneously, we get the confirmation of the procedure used in Roman opera of mixing comic and serious elements and introducing types which Baroque opera was to use constantly until the early decades of the eighteenth century: the parasitic hanger-on Iro in *L'incoronazione*, the nurse (outstanding among them, as we have already seen, Arnalta), the valet, the page, the young woman (already adumbrating the soubrette type), the soldier who grumbles about his wretched lot (*L'incoronazione*), and so on. With Poppaea, we get a rounded sketch of the character of the seductress already present in *La catena d'Adone* of Mazzocchi, and again with Drusilla in *L'incoronazione*, an early characterization of the *ingénue*. Finally, we have the role of Nero, a historical, not a mythological character, given over to a male soprano, whereas even in *Il ritorno d'Ulisse* the protagonist is a tenor. This is the bel canto law of the reworking of historical personages in a mythological setting, side by side with the notion that a love song calls for the flexibility, agility, languor, and timbre of a 'white', stylized voice.

Monteverdi's extraordinary capacity for character-drawing is unfolded not only through recitatives, declamation, melody, and a particular use of coloratura, but also through a shrewd choice of vocal tessituras. The seventeenth and eighteenth centuries were conscious only of the baritone type of tenor; but in *Il ritorno d'Ulisse*, a lower tessitura differentiates the protagonist, a man of mature years, from Telemachus and Eurimaco, juveniles—a notion simply unheard of at the time and positively pre-Romantic in flavour. As regards women's voices, in exactly the same way as both his contemporaries and his predecessors, Monteverdi uses two: the contralto or male alto, and a type of voice which is soprano in name but never sings in very high tessituras or over a very wide range, and in any event simply coincides with the mezzo-soprano voice. Some female figures of the grieving, suffering type, and women of relatively mature age (Penelope and Ottavia) come decidedly into this vocal category. Poppaea, on the other hand, although she sings in a middle tessitura, already suggests what we call a lyric soprano, whereas the young lady Melanto of *Il ritorno d'Ulisse* denotes the soubrette, and Valletto in *L'incoronazione* (a male soprano or a soprano *en travesti*) is a forerunner of the page-boy role. If we now look at the way in which the role of Minerva is written in *Il ritorno d'Ulisse*, we perceive certain features of the 'dramatic soprano with agility'. With regard to the contralto voice, Monteverdi uses it for the role of the nurse Arnalta, having her sing a very low tessitura with a range that for practical purposes is confined to the lowest octave of this type of voice. The principle of the elderly female represented by a very dark voice is another example of Monteverdi's anticipation of notions which later developments in opera were to modify or overturn, but which was to reappear in certain works of Mozart and during the Romantic period. The impression of modernity we get today from listening to a work like *L'incoronazione di Poppea* is also partly due to the use of certain types of voice which are in some respects familiar to us.

It is not possible to isolate from the rather nebulous panorama of the vocal art of the mid-seventeenth century a tradition of interpretation going back specifically to Monteverdi. It can be assumed that the *concitato* style involved extremely rapid, scanned recitatives, and brought out in the performers the typically Italian theatrical manner I have already mentioned. As far as florid singing is concerned, Monteverdi's writing, regardless of the additions probably made by the performers, suggests in *Il ritorno d'Ulisse* and *L'incoronazione* a melismatic leaning which is more accentuated than in Roman opera (longer vocalises, more complex figurations); and this presupposes an improvement in the virtuoso skills of the executants. In addition, it is precisely during this period that we see the emergence of the most famous castrato of the first half of the seventeenth century, Baldassarre Ferri (1610–1680) of Perugia, who came out of the Roman vocal school. Ferri was outstanding for his virtuosity (he was, among other things, a spectacular executant of trills), for his range, and for a quality which after him became one of the features of all the best singers: exceptional breathing capacity. Ferri's career was mostly abroad (Warsaw and Vienna). Notices concerning his Italian activities do not rule out in the possibility of his participation in performances of Monteverdi.

CAVALLI AND CESTI

Francesco Manelli's *Andromeda*, with which the San Cassian theatre in Venice, the first public theatre, was inaugurated in 1637, was famous for the magnificence of the production. Splendid seascapes alternated with woodland scenes; Perseus fought the monster and killed it; Aurora appeared, dressed all in silver, in the centre of a cloud; Neptune was brought on to the stage in a chariot shaped like a shell and drawn by four horses; Juno made her entrance in another chariot to which seven peacocks were yoked; Mercury, wearing a blue mantle, arrived on the wing; Andromeda wore a flame-coloured gown; while a mantle of gold and a mantle of stars enveloped Venus and Jupiter (Giove).

The whole cycle of Venetian opera was characterized by the splendour of the costumes, the stage sets, and the inventive mechanical devices: storms at sea with movements of ships, chariots of war overturned, armies engaged in battle, flights of eagles, elephants, monsters of every type, prisoners thrown down from towers or borne aloft in flight by spirits, ghostly apparitions, troops of dancers. All this had a direct impact on the structure of opera, leading the librettists to devise plots which involved many changes of scenery and fantastic situations. Thus some of the principles of Classical drama were subverted (the unities of time and place, for example), and as the librettist Giacomo Badoaro pointed out, 'inventiveness' triumphed and even the verisimilitude of human types and deeds was sacrificed to that end. Nevertheless, this type of spectacle gave expression to the Venice of the time, a city of luxury and cosmopolitanism, and it exerted a strong influence on Italians from other regions and on foreigners. But it is also true that this spectacle was made generally accessible to all classes of society, since even the common people had access to certain sections of public theatres.

In this climate, a love of opera grew up which extended also to the vocal art, leading, for example, to a gradual increase in the number of arias and also, as time went on, to a more frequent application of standards of virtuosity. Admiration for the castrato voice and the *travesti* was immediate. Among the performers in *Andromeda* there was only one woman, Maddalena Manelli, who played the title-role. The composer, Francesco Manelli, played the parts of Astarco and Neptune; Annibale Grasselli (Perseus and Mercury) and Giovanni Bisucci (Jupiter and Proteus) were tenor and bass respectively; but Francesco Angelelli (Juno), Girolamo Medici (Astrea), and Anselmo Marconi (Venus) were castrati, as also were Francesco Antiguardi and Guidantonio Boretti, though it is not known what parts they played. Nearly all the singers came from the States of the Church. Thus Venetian opera was born out of a sort of emigration of singers from the Roman school, possibly as a result of the spells of bigotry which in those days were inimical to theatrical activity in Rome. For the same reason, two famous Roman singers, Anna Renzi and Caterina Pori, moved shortly afterwards to Venice.

The opera composer most representative of the first twenty years of Venetian opera is Francesco Cavalli. He made his debut in 1639 with *Le nozze di Teti e di Peleo.* His vast production (some forty operas) reflects the new status of the Italian composer, spurred on by the popularity of opera and the constant requests by the theatres for new works, and thus encouraged to write with a certain haste, to accept librettos more or less as fast as they were ready, and to appeal to the taste of the public. This led to a sort of standardization, ups and downs in quality, unevenness of values; but from a practical standpoint, the system undoubtedly worked, since present-day musicology unequivocally recognizes Cavalli as a man of great ability and the composer of very fine works.

Like almost all the opera composers of his time, Cavalli had himself been a singer (tenor), first in the cathedral at Crema , then with the Cappella Marciana in Venice. As far as the vocal art was concerned, he started out from an attitude fairly close to that of the later operas of the Roman school, while not neglecting some experience gained from Monteverdi. Thus in his later works he achieved a type of singing melodically broader and, in virtuoso terms, more ostentatious. An examination of his writing does not give evidence of invention of a decisive kind in the matter of vocal patterns and forms. Cavalli consolidated the principle, already backed by the Roman school and by Monteverdi himself, that if outstanding historical or mythological figures took part in the action as lovers, the roles should be played by castrati. Thus, Jason and Pompey are male altos, exactly in the same way as figures from fable or legend (Lidio in *Egisto*, and Ormindo), whereas Ciro and Scipio the African are male sopranos. Fairly frequently also, rival figures are castrati, particularly if the rivalry is confined to the love theme (Arsamene in *Serse* is a male alto, Servilio in *Pompeo Magno* is a male soprano). Women in love, and their rivals, are as a rule female sopranos. The male altos sing in a very low tessitura covering a range which starts from the g below the stave and hardly rises beyond an octave. The sopranos and male sopranos correspond roughly to the mezzo-sopranos of today, and rarely sing higher than a″. The tenors are of the baritone type, and only one or two of Cavalli's early operas cast them in the role of lovers (e.g. Peleo and Meonte in *La virtú degli strali d'amore*). At times they play the part of the rival of the male lover, but more often they play buffo parts. In the male voice department, Cavalli seems to prefer basses to tenors, in accordance with a taste going back to the polyphonic school. Basses frequently appear in buffo parts, or impersonate kings, fathers, great deities, etc. At times they play the title-roles (Xerxes, Hercules, Mucius Scaevola), and occasionally their vocalism is of virtuoso stamp. Contraltos are as a rule servants, nurses, or at any rate elderly women. Like male altos, they sing in a very low tessitura and cover a very limited range.

Cavalli calls for considerable expressive gifts from his executants. First and foremost, his recitative writing is extremely varied. This is frequently manifested in sequential patterns; it is quite rich in chromaticism, declamatory passages alternating with arioso; at times the central section actually falls into a ternary aria in *ABA* form (for example Sicle's lament in *Ormindo*, 'Chi mi toglie al die'); and not infrequently, although with less nervous tension and a more restricted use of word repetition, Cavalli reverts to the *concitato* style of Monteverdi. Recitative, on the other hand, sometimes in more or less arioso form and sometimes with declamatory force, making the voice hammer on a single note, is present in Cavalli as a fundamental feature of important scenes such as: Dido's dying monologue in the opera *Didone*, and the moment in *Mutio Scevola* where the protagonist puts his hand into the fire. *Concitato* style also appears in arias expressing enchantment (the famous 'dell'antro magico stridenti cardini' sung by Medea in *Giasone*) and of course in monologues of invective and desperation, like the 'Scelerato Troian' sung by Dido in *Didone* and 'Empia, l'empia mia sorte', sung by Climene in *Egisto*.

The vigour of these recitatives and these arioso passages or arias of Cavalli makes for personages of almost epic stature such as the protagonist in *Ercole amante*, and above all, female figures who could be described as heroines in the etymological sense of the word: Dido, Medea, Climene, Doriclea, and others. In today's terms one might speak of a vague anticipation of the dramatic soprano (although they sing in a tessitura nearly always in the middle of the voice), but bearing in mind that these female characters add to their agitation a marked element of pathos. The sadness of the 'lament' is actually the most characteristic note of Cavalli's writing. Monteverdi before him had already carried the lament to great artistic hights (in *Arianna*, *Il ballo delle ingrate*, *Il ritorno d'Ulisse*, *L'incoronazione*), but Cavalli brings to this type of aria a melodic expansiveness and a structural definition (the *passacaglia* rhythm) which make it one of the finest vocal forms of the seventeenth century. Rightly celebrated are the laments sung by Cassandra in *Didone* ('L'alma ria'), by Climene in *Egisto* ('Piangete, occhi dolenti'), by Issifile in *Giasone* ('S'ei non torna mi moro'), and by Dejanira in *Ercole amante* ('Misera, ahimé, che ascolto'). But we would need to quote many other examples, since the lament is a recurring feature of Cavalli's operas. Quite frequently the lament is entrusted even to the lovers, and the lament ('Ah, spirò, mia vita . . .') sung by the protagonist in *Ormindo* over the body of Erisbe, who is thought to be dead, is famous.

Another vocal form which Cavalli develops expressively on a large scale is the duet. The most frequent type is the love duet in a sensuous setting, which in part links up again with the scenes between Poppaea and Nero in *L'incoronazione*. At times these duets have ecstatic outbursts, as in that between Meonte and Eumete in one of the very earliest works, *La virtú degli strali d'amore* (1642); but as a rule the mood is one of languorous abandon, accentuated here and there by a melisma. The less measured and perspicacious use of *fioriture*, intervals, and pauses rules out in general achievements really comparable to those of the duet between Nero and Poppaea in *L'incoronazione*. The fact remains, however, that the spread and the final crystallization of the love duet in seventeenth-century opera are the work of Cavalli. Outstanding successes were also achieved by Cavalli in duets which, while not strictly love duets, come within the sphere of voluptuous tone, starting out from the imitation of nature (the famous 'Musici della selva' sung by Lidio and Clori in *Egisto*), or the description of feminine charms ('Auree trecce inanellate' sung by Erisbe and Merinda in *Ormindo*). Cavalli also launched the duet in other directions. Pathetic farewell scenes between lovers or spouses are quite frequent, and in *Ormindo* we have what is positively an 'agony' duet between the protagonist and his beloved Erisbe.[10] Nor is there any lack of 'scorn' duets, such as that between Venus and Juno in *Helena rapita da Theseo*.

Languor and voluptuousness represent a chord which Cavalli strikes frequently in the arias sung by male and female lovers (one of the prototypes is 'Delizie contente' sung by the protagonist in *Giasone*); but still more characteristic are perhaps the arias and ariettas inspired by the beauty of nature. The best-known examples are 'Hor que l'aurora spargendo fiori', sung by Lidio in *Egisto*; 'Mormorate fumicelli', sung by Prasitea in *Ercole amante*; and 'Zeffiretti placidi', sung by the protagonist in *Artemisia*. In all these pieces, Cavalli's writing calls for delicacy and smoothness, and it is quite understandable that the pathos and languor of the idyllic-style arietta called for the flexibility and delicacy of the castrato and the female soprano voice. In particular, love duets between a male alto and a female soprano had to take advantage of effects bound up with the peculiar sound, rather dark, dense but light in weight, characteristic of the voice of the lover in low tessituras. However, Cavalli's writing, both in cantabile passages expressing voluptuousness and in pathetic and idyllic passages, is deliberately plain. True, melismata and vocalises underline courtly words, or phrases which require an imitative quality in the singing ('Auree trecce inanellate' from the duet in *Ormindo*, for example, or 'Zeffiretti placidi' sung by Artemisia), but as a rule the passages are extremely short and made up of slow vocalises which proceed, both ascending and descending, by adjacent steps. Wide intervals and vaulting leaps are rare, especially in cantabile passages. In short, Cavalli's writing from the point of view of virtuosity is very simple; indeed, he frequently seems to take no interest in melismatic outbursts, leaving the task of 'colouring' to the executant. In his last operas, however, falling in with the

---

[10] In the interests of the happy ending, death was only apparent. The two lovers had not been given poison but a sleep-inducing potion.

general practice, Cavalli increased the number of arias, reducing the recitative sections; and he also wrote passages for soprano with a relatively high tessitura and rich in *fioriture*, such as 'Cara effigie', sung by Elmira in *Erismena*, or 'Alpi gelide', sung by Giulia in *Pompeo Magno*. Another virtuoso aria with rapid vocalise passages of a descriptive nature is the aria sung by Borea (bass) in *Eritrea*: 'Dell'iperboreo ghiaccio'. The aria 'Alpi gelide' from *Pompeo* includes a part for a solo violin, which imitates the soprano's singing. Arias with a concertante instrument are extremely rare in Cavalli and are only found in his very latest works. In *Artemisia* we get an aria with two trumpets ('Trombe a battaglia', sung by Indumano), here again in keeping with a vogue which by that time was gradually dying out. We also find in Cavalli 'sleep' arias ('Mormorate fiumicelli' sung by Prasitea in *Ercole amante*, for example), and some of the earliest scenes in Venetian opera describing ghostly apparitions (Hecuba and Creusa in *Didone*, Iole's father in *Ercole amante*), while in other such arias, but reserved for buffo roles, certain Monteverdian precedents are brought out and codified: grievances expressed by soldiers about their lot, braggadocio outbursts by crippled buffoons, the impudence of aged nurses, the free-and-easy joviality of young page-boys. Nor is there any shortage of 'laughing' arias: 'Affè, mi fate ridere' sung by the Page in *Serse* and 'Io intendo ciò che fu' by the procuress Harpalia in *Pompeo Magno*.

It was with Antonio Cesti that Venetian opera took a decisive step in the direction of the glorification of the art of singing. He increased the number of arias, reducing the number of recitatives. The melody is often more vividly characterized, as compared with Cavalli's operas, if only because it tends more and more to break away from the step wise mode and close intervals, thus achieving greater impetus and variety. But above all, with Cesti, we get a more marked interplay of florid passages, ornaments, and vocalises. The coloratura begins to take on more explicitly patterns inspired by formulas borrowed from the organ, the harpsichord, or the violin. In *Dori*, Mars' aria, 'Questo è il giorno fatale' has the voice perform figurations inspired by the trumpet. The vocalise begins to be fairly often built up on figures, particularly four-note groups consisting of short notes (semiquavers). In *Il pomo d'oro* there are vocalise passages which are not only fairly long, but of a design including wide intervals and leaps (for example, the aria sung by Pallas: 'Non più pugne giocose'; but even the aria by the protagonist in *Argia*: 'Lucimoro godrà calma serena', refers back to this pattern). In some instances the coloratura even extends to buffo parts, as in the aria sung by Momus (bass): 'Da queste aurette volo', again from *Il pomo d'oro*. We are, of course, still a long way from the vocal pyrotechnics set to cause an explosion at the beginning of the eighteenth century, but it is fairly clear that the twenty years during which Cesti worked laid down some of the bases for true vocal virtuosity. This does not mean that in Cesti melismata played a decisive role; but certainly we see a changeover in relation to Cavalli. The tragic-pathetic style loses ground, and we find the emergence, not so much of figures of heroines, but of queens and princesses of an idyllic cast, like Orontea or Semira, more inclined towards the expression of languor or lyrical ecstasy (a good example is the very famous 'sleep' aria sung by Orontea: 'Intorno all'idol mio'). There is no lack in Cesti of quick-moving and vigorous recitatives (for example, the monologue by the protagonist in *Argia*: 'Ah! perfido Selino'), or of languid love duets or laments (such as 'Discioglietevi pure', likewise from *Argia*, or 'Paride, Paride dove sei?' sung by Enone in *Il pomo d'oro*), or the elegiac-nostalgic effusions of lovers. Rather, the sentimentality of some of the love arias ('Afflitto mio core', sung by Semira in *Semirami o La schiava sfortunata*; 'Mi rapisce la mia pace' and 'Rendetemi il mio ben', sung by Oronte in *Dori*) is one of the characteristics of Cesti. Yet the vocal style which derives from the operatic writing of this composer is above all what one might call 'graceful', as mani-fested, for example, in the ternary aria (see Ex. 4) sung in *Dori* by Arsete (tenor). Here we have two distinct effects: in the first two

Ex. 4

bars the effect which derives from the upward movement of the design and its subsequent falling; and in the third and fourth bars the light and rapid tripping of the voice along the wavy pairs of quavers and semiquavers. The rapid movement of very short phrases or fragments of vocalises from the bottom to the top of the stave—or vice versa—is in any case a basic element of Cesti's graceful style, and even recurs in the sentimental arias of the female and male lovers ('Tu credi mio core', sung by Celinda in *Dori* and 'Celar d'amor la arsura' sung by Nino in *Semirami*).

In Cesti at times we come across arias which subsequently have given rise to genres that became very popular. Thus Apollo's toast to Jupiter in *Il pomo d'oro* ('Questo calice spumante') is one which could be defined as a 'doubt' aria—the lover torn between love and fear or between love and duty. A prototype of this is 'Che cruda battaglia', sung by Clearco in *La magnanimità di Alessandro*), where among other things the violins reiterate the *fioriture* sung by the voice.

Cesti's vocal types are not differentiated from those of Cavalli. In one single case (Alidoro in *Orontea*), the tenor plays the part of the lover. Nor do the tessituras present any change, except that the female sopranos are slightly higher. However, Cesti calls for a type of executant who is less passionate and emotional but more agile and elegant than the Cavalli types. Even more than in Cavalli, therefore, the interpreter must be capable of rendering the subtle nuances of characters constantly involved in equivocal and paradoxical situations: women in love who dress up as men and embark on pilgrimages which take them in search of their lovers; continual changes of personality; men and women of humble status who unexpectedly turn out to be kings, princes, or queens. Finally, it is always with Cesti's music that Italian singers— who as early as the beginning of the seventeenth century had already begun to settle in Austria, Germany, and Poland to serve in the court chapels—began to be invited abroad as opera performers as well. The exceptional splendour of the production of *Il pomo d'oro* in Vienna in 1666, on the occasion of the marriage of Leopold I, marked the birth of international grand opera in court circles. The performance took place in an open-air theatre, with about 5,000 persons attending, on two evenings, the entire duration of the spectacle being about ten hours. The plot included a total of 48 characters, and called for 23 changes of sets.

LEGRENZI, SARTORIO, P. A. ZIANI, AND POLLAROLO

Giovanni Legrenzi and Antonio Sartorio give us a type of Venetian opera which in its structures and types is perhaps more authentic than that of Cesti. Both of them set to music librettos which put on the stage figures from ancient Rome or the early Middle Ages, and this creates a climate, especially in Sartorio, which is in its way epic. The plots are always highly complex, and the situations continue to lean more towards invention than verisimilitude; but the *travesti* scenes, the misunderstandings, and the purely fairy-tale element give way here and there to a semblance of historical truth and to violent encounters between the characters. These encounters, even though they are resolved on a musical level with tuneful lyricism (and stage-wise always with a happy ending), nevertheless take place in a framework of battle, siege, and destruction. In short it is a type of 'warrior' opera, if not actually heroic, the campaigners being fierce conquerors, strenuous defenders of all things Roman, and chaste, spirited queens and matronly figures.

The vocal art in Legrenzi and Sartorio aims more directly than that of their predecessors at a confrontation between voice and instrument. Thus we see the development of the aria with a concertante instrument which in the genre in point—'warrior' opera—seems to give precedence to the trumpet. But the aria with trumpet accompaniment is reserved exclusively for royalty or for personages distinguished by exceptional prowess as soldiers. It is significant that during the Baroque period the trumpet is the symbol of royal majesty. Thus in Legrenzi's *Totila*, the protagonist (a male soprano) launches the Gothic warriors against Rome with an aria ('Arda Roma') in which solo trumpet and violin respond to the florid singing of the warriors. In another scene, the great Belisario, personified by a tenor who appears seated on the back of an elephant, with a following of 150 companions-in-arms, sings an aria in plain style ('Coronate di verdi allori'), the vibrant, martial character being suggested precisely by a trumpet. Still more celebrated is the scene in Sartorio's *Adelaide* in which the protagonist, while following the retinue of Beringario II as a prisoner, takes up in jig rhythm the triumphal tune played by the trumpets, singing the virtuoso aria 'Vittrici schiere'. Other arias with trumpet are to be found in *Antonino e Pompejano*, likewise by Sartorio.

Adelaide is one of the figures in 'warrior' opera linked to Cavalli's 'heroines'. Another is the virtuous Giulia in *Antonino e Pompejano*. On the other hand, in Legrenzi's *Totila* one of the campaigners is Clelia, wife of the Consul Pubblicola. In the first scene of *Totila* we get a situation which long afterwards other opera composers were to make famous. As the Goths march into Rome, Clelia debates whether to kill first her son and then herself; but she desists after singing to the sleeping child a nostalgic 'sleep' aria, in E minor ('Dolce figlio che posi e dormi'). Another time Clelia, who is tempted by Vitige, Totila's general, does not hesitate to don a suit of armour and draw the sword. Another heroine is Arianna in Legrenzi's *Giustino*. She is the wife of the Emperor Anastasio, and is lusted after by Vitaliano, a warlike Oriental monarch. The aria 'Caderà, caderà chi mi fa guerra', where the strong-willed Arianna imitates rapid trumpet passages, uses a coloratura which in its rhythm and the length of some of the vocalise passages is one of the most complex in all seventeenth-century opera. Noteworthy are several *p* and *f* markings inserted by Legrenzi in the score. This is one of the earliest instances of marks of expression applied to singing, whereas in instrumental music the practice was of long standing.

In *Giustino*, the character of the heroine Arianna is offset by Eufemia, a feminine figure already sketched out by Monteverdi, Cavalli, and Cesti in the guise of the vivacious, sprightly young lady type. In the operas of Legrenzi and Sartorio she becomes a bewitching and provocative character, but often also shrewd and strong-willed. She is the earliest incarnation of the soubrette soprano, represented in Legrenzi above all in *Totila* by Marcia, a Roman patrician, daughter of a senator. Totila is in love with her, but Marcia provokes him, rejects him, or coquettishly makes fun of him, afterwards preferring him to others who pay court to her. Her most typical piece is the 'villotta' 'Per deridere un cuore amante' (see Ex. 5). This type of aria gave rise to a tradition which, in comic opera particularly, was to persist until the middle of the nineteenth century.

In Sartorio's *Adelaide* the soubrette is Gisilla, whose aria 'Giosci

Ex. 5

alma mia', rather in the style of Marcia's 'Per deridere un cuore amante', has the violins at times imitating the soprano voice.

'Warrior' opera crystallizes a vocal type unknown to earlier composers—the barbarian tyrant who in theatrical parlance is identifiable with the 'villain'. In Legrenzi, one such personage is Totila (male soprano), although he is a versatile character who alternates between arias expressing rage such as 'Arda Roma', or godlessness ('Di voi rido, o numi insani') and the graceful and florid style of 'Son guerrier della beltà', indeed, he is both tyrant and lover at the same time. Another personage of the same stamp is the protagonist of *Odoacre*,[11] who sings of the destruction of Rome in the aria 'Moli eccelse che cozzate', while in *Giustino* the tyrant is Vitaliano.

In Sartorio, a typical tyrant is Berengario d'Ivrea (bass) in *Adelaide*, whose characteristic piece is the 'fury' aria 'Numi tartarei, Stigia Proserpina, Demoni, Furie'. This aria, in plain style, is one of many on the pattern of 'Dell'antro magico stridente cardini' sung by Medea in Cavalli's *Giasone*, but vocally it is reminiscent of 'Flagelli, flagelli, funi, funi . . .' sung by Nero in *L'incoronazione di Poppea*, and it also represents a typical melismatic formula used by Monteverdi, namely, a descending scale fitted to the word 'fulmini' (Ottavia's 'scorn' aria: 'Destin, destin, se stai lassú', again from *L'incoronazione*).[12]

In some of the most representative operas of Legrenzi and Sartorio, the role of barbarian is offset by the champion of the

[11] Some writers attribute this opera to Giovanni Varischino, Legrenzi's nephew. It too has a heroine (Giunia) and a soubrette (Fausta). It was one of the most spectacular works of Venetian opera, with battles and sensational scenes showing the destruction of palaces.

[12] Another 'scorn' aria reminiscent in some respects of the *stile concitato* of Monteverdi is 'Su sbranate, lacerate', sung by Flacco in *Odoacre*, by Legrenzi (or Varischino).

Roman world: Ottone in *Adelaide*, Belisario in *Totila*, the title-role in *Giustino*, Flacco in *Odoacre*. Both barbarian and Roman are at times flanked by warriors of minor calibre (Vitige, Lepido, Teodato in *Totila*, Polimante in *Giustino*) who sing rough, martial arias. A typical case is 'Su, nocchieri, alle navi, alle navi' sung by Teodato (bass), where the voice imitates, but in syllabic style, trumpet figurations including upward leaps of an octave.

In these operas both lovers and 'heroines' are given tunes full of pathos to sing. Thus in *Giustino* Anastasio, male soprano, sings a moving farewell aria ('Ti lascio l'alma in pegno'), and in *Adelaide*, Adalberto, male alto, performs the lament 'Qual colpa mi date, tiranne pupille'. The expression of pathos is occasionally given over in Legrenzi and Sartorio to the soubrette (Marcia and Gisilla in *Totila* and *Adelaide* also have farewell arias and laments) and even to the barbarian warriors. Thus in *Totila*, the aria 'Resta il cuore se parte il pie', is sung by Vitige, one of the few seventeenth-century opera characters whose parts are written in the c clef (mezzo-soprano).

Lovers are also given the sensuous duets deriving from the Cavalli–Monteverdi tradition. (Noteworthy among them is the duet 'Corri, vola tra queste braccia' between Anastasio and Arianna in *Giustino*, and the 'doubt' arias of which we found one of the prototypes in 'Che cruda battaglia' sung by Clearco in Cesti's *La magnanimità di Alessandro*.) These arias, of the type 'Fan con l'armi un'aspra guerra/ nel mio sen sdegno ed amore', sung by Adalberto in *Adelaide*, at times represent, together with trumpet arias, the most advanced form of virtuosity in the operas of Legrenzi and Sartorio. The imitation of alternating states of mind actually leads to fairly complex figurations in which the voice rises and climbs, sometimes by adjacent steps, sometimes by fairly wide intervals, also including irregular groups of notes as well as series of two, three, and four semiquavers. The tradition of shade or ghost scenes, initiated by Cavalli, is carried still further by Legrenzi and Sartorio (for example, the appearance of Vitaliano the father in *Giustino*), and similarly the 'death' aria (cf. *Ormindo*, also by Cavalli) which we find again in Sartorio's *Antonino e Pompejano*. This opera also contains a type of stage scene which was to enjoy great success—the scene where the hero (Pompejano), in chains, bids farewell to his wife Giulia before being led off to his death. This was to give rise to the 'bound in chains' aria.

In Legrenzi's *Totila*, in contrast, we have a prototype of the mad scene. The Roman consul Pubblicola (male alto) goes out of his mind during the invasion of Rome by the Goths on hearing the false news that his wife Clelia is dead. He wants to go down to the nether regions, and he sings 'Aprite i cardini del basso Tartaro'. Actually, the scene is a parody of the 'conjuration' aria 'Dell'antro magico' from Cavalli's *Giasone*, but as time goes on the onset of madness in one of the personages is taken up in a mood of pathos and developed in an atmosphere of virtuosity.

In the operas of Legrenzi and Sartorio, the buffo roles acquire a still broader status than earlier on. At times the buffo sings using melismata for grotesque effects, and they revive and renew a version of the old, intriguing procuress-nurse, a version now entrusted to a man in women's clothes, and nearly always a tenor.

Pietro Andrea Ziani has a much less grandiose notion of the historically-based opera than Legrenzi and Sartorio. Instead, he tends in revamping the ancient world to accentuate the comic element; or he shows us figures of heroes rendered impotent for battle by love. This is true of the protagonist in *Annibale in Capua*, who is languishing for Emilia, a Roman amazon. Ziani's writing is not dissimilar to that of Cesti, Legrenzi, and Sartorio, except for greater melodic characterization and a more marked tendency towards broad legato singing, together with the acquisition of instrumentally-inspired figurations. But he is perhaps closest to Cesti, because his style is decidedly 'graceful'. The mode of expression most characteristic of Ziani seems to be that of the arietta and canzonetta, where among other things he introduces changes of rhythm and tempo, obviously for the purpose of giving greater variety to the singing. This happens, for example, in Annibale's canzonetta 'Son guerrieri Amore e Marte', a 'doubt' or 'inward struggle' aria. Unlike Cesti and Sartorio, Ziani does not give this piece a virtuoso stamp, and he seems to be anxious to concentrate the effect on the low notes of the male alto voice. But he moves from an initial Andante in 3/2 time to an Allegro in 4/4 which is close to being a curious foretaste of the cantabile with cabaletta of Romantic opera. Then there is an apparition scene: the ghost of Amilcare (bass) chides his son Annibale for his indolence. After a recitative we go on to an Allegretto in 4/4 time ('Prigionera del bel crine' and then to an Allegro in 3/4 time ('Troppo, troppo il tuo cor'). If we think of Cavalli's 'apparition' arias, it is clear that the tendency to replace the arioso recitative and declamation by broad legato singing, given variety by changes in tempo and rhythm, is already under way. All this also constitutes one of the earliest manifestations of the free-and-easy manner in which, more and more frequently as time went on, opera was to make cantabile the vehicle through which the more solemn characters express themselves. It may be added that Amilcare's Allegro is somewhat reminiscent of Monteverdi's *stile concitato*.

Again in Ziani we find other examples of arias expressing internal struggle—evidence of the success which this type of cantabile was beginning to enjoy (for example 'Dimmi, Marte, che val la vittoria', sung by the male soprano Seleuco in *Amor guerriero*); while *Candaule* presents one of the first examples of the 'toilette' aria, i.e. a canzonetta sung by a lady while she is dressing: 'Bei fioretti che ridete' sung by Alinda (soprano), who is adorning herself with flowers. Here we are in the graceful style reminiscent of Cesti, but with florid writing of a more marked kind, probably influenced by violin figurations. And again with Ziani (*Semiramide*), we come across the first sketch of what was subsequently to become the 'tempest' aria. Iside (soprano) sings 'Senza scorta e senza stelle/ sembro nave in mezzo al mar/ il mio pianto è la procella/ scogli sono i miei martiri . . .' In Ziani's initial draft, the aria is idyllic and in a deliberately plain style; but gradually the simultaneous imitation of the storm and the internal agitation of the characters brings the vocal writing to express the more arduous forms of virtuosity.

In Ziani we find at times a return to the sensuousness of Cavalli's duets, the most eloquent example being perhaps the aria 'Sí, bella bocca sí' which Candaule (male soprano) sings and his wife Alinda (soprano) takes up. This aria, graceful in style, is defined by the composer himself in the score as 'joyous, affectionate, and bizarre'. This could actually be taken as the hallmark of all Ziani's vocalism, in particular his adventures in the direction of the comic element. Nor is his work lacking in laments, outstanding among them Candaule's Adagio 'Che ti feci, idolo mio', extremely simple in style, like some of those of Cavalli, and accompanied by violas.

The writing of Carlo Francesco Pollarolo does not differ appreciably from that of Legrenzi, Sartorio, and Ziani. Pollarolo tends towards the fairly florid idyllic cantabile, like the aria of the protagonist (a male alto) in *Onorio in Roma*, later taken up by Termancia (soprano): 'Usignoli che cantate', one of the very earliest imitations of birdsong. The accompaniment is given to violins alone, which alternate with the voices and imitate the nightingale with much greater virtuosity than does the singer. The same procedure appears in a 'seduction' aria sung by Termancia ('Chi ben ama dona il core'), without continuo and accompanied only by four violins. Again in *Onorio in Roma* we find a woman contralto in a serious role, that of Placidia; but in this Pollarolo had been preceded, as we shall see, by other composers. Likewise the pathos-filled aria 'In quel pie' legato ho il core', sung by Placidia herself, is accompanied only by a theorbo, two violas, and a double bass imitating the voice; and throughout, strings alone accompany an aria with which Onorio sings himself to sleep ('Vacillante è il regno mio'. Another 'sleep' aria, but in French, is sung by Termancia ('Suivons l'aimable paix').

All in all, the singing in Legrenzi, Sartorio, Ziani, and Pollarolo does not attain a level of virtuosity to compete with that of later composers, but it lays the foundations for them, above all by introducing figurations for trumpet and violin, and discourse between the voices and these instruments. The 'warrior' operas of Legrenzi and Sartorio also present a vocalism with an epic-style background, and even retain something of the courtly-pathetic style found in Cavalli. Ziani and Pollarolo, on the other hand, tend towards the graceful style, at times reminiscent of Cesti. Their writing is richer in melismata for the roles of male soprano and female soprano than for those of male alto or female contralto.

Similarly during this period, changes appear in rhythm and tempo within the aria; we find the first marks of expression (*f*, *p*) given by the composer, and also other signs: the trill indicated by the abbreviation *tr* rather than written out, and the fermata or pause, which leaves the singer free to lengthen the sound at will. In this phase of Venetian opera, arias become extremely numerous, often between sixty and seventy. But even when they have a 'da capo' they are modest in length. The classification of arias and ariettas in general adds to the old forms ('lament', 'scorn', 'conjuration', 'apparition', 'farewell', 'sleep') new types of set pieces: the 'doubt or internal struggle' aria (mostly a virtuoso piece), the 'warrior' aria with trumpet, the 'toilette', 'seduction', and 'mockery' arias (usually sung by the soubrette), and prototypes, for the time being with very simple coloratura patterns, of 'tempest' arias and others imitating birds. Finally, more space is given to buffo roles, including the tenor *en travesti*, playing the part of the old nurse. Obviously, expansion of the categories of arias brings with it an expansion of the field of expression of the interpreter.

CARLO PALLAVICINO AND STEFFANI

In the gradual mastery of consummate virtuosity which was to be characteristic of Baroque opera in the first half of the eighteenth century, Carlo Pallavicino fulfils an important function. In comparison with his predecessors, his writing shows: (*a*) a tendency to accentuate effects bound up with rapidity of execution—to be seen above all in *Gerusalemme liberata* (1687, Dresden version) by way of frequent use of allegro and once even of 'allegrissimo' ('Un motivo d'allegrezza', sung by Tancredi, male soprano); (*b*) rapidity of execution accompanied by greater complexity and longer vocalises. Again in *Gerusalemme liberata* we find Allegros sung by Argante (tenor) and Armida (soprano) containing vocalises of nine and fourteen bars respectively; but the trend towards long vocalise passages is manifest also in the other voices: Goffredo (bass), Clorinda (soprano), Tancredi (male soprano), Rinaldo (male alto); (*c*) vocalises which tend to accentuate certain instrumental patterns and to break away more and more in design from the adjacent style, with narrow intervals, to take on an arpeggio look and at times to project the voice upwards with leaps of an octave or even as much as two octaves (as in Goffredo's aria 'Ove siete, lauri, palme', where the voice takes a sudden leap from C to c'.

Noteworthy also in *Gerusalemme liberata* is a more marked tendency towards *recitativo secco*, on the one hand, and towards strophic melody on the other. The requirements of melody of broader and broader design led the composer to the device of repeating words or phrases. An example is: 'Accheta la tempesta/che l'anima molesta/con tante pene/con tante, tante pene/con tante pene alfin!' (Tancredi, III. xii). This procedure is distinctly different from the iteration devices in Monteverdi and Cavalli, which are limited to recitatives in *stile concitato*. Nevertheless, the arias are still fairly short and extremely numerous. *Gerusalemme liberata* has sixty, plus two duets. Pallavicino also takes over from the composers of the preceding generation the use of certain expression marks: the fermata, *tr*, *f*, and *p*, at times alternating to give an echo effect.

Essentially, *Gerusalemme liberata* is characteristic of the 'warrior' opera of Legrenzi and Sartorio both in the matter of spectacle (cannon-balls and storms) and in regard to vocal types, which, however, become more clearly characterized. The figure of Armida, for example, is made by the virtuoso vocal writing itself to reveal fully the real sorceress within her (see the aria with trumpet 'Fiera Aletto') combined with the allurements and the fickleness of the seductress, expressed alternately in animation and insolence. Clorinda, on the other hand, is akin to the heroines of Legrenzi and Sartorio, and even here the long vocalises which fall on words like *guerreggiar* (I. v) or *lampeggiar* ('Del brando al lampeggiar', I. xvii) have a character-forming function underlining the warlike nature of the personage. Argante, on his side, suggests fairly straightforwardly the truculent, haughty warrior, a figure the tenor was to share with the bass through the whole of eighteenth-century opera. He too gets the aria with trumpet, by now generalized, as well as developments leading the voice to imitate the concertante instrument.

Tancredi, on the other hand, is the pathetic character who sings the melancholy 'farewell' aria ('Partirò, ma teco resta/ questo core incatenato' and who bursts out, on the death of Clorinda, into an aria of desperation ('Tesifoni d'abisso, volatemi nel cor') still partly bearing the imprint of the Monteverdian *stile concitato*. In contrast, Goffredo is the wise, thoughtful general, who nevertheless yields at times to bellicose impetuosity (see the 'vengeance' aria in the finale to act I, with long bravura vocalises). Finally, Rinaldo is the lover torn between passion and duty who alternates between warlike ardour or songs of victory, built up on melismatic patterns, and soulful, sighing tunes.

Other operas by Pallavicino are different in character and vocal content. *Messalina*, for example, which seems to adumbrate the free-and-easy customs of the Venetian aristocracy, sees the graceful style come into vogue through the 'seduction' arias sung by the protagonist (soprano), fairly florid and decidedly vivacious. Here even the 'jealousy' arias—like 'Lasciami gelosia', sung by the Emperor Claudius (Claudio), male soprano—move along at a languid pace, while the expression of pathos is left to the laments of Fioralba, another soprano ('Aure, o voi ch'a fiato lento'; 'Moro sí, moro innocente'), and the tender and moving 'sleep' aria of Tergisto, bass ('Caro sonno, dolce oblio'). However, unlike pieces of this kind written by earlier composers, this has one or two fairly complex vocalises. The level of virtuosity is nevertheless, in *Messalina*, decidedly lower than that of *Gerusalemme liberata*, even though one aria sung by Claudio ('Ho risolto, goder voglio') displays a long vocalise, somewhat difficult, and also sung on repeated ascending scales.

Apart from the title-role in *Messalina*, Pallavicino is particularly successful in his handling of young, vivacious, coquettish women, like Lidia in *Gallieno* and Gilda in *L'amazzone corsara*, to which we owe a typical 'toilette' aria, sung by the soprano as she makes herself up in front of a mirror ('Dite il vero a queste luci'). In similar arias, the singing is mostly syllabic and the tessitura is medium. In others again, Pallavicino harks back to the position adopted by Cavalli for 'conjuration' episodes, giving a declamatory imprint in *Gallieno* to 'D'ombre Stigie ampi volumi' sung by Aristodemo, a bass who is actually baritone in tessitura and even goes up to a top g'. Then in the 'lament' aria, Pallavicino at times uses vocalises in an unusual, graceful style, light, airy, and with pauses which give the singing a sense of trepidation and nervousness. Thus in the third scene of the second act of *Diocleziano*, Rosamunda (soprano) sings 'Mi lasciate speranze' (Ex. 6). And later on again Rosamunda sings a 'doubt' aria ('Voglio morte e voglio vita'); but contrary to the usual practice in such pieces, it is syllabic in style.

Ex. 6

Agostino Steffani, who between 1680 and the early years of the eighteenth century typifies Venetian opera transplanted to Germany, follows a twofold direction along the path of vocalism towards what was to be the most resplendent phase of bel canto singing: virtuoso figurations and melodic resources manifested through a sort of vocal amplification of all the styles which from Cavalli onwards had made up Baroque opera.

Steffani is above all inclined constantly towards taut, vigorous singing, and in that he is more than any other composer of the Venetian school akin to Cavalli. Thus some of his recitatives, while coinciding, sometimes more, sometimes less, with the *recitativo secco* formulas, contain declamatory sections which carry the voice up to a high tessitura, with almost always isolated and sudden rising or falling scales[13] not infrequently reaching notes extremely high for the period. The most significant examples are: in *Marc'Aurelio*, 'Ecco di mie sciagure' (III. ii) sung by the protagonist, a baritone;[14] in the Prologue to *Servio Tullio*, the aria 'Come? Che sento?' sung by Giove (Jupiter), a male soprano; in *Niobe*; 'De' regali fasti' (I. xiii) sung by Anfione (male soprano); in *Henrico Leone*, 'Inferocite, o venti' sung by the protagonist (male alto) in the 'tempest' scene with which the opera opens—a recitative, varied and impetuous, in which among other things Enrico sings at a tessitura which must have been extremely high for a male alto at that period, reaching e″, likewise a very high note for the time. We also have 'Ciò que pensa Giasone' (II. x) sung by Medea (soprano) in *Le rivali concordi*; 'Enea son io' (I. ii) sung by Aeneas (tenor) in *Turno*; and 'A te la prole' (III. viii) sung by the protagonist in *Alarico*, where the voice of the male soprano reaches b″, another extremely high note for the period.

But Steffani goes even further. In the third act of Niobe, the death of Anfione is an 'accompanied' recitative ('Spira già nel propio sangue') in which, among other things, the voice, with brief vocalises interrupted continuously by pauses and descending scales with 'detached' (*picchettato*) sound—an ornament no longer used at the time, this being 1688—imitates agonized panting; and Niobe (soprano) replies with another recitative, vigorous and *concitato* ('Ahi che trafitto, privo d'alma e di vita') before embarking on the Largo in 3/2 time, 'Funeste immagini', a lament to which the chromaticism gives an introvert, gloomy tone.

[13] More often ascending. Steffani and Alessandro Scarlatti are the first composers to use this figure regularly.
[14] Marc'Aurelio is one of the few roles in 17th–18th-c. opera written in the 'baritone clef'.

Steffani's inclination towards the severe, energetic style is to be seen also in the coloratura of the more quick-moving arias, which frequently takes off from a rapid ascending scale and then increases its own impetus with vocalises, short, but in the form of great upward leaps. Thus the 'anger' aria sung by Polifemo (another role written in the 'baritone clef', but with a tessitura essentially bass); 'Fiera Aletto', likewise in *Niobe*; the 'vengeance' aria sung by Semiamira (contralto) in *Alarico* (I. ix); or the 'scorn' aria: 'Le saette del tonante', sung by the protagonist (male soprano) in the same opera—all these arias are allegro, and the expressiveness is given precisely by the speed of the melisma figurations and the impetus of the vaulting leaps. We also come across warlike arias where the vocalise passages are sustained for six or seven bars ('Tra bellici carmi/ risvegliati all'armi', sung by Anfione in *Niobe*, one of the most virtuosic arias composed by Steffani for the soprano voice). But these are rare instances; nevertheless, the reiterated rapid rising scales, carrying the voice higher and higher, give great impetus to the singing.

Steffani's concern for expressiveness leads to expression marks which the other opera composers had hitherto ignored: Allegro non tanto, Allegro con brio, Allegro con fuoco, Con moto passionato, Moto moderato, Con moto deciso, etc. The 'lament' is a basic aria for this composer, but unlike the pieces of the same type in the works of earlier opera composers, he breaks away from the adjacent interval style. He starts out from the lower part of the stave, and climbs up with wide intervals to a higher tessitura, thus giving a more ample line to the melody. This is what happens in the plangent, solemn aria sung by Placidia (soprano): 'Dove mai senza riposo' (*Alarico*); in Anfione's Largo: 'Dal mio petto pianti uscite' (*Niobe*); in the Largo sung by the protagonist (soprano) in *Briseide*: 'Una volta al fin saziatevi', with oboe and violin; and in another Largo, the delicate 'Ogni core può sperar' sung by Tanaquil (male soprano) in *Servio Tullio*. But even in the tender, affectionate, and graceful style, Steffani has a habit of giving the melody the pattern of vaulting leaps and a type of singing which embraces a very large part of the stave e.g. the 'sleep' aria sung by Sabina (soprano) in *Alarico*: 'Palpitanti sfere belle'; in *Niobe* the simple, graceful Andantino sung by Tiberino (tenor): 'Quanto, quanto sospirerai'; in *Il zelo di Leonato*, the 'doubt' aria sung by Clito ('Ondeggiando va quest'alma'), in which Steffani, using vocalises where the design develops in progression, with rising leaps and short pauses, gives a bass voice the waverings and hesitations of uncertainty.

Many of Steffani's arias are in ternary form, and some already show a structure which links them to the great eighteenth century *ABA* type aria, as in the Poco largo sung by Giasone (tenor): 'Deh, tornate, occhi stellanti' (*Le rivali concordi*), outstanding also for the unusual breadth and virtuosity of the central section. Anyone listening after that to the aria with trumpet in *Tassilone*, sung by Sicardo (male alto), 'A facile vittoria', or Adalgiso's tenor aria with oboe, 'Piangerete, ben lo so', will already have noticed an almost Handelian climate in the melodic invention, the behaviour of the concertante instrument, and the actual structure of the piece.

In conclusion, it can be said that Pallavicino, especially in *Gerusalemme liberata* (Dresden version, 1687), in which Armida was sung by the famous Margherita Salicoli, provides evidence of the technical progress made by the singers of the period in the way of speed of execution combined with a broadening of the vocalise passages, anticipating what was to be one of the effects most sought after by the vocalists of the first half of the eighteenth century—spectacular breathing capacity. On the other hand, Steffani, although at times he writes virtuoso passages, has as his basic aim melodies of a varied and quick-moving design, which give evidence of technical progress through the capacity of the executants to sustain tessituras which are probably the highest to be found between the end of the seventeenth century and the early years of the eighteenth century. Furthermore, the expansion of the vocal range introduced by Steffani is a novelty. Agamennone (tenor) in *Briseide* ('Dolce maga è la beltà') reaches b'. The male alto rises to e''; the (female) contralto voice, which following the precedent in Pollarolo's *Onorio in Roma* we find used also by Steffani in serious roles (Drusilla in *Servio Tullio* and Lavinia and Semiamira in *Turno*), sings up to d'', a note unusual at the time for that vocal register, and incidentally initiated by Steffani in *Turno*, with a fairly decided virtuosity (e.g. Semiamira's aria 'Placidette belle aurette', in imitation of the sighing of the wind). The male soprano and the female soprano, finally, while only ocasionally going beyond a'', sing this note more frequently than in the past. But above all, what is striking in Steffani is the grace and elegance with which heavy voices like those of the baritone-tenor and bass are made to perform lightly the graceful, tender type of aria and the accompanying coloratura. I have already mentioned the aria sung by Clito (bass), 'Ondeggiondo va quest'alma' from *Il zelo di Leonato*, which, although a 'doubt' aria, is typical of the graceful type of virtuosity. But even Pisone in *Alarico* (another role written by Steffani in the 'baritone clef', following Marc'Aurelio, and Polifemo in *Niobe*), is often asked for graceful-style singing and fairly rich coloratura. Steffani frequently gives the tenor, apart from the aria 'Piangerete, ben lo so', already cited as sung by Adalgiso in *Alarico*,[15] an elegiac grace (this too is unusual) which allows him to sing love-songs: for example, Tanaqui in *Servio Tullio*, Tiberino in *Niobe*, Almaro in *Henrico Leone*, and even more notably, Giasone in *Le rivali concordi* and Aeneas in *Turno* (cf. the slow-moving duet between Aeneas and Lavinia 'Del bell'idol che adoro'). It is also possible to state, quite apart from what Handel owed to his example, that Steffani, along with Alessandro Scarlatti, is the late seventeenth early eighteenth-century composer closest to the Golden Age of bel canto singing.

SCARLATTI

Between Alessandro Scarlatti and Steffani, although they were working in very different surroundings, there are many analogies to be found. First and foremost, there is a certain affinity in their use of recitative. According to Dent,[16] Scarlatti first used recitative with instruments in *Olimpia vendicata* (1685): ('Quanto, quanto tardate', sung by Bireno, male alto). Steffani uses it, as we have seen, in *Niobe*, produced in Munich three years later. Apart from this, Scarlatti's use of recitative, either accompanied or *secco*, frequently reflects Steffani's leaning towards tautness and vigour. For

---

[15] A gramophone recording version of this aria, by the tenor Peter Schreier, was issued by Telefunken about 1965. Anyone who knows it might have reason to doubt what I am saying if I did not point out that the performance is very poor. Schreier not only shows an extraordinary lack of sensibility towards the variety of stresses, colours, and nuances, but also a dilettante technical approach which makes his voice hard and at times strident, and also runs counter to the correct way of singing vocalises. The fact that subsequently this tenor was able to find admirers even among Italians is due simply to the provincialism of a coterie which kowtows to him as an interpreter of Lieder and a tenor who appears at Salzburg in performances of Mozart. If this is anything to go by, Schreier also sings his Lieder badly and is not fit to sing Mozart.

[16] E. Dent, *A. Scarlatti*, London, 1905.

example, Rosiclea's recitative in *Anacreonte* (a youthful work, written in 1689), beginning 'Destino, amor', uses the same procedure as Steffani of carrying the soprano voice vigorously and with wide intervals from the middle register to the first of the high notes. In recitative, Scarlatti is more varied than Steffani. In *Mitridate Eupatore*, he actually achieves chromatic recitative in Laodice's 'O vacua speme!' (III); but even earlier, in *Rosaura* (1690), after the first part of the Largo sung by the protagonist ('Se delitto è l'adorarvi'), he had inserted the vibrant recitative 'Ma che non hai vendette'.

An even closer analogy between Steffani and Scarlatti is in the similar way they have of starting certain arias. Steffani's practice of starting out, in fast-moving arias ('vengeance', 'scorn', etc.), with an ascending scale is also found in Scarlatti, for example in the Allegro sung by Stratonica (soprano) in *Mitridate Eupatore*, 'Esci ormai'. But even more frequently to be found in both of them is the aria initiated by a very short phrase—a sort of rough statement of the theme—which is then held up for one or two bars of instrumental playing to be taken up again and developed, as in the aria sung by Climene (soprano), 'Un ruscello puro e bello' from *Pirro* (Ex. 7). This opera dates from 1694, but Scarlatti had used a

Ex. 7

Un ru — scel — lo pu—roe bel—lo

un ru — scel — lo pu—roe bel—lo de—stain me

similar procedure, likewise very common in Steffani, as early as 1680, in *L'honestà negli amori*,[17] and he was to use it very frequently until *Scipione nelle Gallie* (1714), in the Allegro 'Amor per sospirar' sung by Marzio (male alto).

Another point in common between Scarlatti and Steffani is their fairly realistic imitation—although only used sporadically—of certain human behaviour traits. In Steffani, as we have seen, a

[17] Steffani too uses it in his first opera, *Marc'Aurelio*, 1681, in Faustina's Larghetto 'Sei si' caro'. Hugo Riemann, referring only to Steffani, speaks of 'Devisen-Arie' in the sense that the first phrase (or, in some cases even a single word, in isolation) acts as a 'motto' or 'signature tune' (*Devise*) (cf. *Denkmäler der Tonkunst in Bayern*, Munich, 1911–12).

typical example is the death of Anfione in *Niobe*, while in Scarlatti, with the help of pauses and repetitions, we get a description of mental confusion in the recitative sung by Valerio (male alto) in *La caduta dei Decemviri*: 'Io/Io/Io vaneggio . . .' (II. xii). Furthermore, in certain arias expressing scorn, vengeance, jealousy, threat, war, Scarlatti equals Steffani in vigour—and perhaps goes beyond him—using fairly similar devices: wide vaulting leaps in syllabic singing and in vocalises; rapid ascending scales; moments when the melody takes on an almost declamatory character; and at times fairly high tessituras. It is mostly in soprano parts that Scarlatti puts these procedures into practice, the result being strong, aggressive female figures. An example is the protagonist in *Rosaura*, singing the 'jealousy' aria 'Per vostro onor, un fulmine' and 'Su, su, mio core, alle stragi', where the coloratura passages have moments of great vehemence, with the help of ascending and descending scales. Similarly, Stratonica in *Mitridate Eupatore* has rapid, excited vocalise passages in the Allegro 'Quante furie', while Isifile in *Anacreonte* is a positively bellicose heroine, as in the aria with trumpet 'Guerra! guerra!'.

Tempestuous recitatives and vigorous and warlike arias are sung fairly frequently also by male characters, and if we relate this to certain features of Steffani's writing and to Pallavicino's *Gerusalemme liberata*, we must assume that in the last twenty years of the seventeenth century and the first few years of the eighteenth century, Italian singers were showing signs of what later became an urge towards a theatrical and in a way emphatic approach. On the other hand, Scarlatti, like Steffani, makes expressiveness the basic aim of opera composer and interpreter alike. Historians who have dealt with Scarlatti's operatic work have made much of a letter of his dated 1706, identifying the purpose of the composer with the desire to 'move and stir the emotions of the listener to the diversity of feelings underlying the various episodes of the drama', and likewise of a *Discorso di musica sopra un caso particolare* (1717) in which the composer stresses the interplay between the tune and the words as the ideal means of 'stirring the emotions'.

Scarlatti expands the horizons of executants in an even more obvious manner than Steffani. Like the latter, he lifts his singers up to higher tessituras because his melodic design is more expansive and varied than that of the opera composers of the preceding generations and hence spreads over a larger area of the stave. But more than Steffani he emphasizes the structure of the aria to obtain variety and to express 'diversity of feelings'. It is understandable that for a long time Scarlatti was regarded as the father of the great ternary aria, although actually he was not the inventor of it. But there is no doubt that among the opera composers of his time he is the one who, both expressively and in substance, gives the greatest variety to this type of aria, with its change of tempo in the middle section, and at times even a change of key, and the other two sections in some instances acquiring an unusual breadth. Scarlatti also strengthens the function of the orchestra. He gives greater breathing space to the ritornelli; he expands the field of the aria with concertante instrument, and he accentuates, in the violins, iteration or virtuoso imitation of the singing. In addition, Scarlatti gives many of the arias breathing space by using phrases stated first in a short and simple form and taken up again immediately afterwards and elaborated both in design and in coloratura, and also by raising the voice gradually in pitch. An example of this is the aria sung by Rosiclea: 'Verrò a tormentarti' (Ex. 8) from *Anacreonte*; but such cases are extremely numerous in Scarlatti both when young and in his mature years.

Ex. 8

Ver – rò   ver – rò a   tor – men – tar – ti   ver – rò a   tor – men –

tar-ti coi   ser–pi d'A – let   –   –   –   –   to

Thus we arrive at a symmetry of design which gives the aria a throroughly rounded character. Scarlatti is also helped to achieve this by making much more use than his predecessors of repeated words or phrases and by releasing ornamentation and coloratura from ties with words having a lyrical or a solemn or a 'tempo' significance. Thus he will write passages with vocalises even on articles, conjunctions, and adverbs. Furthermore, his melismata and vocalises tend towards a less literal imitation of the meaning of courtly words and towards a broader and more complex description of natural phenomena. This is important, because the melody unfolds more freely and fancifully, with melismata not conditioned by rigid imitative formulas but more imaginative, and more in keeping with the actual character.

Mention has been made of the shape of many recitatives, and of the vigour of many of the arias expressing vengeance, fury, jealousy, whether syllabic in style or virtuosic, or a mixture of the two. We must also underline the brilliance of the arias with trumpet, which are extremely numerous; and we must give due credit to a certain trend towards the expression of pathos, from the farewell scene sung by Deidamia (soprano), in *Pirro e Demetrio* ('Germano, germano, addio' (III. xvi) to the lament by Laodicea (soprano) in *Mitridate Eupatore*, which is one of the prototypes of the 'tomb' aria and the 'funeral' aria ('Cara tomba del mio diletto').

But we must nevertheless not forget that Scarlatti lived through the Arcadian epoch, and that this brought about a link between his inspiration and the 'comparison' aria, hinging on pastoral and bucolic elements: flowers, streams, plants, turtle-doves, nightingales. And it is with Scarlatti that the imitation of nature in Baroque opera is accentuated by the vocal melody. In *Carlo re d'Allemagna* (1716) we find one of the prototypes of the 'tempest' aria ('Sono in mar con ria procella', sung by Giuditta, soprano); but the imitation of a storm is already to be found in *Tutto il mal non vien per nuocere* (1681) sung by Doralba (soprano), in 'Son di scoglio se il ciel lo combatte'; and earlier still, in *Honestà negli amori* (1680), sung by Rosmira (contralto), 'Scogli voi che v'indurate/ all'urtar d'onde frementi'). The 'tempest' aria in *Carlo re d'Allemagna* anticipates procedures which soon afterwards were to be used by many composers: vocalises sometimes long, sometimes interrupted by pauses, sometimes stepwise, sometimes characterized by ascending leaps.

But far more frequent are the arias which have rustic, country features as their starting-point. *Gli equivoci nel sembiante* (1679) already presents the delicate, pastoral melody sung by Eurillo (tenor), 'Più del nascente sol vaghi splendori'; but everywhere we come across melodies and coloratura formulas which imitate the wind and streams: from 'Aure leggere, fermate il volo', sung by Lucilda (soprano) in *Tutto il mal non vien per nuocere* (1681) to 'Aure, voi che mormorando' sung by Lotario (male contralto) in *Carlo re d'Allemagna* (1716); from 'Acque limpide che mormorando' sung by Alcidamia (soprano) in *Clearco in Negroponte* (1686) to 'Un ruscello puro e bello', sung by Climene (soprano) in *Pirro e Demetrio* (1694). Or again, ariettas inspired by flowers, like the famous 'Le violette' from *Pirro e Demetrio*, or 'Il giglio nel prato', sung by Beraldo (tenor), in *Carlo re d'Allemagna*. And finally, melodies imitating the flight of the butterfly ('Farfalletta che avvampa le piume', sung by Olindo (tenor) in *Tutto il mal*; the cooing turtle-dove ('Tortorella che d'amore', from *Rosmene* 1686, sung by Rosaura, soprano); the nightingale which pours forth its notes ('O! sentite quel rossignolo,' sung by Avilda (soprano) in *Le nozze con l'inimico*, 1695), and finally, the groans of the thirsty stag ('Come in traccia di fiume distante', sung by the protagonist (soprano) in *Rosaura*, 1690). Still more common in Scarlatti is the 'love' aria or arietta, which ranges from the jocular or capricious ('Se Florindo è fedele' or the Siciliana 'Non mi tradir mai più' sung by Lisaura in *La donna ancora è fedele*) to the pathos of 'Son tutta duolo' (again from *La donna ancora è fedele*) or from 'Vanne crudo e al dolor mio' (*Tutto il mal non vien per nuocere*) to 'S'ha da penare, povero core', in *Scipione nelle Gallie*. Amorous skirmishing, courtship, hyperbole in praise of the beauty of the beloved, take up most of the space in Scarlatti's opera technique, at times taking the form of plain or only slightly ornate melodies, at others of vocalises. This is the sentimental, gallant style that occupies the centre of the stage in Baroque opera and dominates it. At the same time the number of certain types of aria which are extremely common in Venetian opera tends to decline, one reason being that the characters are fewer. The 'sleep' aria and the 'conjuration' aria (of the type 'Orridi spettri di Cocytus', sung by Asteria (soprano), in *Clearco in Negroponte*) are rare, as are also 'doubt' arias, which do, however, retain their virtuoso character: ('Messagiero son di pace' sung by Adrasto (male soprano) in *Clearco*). On the other hand, there is real development in the direction of duets, trios, quartets, and also buffo roles.

With regard to the writing and types of voice, Scarlatti is less prone than Steffani to give the singers very high notes to sing. The a″ for soprano and male soprano, e″ for contralto and male alto, a′ for tenor, f′ for bass are, generally speaking, the ceilings set. The protagonist in *Griselda*, a soprano, who sings a b″, is an exceptional case, related, moreover, to a period (the opera dates from 1721) when lifting the vocal range higher was a fairly general trend. But like Steffani, Scarlatti does raise the tessituras. Moreover, he tends fairly often, in *stile concitato* arias, to make sopranos and male sopranos attack high notes (g″, a″) uncovered. In coloratura, the use of long vocalises is fairly frequent, but not systematic. In the operas of his mature years, however, Scarlatti's writing is more virtuosic than that of Pallavicino or Steffani. This is particularly true of the male alto (Alfo in *L'amazzone corsara*, Elmiro in *Rosaura*, Muzio in *Scipione nelle Gallie*, Adalgiso in *Carlo re d'Allemagna*) and of the female contralto voice which Scarlatti uses in serious roles as early as *Honesta negli amori* (1680, role of Rosmira) and carries to an unusual level of virtuosity for this type of voice with Cunegonda in *La principessa fedele*.

Scarlatti makes a somewhat elastic use of the tenor voice. He uses it for the role of lover in the early operas (Eurillo in *Equivoci nel sembiante*, Rosanno in *Honestà negli amori*, Olindo in *Tutto il mal*, Celindo in *Rosaura*); and in similar instances he too, like Steffani, uses this voice for light, graceful singing and at tessituras fairly high for the period.[18] Love-songs and virtuosity are also asked of some tenors in the later operas (the title-role in *Scipione nelle Spagne*, Berardo in *Carlo re d'Allemagna*). However, already in *Honestà negli amori*, the tenor is used for a buffo role as an old man, and in many later operas he appears *en travesti* as a nurse or old procuress; and in *Anacreonte*, the tenor in the title-role plays the part of a tyrant.

Likewise the bass, who appears in serious roles in the early operas, sometimes with a fairly high tessitura (e.g. Anassacro in *Anacreonte*) subsequently plays buffo parts. Finally, it may be recalled that in Scarlatti's operas written for the San Bartolomeo theatre in Naples, women frequently appear dressed as men: Simando in *Emireno*, the protagonist in *Muzio Scevola*, Evandro in *Il prigionero fortunato*, Oronte in *Gli inganni felici*, Decio in *Eraclea*, Mario in *Tito Sempronio Gracco*, and even Quinto Trebellio in *Scipione nelle Spagne* and Argiro in *Cambise*. Some of these roles were played by sopranos, others by contraltos. The use of *travesti* roles was a feature of the performances at the San Bartolomeo

[18] As regards range, a quite unusual case is that of the tenor in *Honestà negli amori* (Alì), who reaches a‴ on top and touches bottom G in the duet with Elisa, 'Dite amanti'.

theatre until the end of 1730, and this also included operas by Giovanni Bononcini, Porpora, Sarro, Hasse, Vinci, and Leo.

THE GOLDEN AGE: FROM LOTTI TO HANDEL

The explosion of great vocalism in the first half of the eighteenth century involved a combination of factors: the great schools of singing of Pistocchi, Porpora, and Bernacchi; the appearance of librettists like Zeno and Metastasio; and the fundamental and decisive contribution of a few opera composers. At the outset, however, it would be fair to cite as a factor in the initial impulse of this bel canto period the libretto writing of Apostolo Zeno, Pietro Metastasio, and their followers and imitators. The reasons for this can be summarized as follows: simplification of the plots which Roman and Venetian Baroque opera had inherited from the Spanish spoken theatre; a drastic reduction both in the number of characters (as a rule limited to seven in Zeno and to six in Metastasio) and in the number of arias; the tendency to hark back to classical drama; a characteristic solemn and courtly manner, especially in Zeno, with illustrations of moral principles governing in particular the conduct of kings and heroes and with political statements (in both, but more especially in Metastasio) which lean towards the glorification of the reigning dynasties and sing the praise of their loyal and obedient subjects.

This engendered characters more profoundly drawn than those of seventeenth-century opera (with the exception of Monteverdi), or at least more given to analysing their own feelings and their own actions both in recitatives and in arias. This in itself is a good reason for widening the scope of the arias; but above all it should be remembered that, with a reduction of the number of set pieces in Baroque opera of the Venetian school, the aria automatically had to expand its structure and increase its length so as to fill space left empty. Furthermore, the greater psychological insight into situations, the more historical and more courtly stamp put on certain characters, the bitter conflict between duty and personal feelings with which princes and heroes have to struggle before duty wins the day, give arias in particular—but set pieces in general—a charge of pathos which automatically stimulates both the inspiration of the composer and the talent of the interpreter. Furthermore, the greater subtlety in the analysis of feelings has repercussions on the coloratura, rendering it more fanciful in the patterns designed to imitate the emotional ups and downs and the outbursts of passion in the human soul. In addition, the courtly or epic stamp of the personages and the affirmation of lofty moral principles likewise find an outlet first of all in the melody and then in the shape of the melismatic patterns, which become more and more complex and intricate as the state of mind to be expressed is more unusual. In a word, the area where Baroque and Arcadian are assimilated, and specifically the inspiration thus brought to the ecstatic contemplation and imitation of nature, finds expression in Zeno, but still more in Metastasio and other librettists, through the wholesale use of metaphors calculated to depict the state of mind of a personage through comparison with natural facts or phenomena: bird-song and the flight of birds; the colour and scent of flowers; the beauty of a plant, a meadow, a wood; the sighing of the wind; the gentle flow or the flooding of a river; storms and the fate of ships tossed by the waves. We have already seen how metaphors abound in Alessandro Scarlatti; In later composers, metaphor or 'parable' often gives a boost to bolder and more fanciful imitation, arising either out of the poetic text or from the bravura of the new singers—bravura here in the sense also of imagination in improvising and embellishing. There is, after all, no doubt—and we shall see this above all in Handel—that at certain moments fantasy on the part of the composer and fantasy in the interpreter are communicating vessels, as are also, more than ever, instrumental virtuosity and vocal virtuosity.

The new libretto-writing also involves structural innovations. Zeno introduces opera finales with chorus (whereas the chorus is of minor importance in Metastasio); he makes it a general rule to have two pairs of lovers; he classifies arias into three main categories (action-filled, metaphorical, and moral); he assigns to each personage a fixed number of arias; and he stipulates that two arias of the same type may not be sung one after the other, not even by different characters. Metastasio, on the other hand, using the more or less fixed pattern of starting with a recitative and finishing with an aria in any given scene, was to create more emotional plots, constructed by inserting imaginary episodes into historical events. He showed great ability in driving heroes and heroines to the edge of catastrophe only to return to the inevitable happy ending.[19] His penchant was for love episodes and their analysis, whereas Zeno tended to regard love as an effeminate sentiment. He had the determination and the ability to win the plaudits of the public, and was guided by a sound view of the basic characteristics of theatrical poetry and opera, based on the firm conviction that 'enjoyment on the part of the spectators arises from imitation, in other words from admiration of the artful representation of the truth executed in a false setting'. Finally, unlike Zeno, Metastasio wrote verse of such exceptional musical fluency that his very poetry seemed to suggest melodic ideas to the composer.

Three composers form a bridge between Scarlatti and the period dominated by Vinci, Handel, and Hasse, in other words the Golden Age. These are Antonio Lotti, Giovanni Bononcini, and Nicolò Porpora. Lotti is mainly to be remembered for the effectiveness and grandeur of certain recitatives such as 'Preso dal tuo rival per ingannarmi', sung by Teofane in *Ottone* (II. v). In addition, he was one of the earliest opera composers to write, in Venice and in Dresden between 1713 and 1718, for singers who shortly afterwards were to appear with success in first performances of Handel and Hasse: the male alto Francesco Bernardi, known as Il Senesino; the bass Giuseppe Maria Boschi; and the contralto Faustina Bordoni. The group of singers for whom Lotti composed included other historical figures: the soprano Marianna Bulgarelli Benti, the contralto Vittoria Tesi Tramontini, the tenor Giovanni Paita, and the soprano Santa Stella, who was Lotti's wife. Stella was, naturally, one of the interpreters for whom Lotti wrote most frequently. The celebrated flautist Johann Quantz, who heard her in Dresden, noted in a book of reminiscences[20] that Stella was a fine actress and had a robust voice, an excellent trill, and unexceptionable intonation. But her range was limited at the top end. Her strong point was the expression of pathos and adagio singing. Quantz adds that from her singing he heard, for the first time, the use of 'tempo rubato'. At times Lotti wrote, always for his wife, vocalises which covered, with rests, as many as ten bars (as for example in *Ascanio*, where Stella played the part of Silvia), but with figurations mostly in adjacent interval style and sometimes coldly instrumental. More frequent, however,

---

[19] Exceptions are *Didone abbandonata* and *Catone in Utica.*
[20] *Lebenslauf von ihm selbt entworfen*, Berlin, 1755.

among the arias written for Stella are those of a serious, energetic type, occasionally adorned with a rather expressive coloratura (e.g. 'Falsa immagine', sung by Teofane in *Ottone*). Even more expressive is the coloratura in the 'farewell' aria sung by Sallustia: 'Padre, addio, addio' in *Alessandro Severo*, written for Faustina Bordoni. Here, actually, a vocalise marks the main introduction to the long, pathos-filled melody (see Ex. 9). This coloratura, however, is much simpler than would have been devised for Bordoni by Hasse, who was her husband, let alone by Handel.

Ex. 9

Bononcini's vocal writing is exemplified best of all by the Neapolitan version (1697) of one of his best operas—*Il trionfo di Camilla*, produced for the first time in Vienna in 1696. The Naples performance was entrusted to singers who were famous, though not yet inured to the audacious virtuosity of the decades immediately following: Vittoria Tarquini, known as La Bombace, soprano (Camilla); Domenico Cecchi, known as Il Cortona, male soprano (Turno); Barbara Riccione, known as La Romanina, soprano (Lavinia); and Maddalena Musi, known as La Mignatti, soprano (Prenesto). Antonio Predieri, on the other hand, appeared as a buffo tenor *en travesti* in the role of the nurse Tullia. One curious detail: in the score, the names given opposite the individual arias are not those of the characters portrayed but the professional names of the singers.

There was no novelty, as compared with Scarlatti and Steffani,

in regard to tessitura or vocal range. But what is at once noteworthy is the symmetrical shape of the phrases, which often tend
to be of exactly the same length and even to develop in a fairly
rigid system of progressions. Bononcini also has a predilection, in
his melodic design, for adjacent or small intervals, and this is one
of the reasons why his cantabile expresses spontaneity of
utterance and singular elegiac tenderness. Examples are 'Sí sí, mi
basta amor', sung by Prenesto (Ex. 10), and other arias by the same
character ('Io vo' cercando gioia e trovo affanni', 'Cara sí, tu mi
consumi'), or Turno's 'Se vedi il mar senz' onda'. But what

Ex. 10

increases the sense of lightness of touch and pathos in certain
arias of a tender nature is the fact that the melody, largely syllabic,
either goes into short vocalises at the end of each phrase, like an
arabesque left hovering over the singing, or introduces an
'elaborate coloratura', from time to time fitting to each syllable a
triplet, a four-note phrase, or irregular groups of three notes.

Arias in quick-moving tempo and expressing feelings of energy
likewise emerge from the syllabic style, but with rapid and usually
short vocalise passages on typical expressions or words: *saettate,
empietà, vendetta* (in the 'rage' aria 'Tutte armate di flagelli', sung by
Prenesto) or *face, dardo, alma,* as in 'Amore m'infiamma col lampo
d'un guardo', again sung by Prenesto. At times the vocalise is
made more incisive by dotted rhythm ('Tiranna gelosia', sung by
Turno). Even in Allegro passages the coloratura tends to keep the
symmetry of progressions and the stepwise development.
Example 11, taken from the Allegro 'Mi lusingo e l'alma spera', is
typical of Bononcini's writing: triplets on each syllable; ascent in
progression through the first phrase, with a falling interval of a
fifth at the end (on the word 'alma'), which unexpectedly inter-
rupts the uniformity of the melodic line; then descent in progres-

Ex. 11

Mi lu – sin – go e l'al – ma spe – ra
ch'è men fie – ra la mia sor – te in que – sto dí

sion and always in adjacent intervals in the third, fourth, and fifth bars.

If we now move forward twenty-five years and look at Bononcini in London at the height of his fame, we note that his ability to write simple, elegant, tender melodies, and his characteristic way of writing, have in the meantime become refined. But Bononcini is now writing for singers belonging to the *nouvelle vague* and of historic stature. He is writing for Francesca Cuzzoni, the first great high soprano in history and one whose leaning towards sensuous, languid emotion is splendidly echoed in the Andante sung by the protagonist in *Calpurnia*: 'Se perdo il caro ben' (1724). Henceforward tessituras are higher, as compared with *Il trionfo di Camilla*, but in all instances the melody is very legato, sweetly flowing, with the odd wide interval interrupting the stepwise gait and with the vocalise formula at the end of the phrase which, apart from being perfectly in keeping with the melody, hints capriciously at the high 'curtailed note' a. This was a trick typical of Cuzzoni's singing style (Ex. 12).

Ex. 12

Andante con spirito

Se per – do il ca – ro ben ch'è gio – ia
del mio cor. Non bra – mo più ria –
mar

Not even *Griselda*, perhaps the most famous of Bononcini's operas, gets away from this type of writing. The orchestra has ample space in the ritornelli, the ternary aria now shows more typical dimensions, but Bononcini's tender melancholy is expressed through the usual linear type of writing in two arias sung by Ernesto (male soprano), 'Non deggio no sperar' and 'Troppo è il dolore', and in one or two arias by the protagonist, among them 'Parto, amabile ben mio' and the lament 'Dal mio petto ogni pace smarrita'. In turn, gallantry is expressed in the famous aria 'Per la gloria d'adorarvi' sung by Ernesto; the 'sleep' aria sung by Gualtiero ('Dolce sonno deh le porta', with flute) is light and affectionate; and the 'hunt' aria, also sung by Gualtiero (male alto), 'Le fere a risvegliar', is in turn a model of its kind, energetic in rhythm, with robust agility passages kept in strict relationship with the melodic line, and with excellent orchestration. Rambaldo's 'doubt' aria, the Vivace 'Timore e speme', preserves the traditional virtuoso structure, even though given to a bass (who is called upon, among other things, to execute rapid ascending scales in succession); while a tribute to Arcadia is paid, in graceful style, in the duet between Ernesto and Almirena (soprano), 'Quel timoroso cervo cacciato'. Always, however, Bononcini preserves his legato line, its symmetry, and the capacity to cope with the phrasing and pauses, bearing in mind the lung power of the executant. From the strictly vocal point of view, he writes best among the composers of the first half of the eighteenth century, and Handel borrowed from him a number of patterns, and indeed from time to time the odd tune.

Nicolò Porpora is the first of the well-known composers to tackle virtuosity in the grand manner. As one of the most illustrious singing teachers of all time, he had extremely famous pupils, as for example the soprano Regina Valentini Mingotti and the castrati Giuseppe Appiani, Antonio Hubert, known as Il Porporino, Gaetano Majorana, known as Caffarelli, and finally Carlo Broschi, known as Farinelli, regarded as the greatest singer in the whole of operatic history.

Porpora's vocal virtuosity as an opera composer is closely bound up with the exceptional abilities of his pupils and other famous performers; and if the luxuriant coloratura does not succeed in concealing a certain banality, not to say poverty of melodic invention, in the realm of expressiveness, the writing is nevertheless a sort of anthology of patterns of great difficulty as well as a set of stylistic guidelines. In the Largos and Andantes of the best-known operas (which incidentally are few), Porpora adheres to the rule, which later became universal, of keeping the voice in the middle of its range. The melody begins ornate (turns written out, trills and mordents); it proceeds molto legato; and towards the middle of the first section it goes into short vocalise passages, mostly interspersed with a whole series of trills. The second section changes tempo and rhythm. A Lento in common time may, for example, turn into an Andante in 3/8 time. In this second section the style is syllabic, and the ornamentation is reduced to the odd acciaccatura and a few trills. Variations in the da capo section are left to the singer.

As regards marks of expression, Porpora makes frequent use of *p* and *f*. He also codifies the rule of the *messa di voce* at the beginning. On the first note of the Lento 'Alto Giove' in *Polifemo* (the role of Acis was written for Farinelli), Porpora wrote a fermata. This meant that the singer was to execute a full *messa di voce*, attacking the sound pianissimo, gradually swelling it until it reached fortissimo, then in the same way gradually softening it; immediately afterwards, without taking a breath, he had to execute the first phrase, which in the case of 'Alto Giove' consists of five lento bars in 4/4 time (the singers of the school of Porpora may have been the ones who introduced this practice, which was subsequently largely applied even in the absence of indications by the composer).[21] The *messa di voce* was of course also executed on other occasions, and in the eighteenth century its importance was enormous. It was regarded as a demonstration of tenderness, of breath power, and of the volume level of a singer, and it corresponded in some respects to the stroke of the bow (*cavata*) on a bowed instrument.

In rapid tempos, Porpora has recourse to long vocalise passages in which the succession of four-note phrases or irregular groups is studded with trills or interrupted by upward and downward leaps, and by repeated ascending and descending scales. Fairly frequently

---

[21] Later came the introduction, always at the beginning of the piece, of a *messa di voce*, trilled or changed into a trill at the end of the held note. The only singer of the present day with any understanding of this procedure is the mezzo-soprano Marilyn Horne, who uses it in Handel arias and in 'Elena, o tu che adoro' from Rossini's *La donna del lago*.

there are acciaccaturas, simple and double, mordents, and written-out turns. Among the most spectacular Allegro arias in Porpora's works may be mentioned 'Senti il fato', sung by Acis in *Polifemo*, and 'Destrier che all'armi usato', sung by Poro in the opera of that name. Both these arias were composed for Farinelli, but Porpora's tendency to write music of high virtuosity is to be found also at times in arias written for singers who did not belong to his school. For example, in the aria 'Sprezzando il suol' from *Enea*, Porpora writes for Francesca Cuzzoni (who was not an acrobatic soprano in the full sense of the word) a coloratura aria which, for length of vocalises and variety of figurations, is more difficult than any normally designed for this singer by Bononcini or by Handel.

Leonardo Vinci will be remembered, as far as vocalism is concerned, for three things. He was perhaps the most important popularizer of what we might define as 'agitated' style, which represented for the interpreters between 1730 and 1740 one of the high points of expressiveness. It consisted of dotted rhythms associated with a semi-syllabic type of singing, which abounded in acciaccaturas written out and gave the phrasing a syncopated movement and a sense of anxiety. This procedure was common to a number of opera composers in the first half of the eighteenth century, including Pergolesi and Hasse. It is the style that some Baroque opera scholars like to define as 'sensitive'. One of the most striking examples is Arbace's aria 'Per quel paterno amplesso' from *Artaserse*, written for Giovanni Carestini (Ex. 13),

Ex. 13

where in fact the figure ♫ corresponds to ♫. A sense of perturbation and anxiety could also be created by a second form, used in another of Arbace's arias, 'Mi scacci sdegnato' (Ex. 14).

The second aspect of Vinci's composition was incisive, vehement melody even in instances of vocal writing not bound up

Ex. 14

with the 'sensitive' style. *Artaserse* contains many arias of this type, often built up on phrases which start out with stepwise movement, only to rise or fall suddenly with a wide ascending or descending interval. The use of wide intervals was in fact typical of Vinci's 'agitated style'. We may recall, still in *Artaserse*, the Allegro 'Non ti son padre', sung by Artabano (tenor); Arbace's Presto 'Fra cento affanni e cento'; and two arias sung by Mandane (male soprano *en travesti*), the Allegro 'Conservati fedele' and the Andante 'Mi credi spietata'. The same is true of the aria sung by Cleofide (soprano), 'Se il ciel mi divide' in *Alessandro nelle Indie*.

Finally, the third aspect: what was most striking in Vinci was imitative virtuosity, particularly in 'tempest' arias. The Presto 'Vo solcando un mar crudele', sung by Arbace in *Artaserse*, presents a dazzling coloratura in which descending scales alternate with rising leaps, and long vocalise passages in groups of four quavers alternate with others in triplets of quavers, which follow one after another, embellished by trills and interrupted by rests, fluctuating between the upper part and the middle of the stave. Impressive again is 'Navigante che non spera' from *Medo*, an Andante written in a very deep contralto tessitura for Farinelli. The coloratura for the most part occupies the octave f–f' (an altogether exceptional case). The voice descends actually to c flat, and an alternating series of rising and falling scales, upward and downward leaps, and long vocalises in semiquaver pairs and triplets imitates the tempest at one moment and the changing moods of the personage at the next. In both cases (but particularly in the second) we reach the peak of virtuosity, with Vinci quite obviously taking advantage of the exceptional abilities of Carestini and Farinelli.

Johann Adolph Hasse was able, like Vinci, to call upon a standard of singing which from the point of view of technique and expressive capacity was at its very peak. Even more than Vinci, Hasse had the opportunity to write for the best singers of the time, from Bernacchi to Farinelli, from Bernardi to Cuzzoni, from Bordoni (who was his wife) to Amorevoli and a number of others.

But this did not make him push virtuosity to the level of audacity reached in places by Vinci and other composers of the period—most of them minor composers. Hasse is regarded first and foremost as the most fluent and limpid melody-maker of the period following that of Giovanni Bononcini, but with certain differences from Bononcini. First of all, Hasse's way of writing vocal music is less bound up with stepwise, adjacent-interval style, perhaps in part because it is linked to a type of melody which in embryo seems to arise out of the prosody of the poetic text (regularly written by Metastasio). Secondly, the coloratura is more complex and varied. Thirdly, he shares with Vinci the acciaccaturas and the dotted rhythms of the 'sensitive' style.

If we compare him with Vinci, Hasse does not have the same vehemence and passion in his melodies; but he is has the edge in grace and elegance, in the tender, elegiac style, to which frequently he brings a decided sense of nobility. His vocalises, moreover, fairly frequently emanate directly from the melody. This is the case, for example, of the Adagio 'Per questo dolce amplesso' sung by Arbace in *Artaserse* (1730), a famous prototype of the Metastasian 'farewell' aria. The role of Arbace was written for Farinelli, for whom Hasse also composed the aria 'Fra cento affanni e cento' (Ex. 15), a typical melody which at the start follows the prosody of the poetic text.

Ex. 15

Fra cent'af – fan—ni e cen-to   pal–pi–to, tre-mo   e   sen –to

A high level of virtuosity is achieved in another aria sung by Arbace: 'Parto qual pastorello', with great upward leaps and a range which stretches from a to c′′′. Hasse's writing, did not, however, exploit all the acrobatic possibilities of Farinelli, who in the performances of *Artaserse* that took place in London in 1734 inserted arias written by his brother Ricardo Broschi, among them 'Son qual nave' (Allegro assai) which presents a succession of trills, ribattutas, ascending and descending scales, and vocalises running to as many as fifteen bars. Again in Hasse's *Artaserse*, the Moderato 'Conservati fedele' (Mandane), written for Francesca Cuzzoni, exemplifies the noble-pathetic style, while 'Pallido il sole' (written for the male alto Nicolò Grimaldi) is in its extreme simplicity one of the most heartfelt melodies in any opera of the first half of the eighteenth century (Ex. 16).

EX. 16

In *Demetrio* (1732), Alceste's Allegro 'Scherza il nocchier talora' is, like 'Fra cento affanni e cento' from *Artaserse*, an example of an aria which starts out from a syllabic beginning to become a virtuoso piece as it goes along. The coloratura of this 'tempest' aria, written for the celebrated male alto Bernacchi, seems to favour the light, elegant style which some of his contemporaries attribute to him. Noteworthy likewise in *Demetrio* are a number of arias full of pathos, including the Moderato 'Nacqui agli affanni in seno' (Ex. 17), sung by Cleonice and written for Faustina Bordoni Hasse. Here the Bononcini style is recognizable. This aria also

EX. 17

shows what the lament had become in the 1730s since the days of Cavalli: a melody which takes shape immediately and then, instead of vocalises on long notes which unwind very, very slowly in close-knit intervals, shows us a coloratura, at once symmetrical and wayward, built up on a series of short trills (mordents), in ribattuta form, written to show off the lightness and legendary elegance with which Bordoni performed them (Ex. 18).

Another opera to be remembered is *Semiramide* (1744), for the graceful style of the title-role, although sung by a deep contralto (Vittoria Tesi Tramontini, another singer who made history) in the

Ex. 18

Andante 'Non so se più m'accendi'; for the simple elegiac style of
the Adagio 'Ardo per te d'amore', a Metastasian-type 'declaration
of love' aria written to be sung by Scitalci, the character played by
Giovanni Carestini; for the vigour of 'Tu mi disprezzi, ingrato',
sung by Tamiri (contralto); and for the incredible imitative
virtuosity of a 'comparison' aria (the Allegro assai 'Talor se il vento
freme', imitative in its great leaps, its succession of short trills, and
its 'curtailed notes'. This aria, be it noted, is entrusted not to a
castrato but to a tenor, one of the best of the period—Ottavio
Albuzzi (playing Ircano). But much more difficult, for length of
vocalises, rapidity of figurations, wide range (from f to b♭′, almost
certainly sung in *falsettone*), is the 'tempest' aria from *Arminio* (the
Dresden version, 1745), written for Angelo Amorevoli, the
greatest virtuoso among the baritone-tenors of the first half of the
eighteenth century, in this opera playing the part of the father
(Segeste). In *Arminio*, Hasse's solemn pathos found its place in the
'repentance' aria sung by Tusnelda: the Andante 'No, genitor, non
voglio'. Tusnelda was played by Bordoni, who was also given the
languorous Andantino 'Desio che nel seno', another example of
coloratura closely linked to the melody.

In a word, Hasse represents in the vocal art of Baroque opera a
balance between cantabile style and melismatic style. But he is
probably also the composer whose melody-writing best expresses
both the 'imitative' qualities demanded of an opera composer of
his period and the fluency of Metastasio's verses. This is the
general view of his contemporaries, who in Italy and in Germany
placed him ahead of any other opera composer. The clarity and
simplicity of the melodic thinking also made him popular with
many great singers—something which did not always happen, for

example, with Handel—especially on the part of those who were outstanding in the pathetic and graceful style.

An all-round view of the state of the vocal art in the first half of the eighteenth century is provided only by Handel. The reasons are several. First and foremost, the recitatives, the vocal melodies, the instrumental ritornelli, the use of concertante instruments, the accompaniments, in Handelian opera present a variety to which no other opera composer of the period can pretend. Secondly, all Handel's scores are accessible to scholars, and they give an account of the vicissitudes of the art of singing from the earliest works to the last, something which is not true of the other composers. Furthermore, we know all the casts of Handel's London period—and among them we find many of the singers most representative of the time. Finally, Handel is the opera composer who was best able to take advantage of the capacities of his interpreters and cleverest in finding how to exploit them, by frequent changes of pattern and ways of writing. We know—or we think we know—that Bononcini's and Hasse's melodic style and Porpora's handbook of virtuoso formulas pleased the singers better than some of Handel's melodies and patterns, in the twofold sense, we must assume, of being more spontaneous, more attractive and pleasing tunes, and less bound by coloratura of an instrumental type. In spite of this, it is precisely with Handel that, irrespective of the roles involved, Baroque opera achieves the closest possible collaboration between composer and performer. The Italian singers who from time to time visited London, attracted among other things by the fabulous fees paid, brought with them the latest novelties by way of virtuosity and expressiveness gleaned from the vast production of operas 'made in Italy'. These novelties were taken over by Handel, who developed them and elaborated them; indeed, his operatic style might well be seen as the sum of the various vocal styles most in vogue between 1710 and 1740.

In *Almira* (Hamburg, 1705) Handel uses fairly high tessituras for the name part and for the tenor (Osmano) and takes both of them up to the high b natural. *Almira* is also striking for the thrust of some of the 'scorn' and 'jealousy' arias. In *Rodrigo* (Florence, 1707) we find brilliant 'battle' arias sung by Giuliano (tenor) and Rodrigo (male soprano), while *Agrippina* (Venice, 1709) already finds Handel embarking on the pathetic, agitated style with the

great aria by the protagonist (soprano), 'Pensieri voi mi tor-
mentate', and sketching out the first of his seductress figures with
Poppaea, soprano, who sings in graceful style a 'toilette' aria
('Vaghe perle, eletti fiori') and the aria with oboe 'Bella pur nel
mio diletto'. Handel's coloratura tends in these early operas to run
to fairly long and varied vocalise passages, but it is rendered
rather mechanical by the geometrical rigidity of the progressions.
Ex. 19 is a passage from the aria 'Vaghe perle, eletti fiori'. In

Ex. 19

Agrippina, the graceful style with a descriptive setting also takes
this form, which is linked to patterns already to be found in
Cavalli and Cesti (binary designs which some French instrumentalists called *confluences*) specifically for words like 'mor-
morare', 'serpeggiare', 'ondeggiare', as applied to rivers or winds
(Ex. 20). This passage is from Ottone's Andante 'Vaghe fonti che

Ex. 20

mormorando'. Ottone was sung by the contralto Francesca Vanini
Boschi, a 'pathetic'-style singer and one of the best among those of
the end of the seventeenth century and the first few years of the
eighteenth century.

The vigorous and the courtly styles in *Agrippina* are expressed
particularly in vocalises with an arpeggio-like movement (see
Ottone's aria 'Lusinghiera mia speranza'), or with hints of the
leaping style in the singing: intervals of an octave or as much as an
eleventh, upwards and downwards. But this had already been
common in Italian singing for a long time. Similarly, we can trace

back to Monteverdi the pattern used by Handel at the beginning
of the aria sung by Claudio (bass), 'Cade il mondo' (Ex. 21).

Ex. 21

Ca - de il   mon - do

In *Agrippina* there are two bass singers. The first, a basso
profundo, in fact plays Claudio; the other, rather baritone-like in
tessitura and with a range from bottom G to f ', is Pallante, who is
given a vocal line which is distinctly light, and in the Allegro 'La
mia sorte fortunata' fairly melismatic. The role was played by
Giuseppe Maria Boschi, the husband of Vanini. Later on, in
London, he was to become the Handelian bass singer *par excellence.*

In *Rinaldo*, the first opera written by Handel for London, we
find in the title-role Nicolò Grimaldi, also known as Il Cavalier
Nicolino, and with him began the Handelian tradition of
assigning the roles of lover and hero to a male alto. Grimaldi, who
until then had been an interpreter of Scarlatti, had a resounding
success in London, particularly for his expressive gifts and his
mimicry. The languorous aria 'Ogni indugio d'un amante' in the
first act and the semi-syllabic writing and short vocalises of the
Largo 'Cara sposa, amante cara' probably reflect his style at its
most characteristic. The same is true of the delicate duets with
Almirena (soprano), while the agitated style is reflected in the
Allegro 'Abbruggio, avvampo e fremo'. The range is a to e″ and the
tessitura is c′ to c″, which is still very low, but distinctly higher than
that of the male altos in Cavalli and Cesti.

The vocalise passages written by Handel for Rinaldo are mostly
short, with repeated quaver triplets, groups consisting of a dotted
quaver and two demisemiquavers, and groups of four semiquavers, articulated in not unduly complex patterns. In the
vocalises forming part of an Allegro with trumpet ('Or la tromba
in suon festante') we find a fairly intricate style of writing, with
semiquaver figures to be sung at a fast tempo. This piece shows us
the aria with trumpet combined with considerable structural
variety. The orchestral ritornelli are ample and incisive, the

instrument at times imitating the voice, at times independent. The vocal line is bound up with figurations of the trumpet kind (Ex. 22).

Ex. 22

[mi ri-] chia - - - - - - - - - - ma

For the role of Goffredo di Buglione, Handel uses a contralto *en travesti*—Francesca Vanini Boschi, who played Ottone in *Agrippina*. A typical imitative procedure (imitating the jagged contour of a mountain range) is characteristic of an Allegro sung by this personage (Ex. 23).

Ex. 23

So - vra   bal - ze   sco - sce - se e   pun - gen - ti

Argante was played by Giuseppe Maria Boschi, who had already sung Pallante in *Agrippina*. In *Rinaldo*, Boschi is better cast, since his booming voice and impetuosity of temperament made him ideally suited for roles of warrior and tyrant—vicious, arrogant, and somewhat satanical. The Allegro with which Argante first appears: 'Sibilar gli angui d'aletto', calls for verve, skill in executing vocalises, and phenomenal breathing power. It includes, among other things, a passage consisting of groups of six semiquavers articulated in different ways, and notes prolonged by tie-signs, which lasts for a good twenty bars. As Argante too, Boschi confirms his own baritone leanings, and incidentally sings up to a top f sharp (f♯').

The roles of Almirena and Armida bring together two sopranos about whom we know little: Isabella Gerardou and Elisabetta Pilotti. Almirena, innocent and in love, incarnates virtue; Armida is one of those enchantresses and seductresses whose portraits Handel drew with a masterly touch. Almirena's Adagio 'Augelletti che cantate', with flute concertante and an idyllic, pastoral introduction, shows an Arcadian lightness, and the Largo 'Lascia ch'io pianga' is one of the most famous of Handel's laments (actually it is taken from the cantata *Il trionfo del tempo e del disinganno*, Rome, 1707).

Armida's entry is prepared by an electrifying orchestral introduction and an exotic, almost bolero-like rhythm. The succeeding 'conjuration' aria ('Furie terribili') is slow and dignified. It is one of the most brilliant and direct characterizations of a personage in all Handelian opera. Another aria, the Allegro 'Molto voglio, molto spero', illustrates Handel's tendency to carry the soprano voice up to high tessituras, and as far as range is concerned, the high c''' reached by Armida is quite unusual. Like all Handel's sorceresses, Armida also touches a pathetic chord in the fine Largo 'Ah crudel, il pianto mio' and in highly effective accompanied recitatives.

It may be well to emphasize that *Rinaldo* distances itself greatly from the Venetian opera of the seventeenth century in the number of arias—only eighteen plus four duets; in the large number of accompanied recitatives; and in the number of characters—ten, including secondary roles. But by now, even in Italy opera had taken on this shape. On the other hand, its spectacular nature remained intact: sieges, troops on the march, triumphal cars drawn by dragons which spouted flames and smoke from their nostrils, and other monsters, apparitions, and earthquakes.

Amadigi (1715) brings together in four main roles[22] a male alto (Amadigi—Nicolò Grimaldi), a contralto in men's clothes (Dardano—Diana Vico, a good singer, possibly of the Venetian school), and two sopranos: Oriana, played by Anastasia Robinson, and Melissa, played by Pilotti. Various cantabile passages in this opera seem to look back to the simple, elegant style of melody of Bononcini, based on motifs which develop in stepwise intervals. An example is the Allegro sung by Amadigi: 'Non sa temere questo mio petto', which also takes over Bononcini's device of having the vocalise passages and ornaments fall on the final word

[22] Amadigi and Dardano are in love with Oriana, but Amadigi is loved by the enchantress Melissa.

of a phrase. In another Allegro, likewise sung by Amadigi, 'Vado, corro al mio tesoro', Handel introduces, in the manner of Scarlatti and Steffani, the 'catchword', in this case 'vado', following it up with a two-bar rest and then the statement of the entire phrase, this too with a melodic flow reminiscent of the simplicity of Bononcini. Likewise simple and languorous in its melody is the Adagio 'T'amai quant'il mio cor', and it is also marked by great rhythmic variety; while the Largo 'O rendetemi il mio bene' carries a pathos that recalls Scarlatti. Noteworthy too is the variety of some of the *secco* recitatives, such as that describing the meeting between Amadigi and Oriana in the third scene of the second act ('Chi mi sveglia dal sonno?'). Between 1712 and 1714, Grimaldi had sung in Italy, and it may be that he carried with him on his return to London the taste that prevailed, especially at Naples, during those years; while a melodic fluency deriving from the simplicity of the writing (statement of the melody in syllabic style and coloratura understood, so to speak, as a development of the theme) is to be found also in the Allegro 'Ch'io lasci mai d'amare' and the Siciliana 'Gioie venite in sen'. Both these arias are sung by Oriana.

Melissa, the enchantress, fluctuates between the 'pathetic' aria (the Largo 'Ahi spietato!') and the 'conjuration' aria with trumpet ('Desterò dell'empia Dite'); while Dardano is a lively, aggressive character, using an impetuous coloratura (cf. the successions of rising scales in the Allegro 'Agitato il cor mi sento'). Handel fairly frequently gave the contralto *en travesti* a vigorous look.

In some arias, Handel is concerned to establish certain details of the coloratura exactly, a tendency he accentuated still further as time went on. For example, Oriana's Larghetto 'Gioie venite a me' (Ex. 24) contains an ornamental formula in typically graceful

Ex. 24

[bril-la] -   -   -   -   -   - [te]

style. Operatic writing in the late seventeenth century presents successions of trills, but they are confined to the simplest formula of adjacent notes, rising or falling, and without any indication of preparation or closing. This was a matter coming within the sphere of the singer's improvisation. Handel's intervention—a pattern which fuses the *ribattuta*-type trill with the trill 'in progression' and inserts with the two semiquavers the equivalent of a 'closing turn' of two grace-notes—is a significant prelude to the elaborate ornamentation written out in full that was just round the corner.

Handel reached this stage at a time when he had at his disposal singers more up to date than those who trod the boards in London up to the early months of 1720 and who therefore took part in the first performance of *Radamisto*. Maddalena Durastanti, for example, who played Radamisto and had played the name part in *Agrippina* in 1709, was by now a soprano in the old style and not too keen on high tessituras. Anastasia Robinson, who five years earlier had played the part of Oriana in *Amadigi*, had now changed into a contralto, and in *Radamisto* she played Zenobia. The other singers were less prestigious. Hence, even though the protagonist and Zenobia have pathetic or 'agitated' arias of some importance, and even though, with Tiridate, Handel laid down the guide-lines for roles in which the tenor is an arrogant, violent tyrant, the second version of *Radamisto*, with Durastanti as Zenobia, the bass Boschi as Tiridate, and Francesco Bernardi, known as Il Senesino, as the protagonist, is more reliable.

Bernardi was destined to strengthen the tradition of the Handelian male alto as hero and lover. He had previously performed operas by Francesco Gasperini, Carlo Francesco Pollarolo, Alessandro Scarlatti, and Antonio Lotti. He had a voice of fine timbre, powerful and flexible. He was skilled in agility singing, but he was apt to excel in the noble, pathetic style rather than in vocal acrobatics. Also, his manner of recitation and his tall stature singled him out as a fine interpreter of courtly roles. Re-writing the part of Radamisto, Handel appeared to be concerned most of all to bring out both the sonority of Bernardi's low register (see the aria 'Qual nave smarrita', in which the voice often sings phrases below the stave without ever climbing higher than the a♯), and his skill in broad, grandiose phrasing, as in the lament 'Ombra cara' or 'Vile! se mi dai vita' from the fifth scene of the second act. It is with *Ottone re di Germania* (1723), in music written for Bernardi in the title-role, that we get a fairly elaborate coloratura, as in the delicious aria 'Deh! non dir che molle

amante', where the odd vocalise, rather in the manner of
Bononcini, swells out like a direct emanation of the melody.

Another major role written by Handel for Bernardi was the
title-role in *Giulio Cesare* (1724), a figure half gallant, half of epic
stature. The Allegros 'Non è si vago e bello il fior del prato' and
'Se in fiorito ameno prato' find Handel adapting the melody,
whether rising or falling, to the languid nature of adjacent
intervals; while another Allegro, 'Quel torrente che cade dal
monte', is the most virtuosic aria written up to then for Bernardi.
It contains long vocalises as long as eight bars—built up on rapid
six-note groups of semiquavers interspersed with rests, 'curtailed-
note' passages, and arpeggios; while at the level of courtly singing,
Caesar's famous lament over the tomb of Pompey is outstanding.

The role of Andronico in *Tamerlano* reconfirms the fact that in
some arias, such as the Largo 'Bella Asteria' and the Andante
'Benché mi sprezzi l'idol che adoro', Handel took account when
writing for the famous male alto Bernardi of certain devices used
by Bononcini, of whose music, incidentally, Bernardi was an
excellent interpreter. These included keeping the melodic line
simple, and avoiding interrupting a phrase with vocalise passages,
so as to hold the coloratura back until the last word. Ex. 25 shows
how, in the Andante 'Benché mi sprezzi l'idol che adoro/ mai non
potrei cangiare amor', the meaning of the word 'cangiar' is
imitated. It was the moment when the Italian vocal art was
beginning to promulgate as a formula for elegant singing the
short trill on notes in *ribattuta* form. In *Tamerlano*, Handel
prescribes this formula not only for Bernardi but for a bass voice,
obviously taking advantage of the availability of a singer of the
stature of Boschi, who played the part of Leone. Ex. 26 shows a
fragment from a vocalise in the Allegro 'Amor di guerra e pace'.

Ex. 25

mai non po - trei   can - -

- -   giar, _____

Ex. 26

di far pe - nar - - - - - - -

In *Rodelinda* (1725), Bernardi plays the role of Bertarido, one of his greatest successes. Bertarido shows how Handel constructed a great character for a great singer. We find situations with an atmosphere and a pathos which are almost Romantic, as when Bertarido, thought to be dead, enters the sepulchre of the Lombard kings, perceives the urn, and after the beautiful introduction for violin and oboe and the recitative 'Pompe vane di morte', entones the infinitely soft Largo 'Dove sei amato bene'; or again, the prison scene with its 'bound in chains' aria (the Largo 'Chi di voi fu più infedele'), or the elegiac Larghetto, 'Con rauco mormorio'. As a counterpart to this type of vocalism we get the courtly, incisive air of the Allegro 'Vivi tiranno', and arias inspired directly by certain skills on the part of the performer, like the Allegro 'Se fiera belva ha cinto', which through the 'leaping' style of singing shows off the sonority of the low register of a male alto (Ex. 27), or the Allegro 'Scacciata dal suo nido', where the rapid

Ex. 27

Col fre - mi - to ri - chie - de la tol - ta li - ber - tà

trills in the voice part and the violins in unison follow one another with an almost hallucinating effect (Ex. 28).

Ex. 28

[que-] re - le la ron - di - nel - - -

- - - - - - - la

The role of Bertarido, in short, marks one of the high points attained by a composer and an executant in the first half of the eighteenth century. Handel wrote other roles for Bernardi, including in 1726 the title-role in *Alessandro* (where a profusion of trills accentuates the martial vigour of the Andante 'Fra le stragi e fra le morti'); in 1727 the title-role in *Admeto* (with the accompanied recitative in the first scene, 'Orride larve', highly varied in rhythm and emphasis, and the lament that follows, 'Chiudetevi, miei lumi'); and finally, in 1728, the title-role in *Tolomeo*. At that point Bernardi left London, but he returned in 1732, when he played the title-roles in *Ezio* and *Sosarme*. Then, in 1733, he was the protagonist also in *Orlando*. In these operas, Handel once again wrote courtly arias for him: the Andante 'Recagli quell'acciaro', sung by Ezio; the 'prison' aria 'Ecco alle mie catene', likewise sung by Ezio; the great mad scene sung by Orlando, which in its variety of tone and rhythm ranges from leaping song making play with low notes to sighing melodies with adjacent intervals, as for example 'Vaghe pupille' in gavotte time.

As already mentioned, Bernardi seems to be one of the links between Handel and the melodic style of Scarlatti and above all of Bononcini. It may be added that, to judge from the tessituras given him by Handel, Bernardi can also be regarded as a fairly deep male alto. As far as range is concerned, Handel hardly ever took him beyond e', whereas Bononcini occasionally had him sing as high as g'.

Mention has already been made, in connection with *Rinaldo* and *Tamerlano*, of the bass Boschi and his skills both as an interpreter of aggression and violence and as a virtuoso. Handel did not always write great roles for him, but in *Ottone*, as already in the preceding operas, he has him sing a syllabic line here and there on a baritone rather than a bass tessitura (e.g. the Allegro sung by Emireno, 'Del minacciar del vento'); and he does the same in *Rodelinda* (the Allegro sung by Garibaldo, 'Tirannia gli diede il regno'). Again in *Admeto*, in the Allegro sung by Ercole, 'Amore è un tiranno', Boschi's voice is used in a series of vigorous vaulting leaps.

Handel has a predilection for two types of voice: that of the male alto and that of the soprano. The greatest soprano used by Handel was Francesca Cuzzoni, who arrived in London in 1723 and has gone down in history as the possessor of one of the most beautiful voices of the eighteenth century, for its resonance, its evenness, and its sweet and moving timbre. Cuzzoni inflected and softened her tones to produce thrilling effects. While she phrased with hypnotic effect in the languid-elegiac and pathetic styles, she was also clean and flexible in agility passages, although she was not outstanding in rapidly moving coloratura. She had a wide range (apparently from c′ to c‴) and she was probably the first great Italian singer with the characteristics of a high soprano, which was not the case with Durastanti, for whom Handel had written up to then. The first result of Cuzzoni's arrival was that wide rising intervals were no longer reserved mainly for vocalise singing but became a feature of syllabic and semi-syllabic singing, broadening the melodic arch and making it more venturesome. Thus in the Larghetto 'Affanni del pensier', sung by Teofane in *Ottone* (Teofane was the first Handelian role sung by Cuzzoni), we find the initial close-knit melodic line (Ex. 29) taking wing with a new, dramatic surge (Ex. 30).

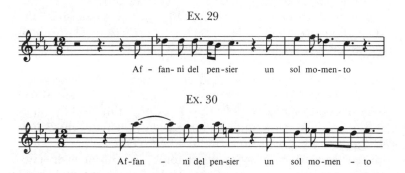

Ex. 29

Af – fan- ni del pen-sier   un   sol mo-men-to

Ex. 30

Af-fan – ni del pen-sier   un   sol mo-men – to

In another celebrated aria sung by Teofane, 'Falsa immagine', Handel introduced, alongside passages of elaborate coloratura characterized also by dotted rhythms and acciaccaturas (the 'sensitive' style which Vinci was popularizing in Italy), airy *fioriture* passages which, by suddenly projecting the voice upwards, underlined the flexibility and grace of the singer. In the case in point, the arabesque on the word 'm'allettò' also has reverberations of sensuousness (Ex. 31). Again in *Ottone* (the Andante 'Gode l'alma consolata'), Cuzzoni's security and verve in the high register were underlined (Ex. 32). There are many phrases in *Giulio Cesare* and *Rodelinda* also where the soaring of the soprano voice into the

Ex. 31

[quel] vol - to   m'al-let - tò _____   e   quel vol - to

Ex. 32

Go - de   l'al- ma   con - so - la - ta   quel - la   [calma]

high regions has a marked quality of voluptuousness or languor
or pathos, especially if we think of it as executed by a singer with a
mastery of airy rising portamento (cf. at the beginning of 'V'adoro
pupille' and 'Piangerò la sorte mia', sung by Cleopatra, the phrases
'Le vostre faville son grate nel sen', and 'Finche vita in petto avrò',
or in *Rodelinda* the Allegro 'L'empio rigor del fato').

Bononcini and Porpora, always with a view to emphasizing the
fascination of certain tricks executed by Cuzzoni in the high
register, wrote for her vocalises which were suddenly cut off on
notes like the a″ and the b″ flat (see p. 71). Handel did not use this
formula, but Cuzzoni carried it to a more marked characterization
of the *fioriture* and ornamentation of the gracious, emotional
style. This is demonstrated by the clever use of the trill (presumably a 'slow trill') alternating with the trill by the flute and violins,
in the melting Largo sung by Rodelinda 'Ombre, piante, urne
funeste'—one of the most beautiful 'tomb' arias of the eighteenth
century—or the interplay of three-note groups (dotted semiquaver, demisemiquaver, quaver) inserted into the semi-syllabic
singing of 'Tu la mia stella sei', sung by Cleopatra, or 'Alla fama
dimmi il vero', sung by Teofane. Finally, although Cuzzoni was not
outstanding in fast-moving coloratura, she was at any rate more
skilled in the virtuoso style popular in Italy in the 1720s than
Durastanti could have been. Hence certain vocalises in
Cleopatra's aria 'Da tempesta il legno infranto', where there is a
succession of 'curtailed' and staccato notes, *ribattuta* effects, and
trills of various kinds. At this point, Handel's writing is distinctly
superior in the boldness and variety of its coloratura to that of his
rival Bononcini; but what is more important, there are soprano

arias with a surge and an imagination that are absolutely new, and along with these, heroine figures like Cleopatra or Rodelinda who are real personages, the one with her voluptuous nature as an enchantress, the other with her melancholy.

The enthusiasm of the London public for Cuzzoni—in spite of her ill temper, poor taste, and somewhat disreputable behaviour—was delirious. But in 1726, London had a second idol in the person of Faustina Bordoni, for whom Handel composed the role of Rossana in *Alessandro*, while Bernardi played the title-role and Cuzzoni played Lisaura, Rossana's rival.

The career of Bordoni, a Venetian, had gone on for ten years, during which, beginning with Gasperini and Lotti and going on to Leo and Vinci, she had become established as the principal female exponent of the new 'brilliant' style. Although some writers described her as a contralto, she was actually a mezzo-soprano with a refined and elegant singing style and extra-ordinary agility. She was particularly outstanding for her rapid execution of vocalises and for the perfection of her trills and her 'beating in the throat'. According to some contemporaries, she also gave great expression to Adagios in plain style, but in this field the palm went to Cuzzoni, who was also superior in regard to the beauty and evenness of her tone.

The roles of Rossana, Alceste, and Elisa, in *Alessandro*, *Admeto* (1727), and *Tolomeo* (1728) respectively, are an indication of Handel's open adherence to the 'brilliant' style. No other com-poser wrote for Bordoni such elaborate, fantasy-filled, and complex coloratura—not even Hasse, who shortly afterwards married her. Trills and *ribattuta* effects were logically the orna-ments on which Handel dwelt most. Thus in the Allegro 'Un lusinghiero dolce pensiero', from *Alessandro*, Handel chose progressions of trills, between each of which he interposed short *fioriture*, according to the notion of the so-called double trill (Ex. 33). Still in *Alessandro*, the Andante 'Alla sua gabbia d'oro' took forms like that shown in Ex. 34, in imitation of the warbling of a

Ex. 33

Ex. 34

Au -gel-lin ca-no

bird. Furthermore, the Largo 'L'armi implora' (a supplementary aria, that is to say, added after the triumph achieved by Bordoni in the first performance of *Alessandro*), contains not only long vocalises articulated on mixed groups of four and six semiquavers and demisemiquavers, but the following example of elaborate *fioriture* with short rests, a testimony to her light, rapid, and clean emission (Ex. 35). But in the arias written by Handel for Bordoni

Ex. 35

[beltà]

we have to distinguish between vocalise singing and syllabic and semi-syllabic singing. The speed of her articulation and her exceptional agility allowed Bordoni to insert trills even in passages of syllabic singing (as in the Andante 'Dica il falso, dica il vero' from *Alessandro*), and in Allegro passages, to cope with short but fast melismata and series of trills inserted in 'leaping' style. Ex. 36 is taken from *Tolomeo*: 'Il mio cor non apprezza'.

Ex. 36

che   tutt'   o - sa e   tut – to   spez – za

né   ra –   gion, leg –   ge o ri –   spet – to

The arrival of Bordoni left definite traces on Handel's manner of composition. For Cuzzoni, Handel made use more frequently from then onwards of trills, at times in *ribattuta* form similar to those written for Bordoni. This occurred, among other places, in the Allegros sung by Antigona in *Admeto*: 'S'en vola lo sparvier' and 'La sorte mia vacilla'. In addition, in the vocalises of arias written for Cuzzoni, the athletic singing passages were accentuated, while Handel kept the short friezes with a large element of whimsical or voluptuous singing (cf. the Allegro sung by Lisaura: 'Sí, m'è caro imitar quel bel fiore'). Naturally, Handel also wrote Adagios and arias in *stile concitato* for Bordoni, for example, the Allegro 'Gelosia, spietata Aletto', sung by Alceste in *Alessandro*; but in this genre the tunes composed for Cuzzoni are more expansive and tender.

In the period between *Ottone* and *Tolomeo*, Handel also used women contraltos for all his operas. As a rule he did not have great stars, and he composed arias with a more all-purpose type of coloratura. Nor did he have notable tenors—indeed, often he had none at all—until 1724, when he engaged Francesco Borosini as Bajazete in *Tamerlano*. Borosini came from Vienna and was decidedly of the baritone type (Fux wrote for him in the bass clef). In Handel, his tessitura runs from g to e', and the range from c to a'. Bajazete is, all in all, an epic-style personage and a noble father, and in some of the 'scorn' arias we find passages of 'leaping' syllabic singing and arpeggio-type vocalises characteristic of the heroic tenor up to the beginning of the nineteenth century. Thus we have the Allegro 'Ciel e terra armi di sdegno' (Ex. 37). Still in

Ex. 37

[Ciel e] ter - ra ar - mi di sde - gno, mor - rò in - vit - to

robust singing with wide intervals we get the more typical arias sung by Grimoaldo, a villain-type rival character in *Rodelinda*—the Allegro 'Io già t'amai' (Ex. 38) and the Allegro 'Tuo drudo è mio rivale' (Ex. 39).

With *Lotario* (1729), circumstances amounting to *force majeure* revolutionized Handel's casting. Another famous male alto arrived in London to replace Bernardi—the Bolognese singer

Ex. 38

Ex. 39

Antonio Bernacchi. He had begun his career at the very beginning of the century and was already 44 years old—an advanced age for a castrato. He is usually looked upon as the first champion of the style between the acrobatic and the brilliant in which Bordoni was outstanding among the singers. If we examine the role of Lotario, we find the odd vocalise passage of some difficulty, although it is kept within a restricted range (c′ to e″), and also of considerable length (twelve bars in the Allegro 'Vedrò più liete e belle'). But more indicative, if we wish to understand Bernacchi's style, are some phrases from the Andante 'Non disperi peregrina', in which Handel writes elaborate *fioriture* in graceful style (Ex. 40). Bernacchi was also a stylish, expressive singer. He is given credit for the sonorous, vibrant production (*di petto*) which was immediately afterwards taken up by Farinelli and Carestini, and he was also said to be capable on occasions of singing in a

Ex. 40

simple, touching style. *Lotario* contains pieces like the Adagio 'Rammentati cor mio', in which this second aspect of Bernacchi's singing could be properly exploited. But he was a singer already past his best, and he was not a success in London.

The tenor voice, generally not very popular with London audiences, is not used at all in quite a number of Handel's operas. In *Lotario*, however, there appeared the greatest Italian tenor of the period, the Bolognese Annibale Pio Fabri. The role of Berengario has a higher tessitura than that which Handel had in mind for Borosini previously, and the writing is decidedly more virtuosic, with trills, 'curtailed' notes in Allegros syllabic in style, *ribattuta* effects inserted into passages of 'leaping' style singing (e.g. the aria from the third act, 'Vi sento, vi sento'), and in particular, long vocalises, especially in the Allegro arias, from which it is evident that the Italian vocal school was tending more and more towards the robust acrobatic style of Farinelli and Carestini. Look at the three bars of 'leaping' vocalise (Ex. 41) from the Allegro 'Regno e grandezza', bearing in mind that the leaping style was always regarded by bel canto specialists as more difficult than any other. All in all, with the way in which the role of Berengario is written, we have reached a standard of virtuosity which was only to be exceeded, as far as the tenor voice is concerned, by one or two pieces written a few years later by Hasse for Angelo Amorevoli.

Ex. 41

[in-vo] - - - - - - [-la-mi]

By the date of *Lotario*, Handel had lost not only Bernardi and the bass Boschi but also Cuzzoni and Bordoni. He replaced both these latter singers by Anna Strada, a good Italian soprano, possibly from Bologna, who had begun to make a name for herself in Venice in 1720–1 in works by Vivaldi, and had later made a hit at Naples in works by Vinci and Porpora. Handel transferred to Strada the type of writing inspired by Cuzzoni and tunes broad in design and rendered quick-moving and varied by high tessituras and rising leaps. In *Lotario*, the role of Adelaide includes

arias of a languid elegance such as the Allegro-Andante 'Quel cor
che mi donasti', Vivace arias like 'Scherza in mar la navicella', and
impetuous arias like the Allegro 'Non sempre invendicata'. In the
Andante 'Una torbida sorgente' we also find elaborate coloratura
formulas which in part recall the style of Bordoni. *Sosarme* can
pride itself on the delicious Largo sung by Elmira, 'Rendi sereno al
ciglio', and *Arianna* on the pathetic Andante-Larghetto sung by
the protagonist, 'So che non è più mio', as well as on one of the
arias in imitation of bird-song in which Handel had specialized
after the enormous success attained by Bordoni in *Alessandro* with
the Andante 'Alla sua gabbia d'oro'. The piece in question is the
Andante 'Se nel bosco resta solo/ rusignolo col suo canto', and the
imitation is particularly marked in the passage in Ex. 42:

Ex. 42

Strada collaborated with Handel for a long time. She played the
part of Ginevra in *Ariodante* in 1735 (particularly noteworthy is the
Larghetto 'Il mio crudel martoro'), and in the same year she
played the title-role in *Alcina*, another enchantress figure
splendidly portrayed by Handel and very ably adapted to the
possibilities of a high soprano voice—from the Allegro 'Ma
quando tornerai' to the Larghetto 'Mi restano le lacrime' and to
another Allegro 'Tornami a vagheggiar' (Ex. 43), one of the most

Ex. 43

sensuous arias written by Handel, if only for the wayward energy of some parts of the coloratura.[23]

In *Atalanta* too, with the Allegro sung by the protagonist, 'Al varco pastori', and the Adagio 'E son quell'augelletto', where the imitation looks like this:

Ex. 44

Handel finds in the soprano voice the inspiration to write highly imaginative melodies (cf. also, in *Giustino*, two Allegros sung by Arianna, 'Quel torrente che s'innalza' and 'Ti rendo questo core').

Giustino (1727) was the last of Handel's operas in which Strada appeared, but again in *Serse*, 1738, Handel treated the soprano as no other composer in the first half of the eighteenth century had done; and the part of Romilda, from the nostalgic 'O voi che penate' to the voluptuous 'Vo godendo, vezzoso e bello'—a delicious Arcadian melody with flute, supported by mysterious instrumental echos—is a fitting conclusion to a cycle which established a flexible and modern view of the soprano voice.

The change of status which occurred in 1729 put Handel into contact with various other new singers. In *Lotario* he had as Matilde the contralto Antonia Merighi, for whom he composed, among other things, the tender-style Andante 'Vanne a colei che adori', with a light and graceful type of coloratura, and the Allegro 'Arma lo sguardo', in which, with the help of an arpeggio, Handel for the first time took the contralto voice up to f″. Typical also is the obbligato recitative in the thirteenth scene of the third act, for its variety and the changes of tempo prescribed by Handel: 'Concitato, ma non furioso—Furioso—Adagio e piano'.

---

[23] The soprano Joan Sutherland has given a superlative performance of this on gramophone record.

Outstanding among the arias for contralto written by Handel in the later operas are the Larghetto 'Come alla tortorella', sung by Irene in *Atalanta*, for a realistic imitation of the word *languir* (the syllables are separated by rests), and the Allegro 'Voglio che ancora', sung by Gernando in *Faramondo*, for the presence of rising and falling chromatic scales. Distinguished too is the character of Amastre in *Serse*, for its excitement and ferocity (the Allegro 'Saprà delle mie offese') which, however, often gives way to delicate, gentle melodies ('Speranze mie, fermate' and 'Cagione io son del mio dolor'). Nevertheless, the contralto voice does not seem to inspire Handel to the same extent as the soprano voice; even the coloratura is quite often conventional and mechanical.

An event of some importance was the engagement of the bass singer Antonio Montagnana, who made his debut in London in 1732, singing Varo in *Ezio*. The flexibility and agility of his voice are highlighted in various passages of the opera, particularly in the Allegro with trumpet 'Già risonar d'intorno' (Ex. 45).

Ex. 45

With simple and light semi-syllabic *fioriture*, interrupted by quaver and semiquaver rests, Handel had even the robust voice of Montagnana in *Sosarme* imitate the capricious flight of a butterfly (the Larghetto sung by Altomaro, 'Fra l'ombre e gli orrori'); and in this essay in the graceful style he made use of a range of two octaves, F to f'. Another virtuoso aria was written by Handel, again for Montagnana, in *Orlando*: 'Sorge infausta una procella', sung by Zoroastro. Later on, Handel too seemed to share the new trends of the Italian vocal school, which until the beginning of the nineteenth century relegated the bass voice in serious opera to more and more secondary roles.

With *Arianna* (1734), Handel came into contact with Carestini, the singer who after Farinelli was at the time the most illustrious representative of acrobatic vocalism. Carestini did not possess the exceptional range of Farinelli, whose voice combined the deep contralto and the high soprano, but he nevertheless had a range in both the high and the low register which was exceptional for the period. Starting out as a male soprano, he went over to the contralto register, but to judge from the music written for him by Handel, we can define him today as a high male mezzo-soprano. Later on, in the final phase of his career, he sang in a true contralto tessitura.

In composing the role of Teseo for Carestini, Handel wrote a less elaborate coloratura than that used by Vinci in his day in *Artaserse*, but in the Allegro 'Nel pugnar col mostro audace', he brought out the singer's ability to execute vocalises with an *arpeggiato* movement, interspersed, without rests, with trills, sometimes rapid, sometimes long, in a range stretching from b to g″. Later, in another series of vocalises in the same aria, Handel used groups of four semiquavers often so arranged as to form ascending and descending runs, with a fairly central tessitura and passages of as many as eleven bars. Highly virtuosic too is the aria 'Salda quercia in erta balza', but the role of Teseo also shows off more specifically expressive gifts in Carestini. Worth singling out is the obbligato recitative 'O patria! o cittadini', from the beginning of the second act, followed by the heartfelt Larghetto 'Sol ristoro di mortali'.

Of great importance is the labyrinth scene (III. iii), with the accompanied recitative 'Ove son? qual orror' (note that Carestini was among other things an extremely impetuous actor) and the succeeding Allegro 'Qui ti sfido, o mostro infame', where on the phrase 'Non pavento la tua rabbia', Handel writes at one point vehement successions of rising scales which carry the voice from b flat to a″ flat. Still more virtuosic was the title-role in *Ariodante* (1735), if only because Handel had to face with Carestini the challenge issued by his rival Porpora, who had brought Farinelli to London. Thus in *Ariodante*, Handel inserts long vocalises (lasting at times for thirteen bars), and in the third act aria 'Dopo notte atra e funesta' he takes the voice down to an a after having called upon it to execute *ribattuta* figures on a″.

We nevertheless have the impression that Handel paid less attention to Carestini's acrobatic gifts than Vinci had done some ten years earlier, and that on the contrary he had concentrated more on the moving purity with which the famous castrato executed cantabile passages. In *Ariodante* itself we find the languid Larghetto 'Se tanto piace al cor', with an extremely appealing coloratura (Ex. 46), and the noble, plangent aria 'Numi! Lasciarmi

Ex. 46

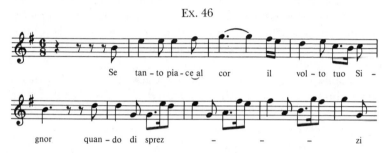

vivere'. But the Andante 'Dopo notte atra e funesta' mentioned above stands out above all for the solemn opening melody which gradually becomes more cheerful and expresses joy through vocalise passages, where the figures rising and falling in progression (pairs of quavers, groups consisting of a quaver and two semiquavers, and groups of four semiquavers) and *ribattutas* as the culmination of the upward leaps, have a syncopated rhythm. The final passage on the word 'gioia' (joy) (thirteen bars of Andante in 3/4 time), with its leap from an a' to four notes on a", in *ribattuta*, syncopated form, followed by a descent to a and a new rise, in arpeggios, to g", is electrifying (Ex. 47).

Ex. 47

In a word, this is the period when Handel shows a very marked leaning towards the Arcadian melody. Carestini was called upon to give expression to this trend both in *Ariodante*, with the Andante-Larghetto 'Qui d'amor nel suo linguaggio/parla il rio, l'erbetta, il faggio' and in *Alcina*, with the famous, very simple Larghetto sung by Ruggiero, 'Verdi prati, selve amene'.

In 1736, with *Atalanta*, the famous Gioacchino Conti, known as Il Gizziello, visited London, and for the first time Handel was able to write for a male soprano of the new school, i.e. with an extremely wide range. In fact, in the Allegro sung by Meleagro, 'Non sarà poco se il mio gran foco', the voice climbs to c'''. The same occurs in *Arminio*, where Sigismondo reaches c''' in the Allegro 'Quella fiamma che il petto m'accende'. Conti has passed into history as a singer of great feeling, smoothness, and grace. Burney attributes the enchanting simplicity of the aria 'Care selve' from *Atalanta* to his influence. That Conti was definitely inimical to the acrobatic, robust singing of singers like Farinelli and Carestini is often evident from the music written for him by Handel in *Atalanta, Arminio*, or *Giustino* (the role of Anastasio). Passages of robust singing are few and far between, and even in vocalises, apart from the syllabic and semi-syllabic ones, there is a tendency for the voice to rise and fall gradually, with a legato movement.

Another singer of notable talent used by Handel in those years was the male alto Domenico Annibali, who among other things sang the title-role in *Arminio* and *Giustino*. The most virtuosic aria written by Handel for Annibali was perhaps the Andante sung by Arminio, 'Fatto scorta al sentier della gloria', in which incidentally the voice reaches g''—an indication of the greater range in the high register that even male altos were achieving. In 1738, finally, Gaetano Majorana, known as Caffarelli, visited London, Handel having written the title-roles in *Faramondo* and *Serse* for him. The writing, whether in the details of coloratura or in the placing of the passages, their length and their range, cannot be defined as particularly virtuosic, with the exemption of Faramondo's Largo, 'Perché pria di morire', where among other things we get a chromatic rising run starting at e' and reaching d''. Here we have one of the first manifestations of the pattern, and, as I have already recalled, in *Faramondo* the Allegro sung by Gernando, 'Voglio che mora', contains rising and falling chromatic scales. *Faramondo* is also the opera in which Handel requires a soprano to execute an ascending scale, not in vocalise but syllabic, stretching from c' to b'' flat. The phrase appears in Clotilde's Allegro 'Mi parto lieta', written for Elisabetta Duparc, known as La Francesina.

In the Largo just mentioned, 'Perché pria di morire', from *Faramondo*, Handel includes a somewhat whimsical passage (the rhythm recalls the 'sensitive' style), fairly elaborate in coloratura, one of the few in that opera which give us an inkling of the complex style of Caffarelli's singing, so much lauded to the skies, or so much inveighed against, according to the circumstances, by his contemporaries (Ex. 48). Equally evident in *Faramondo* is the

Ex. 48

tendency to keep Caffarelli within the confines of the 'graceful' style. This applies also to the title-role in *Serse*, where later on we get an Arcadian flavour (the famous 'Largo', 'Ombra mai fu'), together with a noteworthy characterization of the personage. The Andante 'Più che penso alla fiamma del core' is a broad, noble aria, with a varied and inspired accompaniment, while the Allegro 'Se bramate d'amar', in agitated style, underlines once again the regal nature of the personage. Both in *Faramondo* and in *Serse*, the voice is used over a range and tessitura which make one think of a male mezzo-soprano. Some years later, however, Caffarelli in reality became a soprano, and Gluck, in *La clemenza di Tito*, repeatedly took the voice up to c′′′.

Two of the most beautiful arias in *Serse* were written by Handel, at the end of his opera cycle, for the character of Arsamene, played *en travesti* by Antonia Marchesini, known as La Lucchesina (a dark-voiced soprano, actually a mezzo-soprano), who had to perform the melancholy Siciliana 'Quella che tutta fe' and an aria full of pathos, 'Per dar fine alle mie pene'.

The period ending with Handel and Hasse, and begun with Scarlatti and Steffani, was the one that saw the triumph of the vocal melody, the instrumentation applied to it, and the 'personage'. To some extent, spectacular scenic effects had lost their charm, and plots relying on machinery had been discarded, along with the multitude of executants, the plethora of arias and ariettas which fragmented and diluted the composer's inspiration and even the emotive force of the stage action. Everything was to be thrown into the melting-pot to be judged by the standards of the day. The spectacular nature of Roman and Venetian Baroque opera had manifestly borne fruit, but it no longer possessed carrying power when first Zeno and later Metastasio appeared on the scene. Both these libretto writers concentrated on the stage character. The accusation made against eighteenth-century Italian opera by the idealist critics of the time (and by others after them) as being 'opera-concert' is, as so often happens, a matter of form rather than of substance. It amounts to saying that an aria, after an introductory recitative 'setting the stage', lacked the power—perhaps because this power was thought to be exclusive to the uniform and repetitive declamatory 'tirades' of German music-drama—to portray a feeling or a state of mind. Everything depends on whether an aria succeeds or not, or to put it more crudely, whether it 'works'. A character is nothing more than the exposition of feelings and states of mind seen as they evolve through the stage action, and there is no doubt that Zeno and Metastasio provided composers with everything they needed, given the taste and sensibility of the first half of the eighteenth century, to portray true-to-life characters melodically. The fact that the actions and the language of such personages were, or later on seemed to be, commonplace and stereotyped, means nothing. Humdrum, stereotyped episodes are the cornerstone, the strength, and the boast of any artistic cycle in its moment of glory, while incurring the danger of becoming its weakness and its stigma in its obsolescent phase. Some of the characters in Zeno's *Griselda* or *Alessandro Severo*, and the many characters made popular by Metastasio in episodes ranging from *Didone* to *Il trionfo di Clelia*, were the connecting link between composers and singers during the Golden Age of bel canto, the epicentre of a movement which found its *raison d'être* in the imitation of emotions, stylized or fairy-tale. This imitation was inherent both in the orchestral ritornello and in the vocalise, in the evolution of the concertante instrument and in plain, cantabile singing. The fascination of the character—precisely the thing that led dozens and dozens of composers to set one and the same libretto by Metastasio to music—rebounded from the melody to the interpreter and from the interpreter to the melody, as in a hall of mirrors. But what in a composer like Handel also became part of the treatment of feelings and states of mind, environment, and hence characterization of personages was a certain atmosphere he established with the instrumental introduction to an obbligato recitative or an aria; a certain local and temporal colouring evoked by his orchestra, not being content merely to furnish a harmonic support for the voice, but ensuring autonomy of invention to the instruments; the use of courtly dance rhythms in arias sung by interpreters in modern dress to bring up to date heroes and heroines of antiquity and to crystallize certain immutable features of the human condition. At a given moment, however, the extraordinary bravura of certain interpreters and the intensity of emotion aroused by them in an audience which was itself highly emotional (cf. the famous occasion when an English lady shouted, 'One God, one Farinelli!'), ensured that above all else the singer became identified with the personage. It was the triumph of voice; but the primary consequence of this was the subordination of the instrumental effect to the vocal effect characteristic of the immediate successors of Handel, not excluding in some respects even Hasse.

It may be that this was the first breach in the wall of that balance struck in the heyday of bel canto by composers and singers—a balance between the search for expression and the search for virtuosity, both directed towards the common goal of imitating emotions. But other motives, too, appeared after Handel and Hasse to widen the breach. Certain basic principles of Italian opera, from the mythology of the stylized timbre of the castrati to that of a fantastically distorted view of the world of feelings, were losing their vitality. Bound up as they were with an aesthetic, that of the Baroque, by now a thing of the past, these principles began in the second half of the eighteenth century to arouse opposition and aversion. The art of bel canto had been able to express the exaggerated emotions which the Baroque period loved, above all when the development of vocal technique had broadened the range of intensities and colours. Performers could now sustain tessituras in keeping with the new developments of melody and with the insistence of librettists on inserting into operas episodes to their own liking, highly coloured and full of pathos. This explains, for example, the popularity of prison scenes and mad scenes, and arias of the 'tempest aria' kind, portraying inner struggles. In the second half of the eighteenth century such typical episodes survived, but in a more and more spent and exhausted form. Above all, the unconditional acceptance of a type of musical theatre in which abstraction and fiction were emotional elements came to an end.

Enlightenment led simultaneously to a search both for dramatic truth and for realism. Italian serious opera was thus caught in the web of music-drama and comic opera. The very triumph of comic opera underlines the fact that Italian musical theatre felt the need in the second half of the eighteenth century to become realistic, and side by side with this to become involved through satire, even veiled satire, in the social and political situation of the day. This involvement was more or less consciously targeted on an overturning of hierarchies and values—first among them the glorification of monarchy—which Baroque opera had accepted without any misgivings whatever, following in the wake, incidentally, of Corneille and even of Shakespeare.

With regard to music-drama, the fact that composers like Jommelli or Traetta gave some warning of its influence led to a change in the pattern of certain scenes, certain recitatives, certain choral interventions, certain types of accompaniment, but not to a really substantial renewal of vocal language. Nor could it be otherwise, since the function of broad and strongly characterized melody was anything but exhausted; it still had before it a long period of flourishing life. Nor had the function of florid singing ceased (it was to go on until Rossini and beyond), because the idealization of certain figures, the 'exceptional' status of a hero or a heroine, was still bound up with allegorical portrayal; indeed the markedly virtuoso writing of Jommelli and Traetta goes to prove this. However, composers of this type could not fail to act as a warning of the drawbacks of a compromise situation.

With other opera composers like Piccinni, Cimarosa, or Paisiello, it was quite clear that their true vocation was the realistic portrayal of character and environment, and that their comic vein, blending with a lyricism derived from the experience of Scarlatti, Bononcini, Vinci, Leo, Pergolesi, and Hasse, could not find a more concordant expression than in the simplicity of *mezzo carattere* opera and *larmoyant* sentimental drama, which expresses the taste both of a bourgeois class in the ascendant and of an aristocracy which was beginning to look at the future with melancholy disquiet. Thus even composers like Piccinni, Cimarosa, or Paisiello find themselves distanced from serious opera in its true sense. In the final analysis, a strong influence is exerted on this by composers whose status as unpretentious imitators prompts them to seek refuge in certain degenerate forms of bel canto. This degeneracy was not a matter of lack of technique or of vocal quality; it had to do with taste. The singers reacted against the gradual weakening of the creativeness in the composers of serious opera, the natural consequence being a weakening of the personage by employing virtuoso formulas more and more spectacular and acrobatic but in many respects superficial. There was no lack of expressive interpreters, since even the second half of the eighteenth century had great and even very great ones; but features crept in which in a general way changed the direction of singing. A mythology grew up, for example, calling for breakneck speed of execution and the extension of the high register. The phenomenon of sopranos and male sopranos succeeding in reaching e‴, f‴, or even c‴‴ (e.g. Lucrezia Agujari, known as La Bastardella, according to a famous statement by Mozart) unleashed a frantic competition to reach exceedingly high top notes. This competition involved the other voices as well, particularly the male alto and the contralto, with the result that singers possessing these registers and capable of sustaining the low tessituras of bygone days disappeared, while inevitably others came along with clear, slimmed-down voices. Inevitably, I say, because this is the price that any singer has to pay when the objective to be attained is a mastery of the very high register and acrobatic coloratura. A letter sent by Metastasio to Saverio Mattei on 25 April 1770 describes the situation in the clearest possible way, and equally clearly bewails the lost vigour of the interpreters of thirty or forty years earlier. Metastasio writes that nowadays, instead of 'striving to make their voices firm, robust and sonorous, singers are trying to make them light and flexible. By following this new method they have achieved quite incredible feats of speed and technical virtuosity, which amaze people and call forth deafening applause from the audience. But a voice which is whittled down and hence rendered incapable of arpeggios, trills, and runs may well give the pleasure that is caused by astonishment—an automatic, purely reflex response but not the pleasure produced spontaneously by the physical, vigorous impression of a clear, firm, and robust voice, which strikes the listening organs of the audience with a balance of strength and delight and produces its effect, penetrating deep into the heart.'[24]

In short, the second half of the eighteenth century, while belonging squarely to the bel canto period, attenuates one of its characteristic features, namely expressive ardour and sensibility, making up for these with a frenzied technical prowess. It was only towards the end of the century and during the first years of the nineteenth century that passion and vigour reappeared—in a number of exponents of the last generation of castrati, like Girolamo Crescentini and Gaspare Pacchierotti, tenors like Ettore Babini, Giovanni Ansani, and Giacomo David; in a few prima donnas like Brigida Banti, Luísa Todi de Agujar, or Giuseppina Grassini; and lastly, the art of bel canto was to experience its grand finale with Rossini.

---

[24] Metastasio also wrote to Farinelli in 1756, after hearing the first performance of Gluck's *Il re pastore* in Vienna: 'The first soprano is Signor Mazzanti, a great "violinist" in the falsetto register. He will not lack admirers, because there are palates for every sauce. When I myself hear singing I am not content just to be amazed; I also want my heart to share the enjoyment given to my ears. But this is an endowment given to few singers, and nature does not often make the effort it takes to produce a Farinelli.'

III

Particular Aspects of Baroque Opera

THE CASTRATO AND THE ART OF SINGING IN HIS DAY

The reason why the castrato voice began to be used is well known. Since women were forbidden to 'exhibit themselves' in sacred vocal music, parts in polyphonic sacred compositions written for 'white' voices were entrusted to boy singers or to men artificially imitating the sound of the female voice (artificial falsetto singers, today known as counter-tenors). But boys were very unreliable, and furthermore, they could no longer be used after the beginning of adolescence when the 'break' in the voice occurred. Artificial falsettists, on the other hand, frequently made unpleasant sounds. The castrato voice offered a solution to this difficulty facing the papal and court chapels. The practice of castration (orchiectomy) was imported from the East via Spain, which was then a Mozarabic country. The earliest castrati to arrive in Italy were in fact Spaniards: Francisco Soto, who joined the papal chapel in 1562, and Hernando Bustamante, who about twenty years later was in the service of the court of Ferrara.

The castrato has to be seen as a 'singing machine' constructed simply and solely by making use of the laws of biology. The underlying principle was that of exploiting and strengthening in adult human beings certain features characteristic of the boy's voice. Among 'white' voices, the boy's voice is that which in the natural range known in vocal jargon as 'chest voice' has the largest number of notes: from b flat to d″ or e″. Fairly often, therefore, the range is a to f″, which means that from ten to thirteen notes can be sung with full voice in the chest register, as against approximately half that number in the female soprano voice. The advantage is obvious if we consider the strength, the fullness, the 'bite' of the chest or 'natural' voice as compared with the more penetrating but less vibrant and rounded sounds of the female 'head voice'.

Thus orchiectomy inhibited the growth of the larynx before the voice broke, in other words before the boy, because of the lowering of the sounds by an octave which takes place in the adult, took on the characteristics of a man's voice. An operation was therefore carried out on the testes (by binding the testicular cord and possibly even by removing the testes in certain cases), the result being—the effect was known at the time but not the cause—a stoppage of the secretion of testosterone, the hormone that causes the growth of the larynx.

Orchiectomy took away the ability to procreate, since the testicles were atrophied and no longer secreted spermatozoa, but it left the possibility of coitus, since the germinal fluid arises in the prostate. Hence the amorous exploits of certain famous castrati. However, the absence of testosterone could cause premature aging, early weakening of the erection capacity of the male member, and forms of senile melancholia in still relatively youthful individuals.

Through the effect of orchiectomy, the castrato voice retained the ring, the freshness, and the carrying power of the boy's voice. Among the secondary manifestations was the appearance of pseudo-feminine characteristics (inhibited growth of the beard, for example) and the so-called keel chest (*pectus carenatum*), with expansion of the rib-cage, leaving more space for the development of the lungs. Subjected as he was to assiduous and extremely strenuous vocal exercises,[1] the boy castrato acquired an abnormal lung capacity, which had a direct impact on his ability to hold his breath for a long time, and on the power of his tone. This exceptional mastery of breath control and breathing power, combined with his assiduous training, was responsible for the flexibility, the soft edge, the agility, the wide range, the ease of legato, and other qualities which, although common to all the great singers of the eighteenth century and the early nineteenth century, were nevertheless present in a more spontaneous and marked way in some castrati.

In particular, the castrati took great pains with the so-called

---

[1] In the Roman schools during the 17th c., 3–4 hours daily, plus as many again devoted to the study of theory of music, counterpoint, composition, and harpsichord.

'singing on the breath' method, adumbrated by writers on singing like Tosi and Mancini,[2] both of them castrati, with empirical jargon terms like 'chest resistance', 'supporting the voice with the natural strength of the chest without tightening the throat', and thus preventing the sound from becoming 'wrongly placed and heavy'. Actually, 'chest' here is synomymous with 'breath', and the notion that the two writers are trying to convey is that in correct phonation a sound is attacked, sustained, amplified, whittled down exclusively on the basis of the amount of breath which the singer, by regulating the action of the diaphragm and making use of the resistance between the breathing-in and breathing-out muscles, decides quite deliberately to allow to escape from the lungs. All this involves an absolute ban on constriction of the larynx ('tightening the throat') which is typical of those who do not know how to sing on the breath and hence emit forced, guttural or nasal sounds. In short, the flow of the breath, which causes the vocal cords to vibrate, corresponds to the action of the bow which makes the strings of a bowed instrument vibrate. Singing on the breath is like the 'bowing' of a good violinist, viola player, or cellist who obtains sostenuto sound in his playing, as well as variety of colour and intensity, by deliberately regulating the speed and pressure of the bow.

Bound up with the notion of singing on the breath, however, is also that of the correct place of resonance. To put it in empirical terms, just as the sound of a bowed instrument is amplified by the resonance chamber, so the singing voice is amplified by the cavities in the thorax and the head, particularly those in the upper part of the face. A sound which is not properly sustained by the breath fails to take full advantage of the resonance cavities of the head or to coordinate their activity with that of the resonance chamber of the thorax—with an adverse effect on the timbre, evenness of tone, softness, flexibility, legato, and capacity to alternate forte and piano and to emit penetrating high notes without effort. The voice of a performer singing on the breath gives the listener a feeling which is not easy to describe, but which is perfectly clear to a practised ear. First and foremost, we get the impression that the sound is formed in the upper part of the face ('dans le masque', to use the jargon term). Furthermore, the tone

---

[2] P. Fr. Tosi, *Opinioni de' cantori antichi e moderni*, Bologna, 1723; G. B. Mancini, *Pensieri e reflessioni pratiche sopra il canto figurato*, Vienna, 1774.

passes from piano to forte and to all the intermediate gradations, or vice versa, with such ease and spontaneity as to give the sensation that it is 'floating' on the breath of the singer emitting the sound. In high notes, then, the emission of the voice on the breath and 'dans le masque' is reflected in spontaneous, intense vibrations, good timbre and ringing tone.[3]

The castrati were in all probability also in the front rank in research on the so-called *passaggio* or change of register. The question is somewhat complex and anyhow bound up with physiological principles. The voice which Tosi and Mancini called 'natural' or 'chest' voice included, in the case of sopranos (this is stated by Tosi) the part of the range between c′ and c″–d″. Beyond d″, with few exceptions, if the voice continued to climb, the sound became forced, muffled, veiled, or even strident. To avoid this drawback it was necessary, after c″ or d″, to change over to the falsetto register, as it was then called. Today we know that the passage of the register consists of bringing about by a variety of devices, but particularly by darkening the sound of the vowel, a tilting or lowering of the larynx. Without this the singer cannot reach the high notes or his voice grows hoarse or becomes strident and edgy, as already mentioned. At the time of the castrati, nothing was known about the physiological basis of the *passaggio*, but the technique had been found which made the change possible. We still have the impression, however, that the practice of register change only became general towards the middle of the seventeenth century, and that it was only applied to one or two types of voice.

The tessitura and the range of the (female) contralto, for

---

[3] The difference between singers using production 'on the breath' and 'in the mask' and others, even though it is unknown to the vast majority of those who teach singing today, is easily perceptible on gramophone records. Recordings by the best prima donnas of the last 30 years (provided they represent the best period of these singers) reflect the return to classic voice production—which had virtually disappeared among sopranos and mezzo-sopranos of the preceding period—to be found in Callas, Tebaldi, Olivero, Simionato, Schwarzkopf in the immediate post-war years, and later Gencer, Sutherland, Horne, Caballé, Freni, Verrett, Kabaivanska, and a number of others. Actually, it is not difficult to hear good singing today even from sopranos and mezzos who are by no means celebrated. In the last 30 years, however, the opposite phenomenon has taken place among male voices, which have decidedly deteriorated from the technical point of view. Hence the best tenors, baritones, and basses are those of the 1920s and 1930s, who provide the most authentic examples on records of emission on the breath and 'singing in the mask'.

example, during the period when this voice was used exclusively for buffo roles, would suggest that only the chest or 'natural' register was used. (Incidentally, it was well suited to grotesque effects, if we think of the resonant but hollow, coarse sound which the French call 'poitriné'.) With regard to the emasculated male altos, it seems not unlikely that until the beginning of the eighteenth century they used only the natural or chest voice (hence their limited range on top), about which Tosi has the following to say: 'Many teachers make their pupils sing "contralto" because they do not know how to make them sing a falsetto, or else in order to save themselves the trouble of looking for it.' Tosi also complained that in his day—again because of the inability of teachers to show their pupils how to manage the register change from chest voice to falsetto—there was a great shortage of male soprano singers; or else there were male sopranos who were obliged to change over to male alto, while continuing 'out of foolish vanity to call themselves sopranos'. But in actual practice, these had to request composers not to write arias for them in which the voice had to sing above c″.

Neither Tosi nor Mancini is concerned with any type of voice other than the castrato. But it is obvious that no type of voice, from bass to soprano, is able to sing up to the high notes correctly without changing register. This was true both for the seventeenth century and for the eighteenth century, and probably following the principles which only the theorists of the early nineteenth century, in particular Manuel Garcia the Younger, took the trouble to expound.

The term 'falsetto register' used by Tosi and Mancini can give rise to error. Obviously it was not a question of thin sounds, since both writers make it clear that the purpose of the register change was to fuse the characteristics of the chest voice (bigger, broader, and more sharp-edged) with the falsetto voice, which is more nuanced, more carrying, more suited to flexibility and agility singing. The trouble is that in the type of singing about which Tosi was writing we have the impression that the teaching was designed first and foremost to give the student the 'falsetto' voice and then, bringing it downwards, to blend it in with the chest voice, adding to this the flexibility and agility of the high register. Hence it could be presumed that until the beginning of the eighteenth century, the castrati had used for their high notes a sort of reinforced falsetto or *falsettone*, sufficiently round and bright (at any rate as round and bright as the falsetto tone of the tenors of the first few decades of the nineteenth century were); furthermore, that they adjusted the intensity and strength of the chest notes to bring them to some extent into line with the *falsettone*. But with the Bolognese school,[4] and perhaps also with the Neapolitan school of Porpora from which Farinelli came, people began to speak of chest voice production even in relation to the higher-register and agility passages. Here, however, the old teaching theories (in particular that of Mancini) went wrong, exactly in the same way as the theorists of the nineteenth century likewise went wrong apropos of the tenor's 'top c in chest voice' (*do di petto*). The fact is that the Bolognese school blended into the falsetto register certain characteristics of the chest voice, obtaining full, ringing sounds on high notes. But to achieve this, it had always to use the change of register and always to make use of 'mixed voice' (*voce mista*), since high notes 'in chest voice' do not exist. The only ones that do exist are the coarse, timbreless, opaque, guttural, forced, and strident high notes of singers who do not really know how, when the occasion arises, to execute the *passaggio* from the chest voice mechanism to that of head voice. In fact the *do di petto* of the tenor is really a 'mixed' note; and so is the g of the baritone and the f of the bass.

From what has been said here it is possible to deduce:

—That in the final phase of the polyphonic period, the 'ars suaviter et eleganter cantandi' which embodied Finck's theories[5] was not backed up by a really sound voice production technique, but was founded mostly on fine natural gifts (the *disposizione* of which some of the writers of the period speak), characterized above all by the capacity to sing sweetly and to execute agility passages in mainly middle tessituras. These qualities are also

---

[4] The founder of the Bolognese school was the male alto Francesco Antonio Pistocchi (Palermo, 1639–Bologna 1726). His most famous pupils were the castrati Antonio Bernacchi and Giovanni Battista Minelli and the tenors Annibale Pio Fabri and Antonio Pasi. His successor was Bernacchi, who is more specifically credited with the dissemination of 'chest production'. Bernacchi's most important pupils were the contralto Vittoria Tesi Tramontini, the castrati Giovanni Tedeschi, known as Amadori, and Tommaso Guarducci, and the tenors Carlo Carlani and Antonio Raaf, as well as the musicologist and teacher Giovanni Battista Mancini.

[5] See p. 14.

bound up with a high level of musical education, since in almost all instances the singers were also composers.

—That no theoretician of the period speaks of the register change. A few (Zacconi, Caccini) contrast the roundness and the strength of the natural or chest voice with the strident sound of the falsetto emitted by male voices. Exceptionally (this is stated by Zacconi and above all in Domenico Cerone's *Melopeo*, 1603), singers could be found who had a *mezzana* (medium) voice: these were probably the ones in whom the register change had come about spontaneously and unconsciously.

—That in the earliest operas, all the voices took off from the vocalism of the final phase of polyphony, including the castrati, who were, however, because of their orchiectomy, endowed with a greater measure of *disposizione*.

—That between 1630 and 1650 the castrati, particularly those of the Roman school, which at the time was in the forefront, began to practise singing on the breath and changing register, and that gradually other singers adopted their methods, apart from the doubts already raised about male altos and female contraltos. Symbolic of this leap forward in technical skill is the male soprano Baldassarre Ferri.[6] The range of two octaves he is said to have had, the length of time he could hold a breath, and his habit of executing the most complex agility passages without the slightest movement of his face muscles and without varying the opening of his mouth, are indications of extremely elaborate phonation. Nevertheless, none of the theoreticians of the time (not even the Frenchmen Bacilly and Mersenne) mention the register mechanism. The first person to speak of it was Tosi (who presumably began his studies about 1660), in his book *Opinioni* (1723).

—That up to the end of the seventeenth century and the first few years of the eighteenth century, as Tosi maintains, the elegiac-pathetic style prevailed, and that this particularly favoured the castrati, with their ease of production and reinforced falsetto (*falsettone*) in agility passages.

That the years 1715–20 or so saw the beginning of the sonorous chest-tone production, particularly in the *passaggio* region, in Bernacchi, Farinelli, Carestini, and others, but without this affecting agility, flexibility, and soft tones. It marks the triumph of

[6] See pp. 37–8.

vigorous vocalism, of the 'sensitive' style, and also of so-called bravura singing, which consists specifically in the execution of full-voice coloratura, as opposed to plaintive, flute-like execution known as graceful or 'mannered' agility.

—That in the second half of the eighteenth century, the vogue for high and extremely high notes and for agility passages executed with lightning speed led male sopranos—and in their wake male altos and (women) sopranos and contraltos—to lighten and clarify the sounds, turning to the falsetto (or *falsettone*) production lamented by Metastasio and leading to overdone virtuosity, to the detriment of expressiveness.

But leaving aside the technical advances which the castrati helped to popularize, they must be given the credit for having introduced and developed the taste which governed the best singing of the Golden Age, and the inventor of which, according to Tosi, was Pistocchi. The best concise and accurate definition of this taste is probably that given by Tartini in his *Trattato di musica* (1754): 'It consists first and foremost in the voice of the singer being produced and used with sweetness, control, power, sostenuto when required, etc. Secondly, it consists of appoggiaturas, trills, rubato and protracted sounds, and methods of singing, natural and artificial, adapted as required to cantilena, etc.'

'TEMPEST' ARIAS

Simile, metaphor, figurative language were elements of which Italian poetry in the sixteenth century, lyric or tragic, made a somewhat excessive use, and this continued also in the succeeding two centuries. But Italy was not alone. The love of far-fetched simile was an aspect of Spanish tragedy too; nor did the French tragedy of Racine and Corneille, or even English tragedy, remain impervious to the cult of the metaphor. On this, or rather against this, rivers of ink have flowed, the main arguments being three: (*a*) tragedy hinged on human emotions, and human emotions called for simplicity of ideas; (*b*) the introduction of the simile or metaphor put into the mouth of a character at a moment of crisis interrupted the thread of the action; (*c*) metaphors and other figures of speech, especially if they were tinged with 'marinism', were distorted and forced.

In spite of this, the simile and the metaphor remained un-
disturbed throughout a good part of the eighteenth century and,
naturally, found their way over into opera when music captured
and absorbed—unlike what had happened in Spain, France, and
England—most of the theatrical energies and characteristics of
Italy. Hence the 'comparison' aria was one of the landmarks of
opera, an immovable institution. Among the comparison arias,
the 'tempest' aria occupied a very important position. This is the
aria in which a particular state of mind or a particular stage
situation induces one of the characters to make observations of a
moral nature (for example, the changing motion of the sea is
likened to change of fortune or of human nature) or leads the
character to compare the tumult of his passions to the fury of the
waves.

Basically we are faced here with an outlook which is typically
Italian, or if you like, typically one of fantasy: music seen not
merely as the reflection of feelings, but as a representation of
natural phenomena. 'The Italians want tunes of every description
which will reproduce the various types of image that music is
capable of depicting.' Thus wrote de Brosses, one of the
eighteenth-century chroniclers who came closest to the world of
Italian opera. But the notion needs to be rounded off. That instrumental music can describe a battle or a storm was a notion
accepted and practised in the seventeenth century universally.
But what the Italians tried to do, and basically succeeded in doing,
was to make singing participate in such descriptions. This trend,
before it reached opera, was to be found in the madrigal, and here
the phenomenon was not exclusively Italian. For substantives and
adjectives expressive of darkness, fog, mist, etc. to find their vocal
equivalents in the lower parts of the stave, where the sound is
dark and obscure, was commonplace throughout the madrigal
period; and similarly for the voice to rise in keeping with words
like 'sky', 'firmament', etc. But in the transition from the a cappella
period to the monodic madrigal, and thence to opera, the descriptive trends crystallized and became more precise, turning into a
typically Italian phenomenon, since the means of expression, in
other words virtuoso vocalism, had become typically Italian.

Let us now turn to literature. In 1515, when opera had still not
arrived and Italy was involved in its first attempts at theatre in

prose, Sofonisba, the protagonist in the well-known tragedy of Gian Giorgio Trissino, speaks as follows:

> Turbato è il mare e mosso un vento rio.
> Purtroppo oimé par tempo
> che la mia nave disarmata iscoglia.

(The sea is wild and the wind is fierce. Alas! I fear that ere long my boat will be wrecked.)

But more important for our purposes is the passage spoken by Oronte in *Orbecche*, by Giovan Battista Giraldi, a tragedy written in 1541. Orbecche, the daughter of the Persian king Sulmone, has married Oronte without her father's knowledge. Naturally, this causes all kinds of trouble and vicissitudes for the young couple. This is how Oronte philosophizes on his misfortunes:

> Difficile è nell'onde acerbe, e crude
> quando l'irato mar poggia e rinforza,
> tener dritto il timone: ma non deve
> però esperto Nocchier perder sí l'arte
> che dall'ira del mar rimanga vinto.
> senza opporsi al furor: che spesse volte
> vince il altrui valor l'aspra tempesta
> e s'avvien pur che'ei si sommerga in mare,
> gran parte di contento è non avere
> lasciato cosa a far per sua salvezza.

(It is difficult in the fierce, cruel waves, when the angry sea is tossing and raging, to hold the tiller straight. But the skilled mariner must not lose his head and give in; he must resist the sea's fury. For often the wild storm prevails, and the sailor is drowned. It is a great source of comfort to have left nothing undone to ensure his safety.)

These are notions typical of the 'tempest' aria. Indeed if it were not for the metre (hendecasyllabic verse was certainly not made for opera), we would have here, from the librettist's point of view, a regular 'tempest' aria. The only trouble is that this is 1541, and opera had not yet come into existence; but even when opera was born, let it be said, the 'tempest' aria needed some time to take shape. The reason is probably a simple one: vocal technique had not yet evolved sufficiently to suggest the acrobatic, imitative effects that subsequently brought this type of metaphor into prominence. Opera in the seventeenth century confined itself in general to an embryonic fashioning of individual elements or sections of what was to be the 'tempest' aria. Furthermore, the taste of the opera composers and librettists of the seventeenth century seems to have been drawn not so much towards tempests as towards idyllic descriptions of the sea, and above all of rivers: the peaceful flowing of the waters, the rippling and sheen of the waves. And even in describing the wind, they preferred caressing breezes and the gentle rustling of the leaves to the whistling and howling of the gale. Furthermore, in the second half of the seventeenth century, the nascent vocal virtuosity found its stimulus in other types of arias: those with trumpet accompaniment, for example, or the earliest imitations of bird-song, or scenes of fury, vengeance, and jealousy. When, later on, seventeenth-century opera wanted to depict the contrasting passions of a character, it did so—as has already been pointed out in connection with Cesti, Legrenzi, Sartorio, and Pietro Andrea Ziani— with the 'doubt' aria which, from the purely vocal point of view, but also to some extent on psychological grounds, constitutes the most immediate precedent to the 'tempest' aria. We have seen, however, that Ziani, in *Semiramide*,[7] finding himself in a situation typical of a librettist of a 'tempest' aria, solves the problem with vocalism which is deliberately plain and unadorned. On the other hand, Steffani, when he had to face 'tempest' aria situations, as in the first scene of *Henrico Leone*, found solutions which were confined to devices such as emphasizing the word *vènti* with an ascending scale. It was to Scarlatti, in his first opera (*Gli equivoci nel sembiante*, 1679) that it fell to set to music, on the basis of a libretto by Contini, an embryonic 'tempest' aria dealing with sudden changes in nature and in men:

> Un'aura soave
> crudel gli diventa
> e in porto paventa
> di franger la nave

(A gentle breeze turns into a gale and threatens to destroy the vessel in the habour.)

But the vocal writing (it is sung by a tenor, Armido, in III. i)

---

[7] See p. 51.

makes no attempt at imitation. The melody is idyllic in character and presents languid *fioriture* which fall, with identical figuration, both on the word 'crudel' and on the word 'soave'. In *L'honestà negli amori*, written in the following year, the aria 'Scogli voi che v'indurate', sung by the contralto Rosmira, has the outline of a coloratura in the phrase 'All'urtar d'onde frementi'. But already in *Tutto il mal non vien per nuocere* (1681), the sentence 'Son di scoglio se il ciel lo combatte' is elaborated boldly on the word 'combatte'. Later on, at a time when the 'tempest' aria was on its way to becoming an institution in opera writing, Scarlatti wrote a fairly long vocalise to render the meaning of the verb 'errando' (wandering helpessly): 'Cosí la navicella/ chi perde la sua stella/ scherzo dei sordi venti/ errando vassi'—*Scipione nelle Spagne*, 1714, the Allegro sung by Sofonisba (soprano); or again, describing the turbulence in the mind of Giuditta (soprano) in *Carlo re d'Allemagna* (1716), he attempted to reproduce by means of sudden swoops in the voice and a rapid series of two-note groups the tossing of a vessel by the sea (Ex. 49).

Ex. 49

It is precisely between 1715 and 1720, coinciding with the first real period of acrobatic vocalism, that the 'tempest' aria takes on definite features, both literary and musical. Fairly typical is the aria that occurs in *Amor di figlia*, by Giovanni Porta (1718) to a libretto by Domenico Lalli. The 'simile' procedure has by now attained full development through a fairly specific description first of all of the waves beating against the rocks, then through the second term of the comparison—the beating of the human heart.

> Mobil onda
> che rupe circonda,
> spuma e piange,
> in se stessa si frange
> e del vento la scuote il furore.
> Tace il core sol cinto d'amore,

si raggira e nel seno vien meno
palpitando fra rabbia e rancor.

(The hurtling wave frothing and moaning round the rocks breaks on itself
and is caught by the fury of the wind. Only the heart surrounded by love
is quiet and composed, no longer throbbing with rage and bitterness.)

In this aria we have relatively simple melismatic circumlo-
cutions, bearing of course on specific words: 'si frange', for
example. But above all, the first part imitates the notion of the
waves billowing, then falling back; and this is accomplished by
plunging leaps from high notes to low notes, emphasized by the
fact that the aria is written for a contralto, the ideal voice for such
effects. The tessitura, incidentally, is extremely low and the range
is for the most part contained between a and b♭' flat.

In Handel's *Agrippina* (1709) we have the beginnings of a
'tempest' aria in the Allegro by the protagonist 'L'alma mia fra le
tempeste/ ritrovar spera il suo porto'. I say beginnings, because
the description and the comparison are not expressed in depth or
developed as in Porta's aria, and the coloratura, essentially based
on progressions of four-note semiquaver groups, does not imitate
billowing waves, but accentuates fairly generally words like 'alma'
and 'ritrovar'. One of Handel's first 'tempest' arias in the true
sense of the term is to be found in *Radamisto* (1720). It is the
Largo sung by the protagonist (in the first version the soprano
Durastanti), 'Qual nave smarrita tra sirti e tempesta'. Written in
syllabic style, this piece makes use of the well-known imitative
procedure of periodic ascending and descending leaps. Again in
the syllabic style is the Allegro sung by the protagonist in *Ottone*
(1723) 'Dell'onda i fieri moti'. A highly virtuoso aria is the Allegro
sung by Cleopatra (Cuzzoni) in *Giulio Cesare*: 'Da tempeste il legno
infranto/ se poi salvo giunge in porto/ non sa più che desiar'; but
the long, varied, elaborately worked out coloratura of some of the '
passages underlines especially words like 'desiar' or 'bear'.

Still more typical, as a 'tempest' aria, is the Allegro sung by
Adelaide (the soprano Strada) in *Lotario* (1729):

> Scherza in mar la navicella
> mentre ride aura seconda,
> ma se poi fiera procella
> turba il ciel, sconvolge l'onda
> va perduta a naufragar.

(The boat rides playfully on the waters while the gentle breeze is smiling. But if a raging storm darkens the sky and lashes the waves into a frenzy, the boat will sink and be lost.)

The imitative procedure is obvious. The style is graceful to begin with, then the storm is suggested by the usual rising and falling leaps (Ex. 50). A long vocalise passage, fairly varied in its figures and characterized again by soaring leaps, then unwinds on the word 'naufragar'.

Ex. 50

In *Ezio* (1732) we find a 'tempest' aria written for tenor voice. It is Massimo's aria 'Il nocchier che si figura/ ogni scoglio, ogni tempesta'. The style is syllabic and full of leaps, the tempo is Andante, and the tessitura is very low. Even in later operas, Handel tends in his 'tempest' arias to fall back on fairly well-worn procedures. Meleagro's Allegro: 'Tu solcasti il mare infido' (*Atalanta*, 1736), written for the male soprano Conti, known as Il Gizziello, begins with upward vaults followed immediately, on the words 'agitata navicella', by the pairs of notes used also by Scarlatti for the same words in *Carlo re d'Allemagna*, except that in Handel—a sign of the development of virtuosity that came about between 1716 and 1736—the pairs of notes are semiquavers (Ex. 51).

Ex. 51

Similar figures, but in quavers, alternating with groups of two semiquavers and a quaver, are characteristic of the beginning of the Allegro sung by Leocasta, 'Sventurata navicella', in *Giustino*.

Actually, if we take the Allegro 'Da tempesta il legno infranto' from *Giulio Cesare* and the other Allegro 'Scherza in mar la navicella' from *Lotario*, the 'tempest' arias in Handel do not seem to call for the same acrobatic vocalism as in the operas written in Italy between 1725 and 1750. Apart from anything else, the libretto writing from now onwards, still in Italy, is under the aegis of Metastasio, who was extremely adept in handling both the rapid passage of violent squalls and high moralizings and exhortations to be drawn from them.

> Benché turbato e nero
> il ciel si vegga e il mar,
> non teme il buon nocchiero
> né lascia di sperare tranquilla calma.

(Although the sky and the sea are turbulent and dark, the stalwart mariner is not afraid, nor ceases to hope for calm and tranquillity.)

The above is from *Siface*. The following is from the *L'eroe cinese*:

> Quando il mar biancheggia e freme
> quando el ciel lampeggia e tuona
> il nocchier che s'abbandona
> va sicuro a naufragar.

(When the rough sea grows white with spume and the sky flashes with lightning and roars with thunder, the sailor who gives up the struggle will surely be shipwrecked.)

Apostolo Zeno too conceived the notion of the 'tempest' aria:

> Son qual nave in ria procella
> quando Borea più l'incalza
> ch'or l'affonda ed or l'innalza
> or la porta a naufragar.
> Splende solo in ciel mia stella
> perché io vegga il mio periglio,
> ma senz'arte né consiglio
> ho la tomba in mezzo di mar.

(I am like a ship in a raging storm, when the north wind is at its fiercest, now lifting the craft out of the water, now plunging it into the depths and threatening to wreck it. My star alone gleams in the sky, warning me of my danger. But without skill and good guidance I shall find my grave at the bottom of the sea.)

This is one of the arias sung by Decio in *Zenobia in Palmira*, an opera produced in 1725, with music by Leonardo Leo. The part of Decio was played by Farinelli. Here too, the wide intervals, rising and falling, are the basic imitative element, but made more urgent and more exciting by the dotted rhythm and the trills (Ex. 52).

Ex. 52

The same tension, but with different figurations, marks the effects describing the word 'naufragar' (shipwreck) (Ex. 53). But these are

Ex. 53

merely fragments of the aria. Even though there are only eight lines of verse in all, section A (the first four verses) was repeated twice before going on to section B, which begins with 'Splende solo in ciel mia stella', and this is in turn prolonged at the end, by repetitions of the sentence 'ho la tomba in mezzo al mar'. Then section A is repeated in its entirety with the variations added by the singer. Nor is this all; the singer had to insert a cadenza at the end of section A, another at the end of section B, and a third, long and elaborate, to conclude the da capo. Thus it amounted to a bewildering succession of vocalises and passages of syllabic writing with sudden leaps upwards and downwards, in both cases with continual changes in figuration and ornamentation.[8] This will give some idea of the difficulties the executant had to cope with.

Mention has been made[9] of the aria 'Vo solcando un mar crudele' from Vinci's *Artaserse* (1713), written for Carestini. Note the vocal line, in syllabic style, carried in a gradually upward movement on to a high tessitura, and then the imitation of the vessel, its mast gone, now rising high out of the water, now plunging into the depths (Ex. 54). What is also interesting in this

Ex. 54

aria is the imitation of the gathering windstorm. The two trills at the beginning of Ex. 55 almost certainly called for a gradual crescendo, after which the singer attacked the vocalise, without taking a breath. Note also that Carestini, even during the period when he was singing as a male soprano, possessed bass notes of

Ex. 55

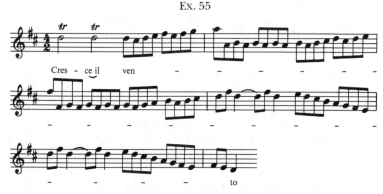

---

[8] This configuration was of course not used only for 'tempest' arias but for all the main ternary arias, whether cantabile or fast-moving. However, from 1725 onwards—or even before—'tempest' arias rose to great heights of virtuosity.

[9] See p. 75.

unusual sonority, and their effect, contrasting with the high notes, is clearly used by Vinci to imitate at one moment the violent whistling and the next the deep grumbling and moaning of the wind.

I have already mentioned[10] another 'tempest' aria by Vinci, impressive both for its exceptionally low tessitura and for the length of the vocalise passages and the variety of the coloratura. This is the Andante 'Navigante che non spera' sung by the protagonist in *Medo* (1728), a role written for Farinelli. In the example below (Ex. 56) the voice goes down—probably the only instance in the whole history of opera—to C.

Ex. 56

Na - vi - gan-te che non spe-ra   più toc-car lon - ta - na   ter - ra

Very different is the manner in which Hasse in *Demetrio* (1732) dealt with the word 'tempesta' in Alceste's Allegro 'Scherza il nocchier talora'. He had recourse to a graceful vocalise built up on short *fioriture*, interrupted by rests. Here is the model, which seems to look for inspiration to the patterns dear to the male alto Bernacchi, who in fact played Alceste. It must be remembered, however, that in 1732 such figurations could appear antiquated in comparison with the new devices introduced by Farinelli and Carestini (Ex. 57).

Ex. 57

Allegro

The vogue for the 'tempest' aria became more pronounced after 1730, and Hasse's *Demetrio* contains another, 'Non fidi al mar che freme', sung by Olinto and written for the male alto Appiani. Vivaldi's *Griselda*, dated 1735, contains no fewer than three

---

[10] See p. 75.

'tempest' arias: 'Se ria procella', sung by Gualtiero, 'Vede orgo-
gliosa l'onda', sung by Ottone; and 'Agitata da due vènti', sung by
Constanza. Also by Vivaldi is one of the most beautiful arias in
this style ever written: the Presto 'Sorge l'irato nembo', sung by
Pompeo (male alto), in *Farnace* (1726), and noteworthy not so much
for the complexity of the coloratura as for its melodic inspiration
and for the accompaniment, given over to the strings.[11]

'Tempest' arias were normally entrusted to 'white' voices, but as
we have already seen, in particular cases they could be assigned
also to tenors. Segeste's Allegro, 'Solcar pensa un mar sicuro' from
Hasse's *Arminio* (the Dresden version of 1745) is one of the most
virtuosic arias written for this voice, intended as it was for the
greatest tenor of the first half of the eighteenth century, Angelo
Amorevoli. But the most frenzied instance of vocal acrobatics was
reached in Arbace's aria 'Son qual nave che agitata' (Allegro assai,
in 4/4 time), composed for Farinelli by his brother Riccardo and
inserted into Hasse's *Artaserse*. The researches of Franz Harböck
(*Gesangskunst der Kastraten*, Vienna, 1923) also provide us with the
ornamented version, with one vocalise which, among other
things, goes on without a pause for twenty bars and presents on
the word 'mare' a terrifying complex of series of runs and trills.

The vogue for 'tempest' arias gradually died down towards the
end of the eighteenth century; but Anfossi's *Antigono* still contains
one sung by the protagonist (tenor) and sustained by the elegance
of Metastasio's verses:

> Va scherzando sulla sponda
> fresca auretta e il mar è in pace,
> ma se il vento incalza l'onda
> trema il lido e freme il mar.
> E il nocchier che sulla prora
> già cantò dell'onde in seno,
> si confonde, si scolora
> di quel vento al sibilar.

(Playfully along the shore a fresh breeze blows gently and the sea is calm.
But if the wind stirs up the waves, the shoreline trembles and the ocean
roars. And the mariner who sang on the prow as he rode the billows is
alarmed and turns pale as the wind begins to howl.)

---

[11] This aria is included in the recorded edn. of Vivaldi's *Orlando furioso* issued in
1977 by Erato. It is performed by Marilyn Horne (II. ii).

BUFFO ROLES

The introduction of comic episodes into serious opera during the seventeenth century is the outcome of the vogue for Spanish drama, but it also illustrates the distrust felt by the seventeenth century for so-called unity of tone, which often turned out to mean uniformity, tedium, monotony. Frivolous episodes alternating with moralistic preaching, grotesque characters side by side with tragic personages, thus became the rule, significant features in a game of relief and diversion aimed specifically at variety. That this in turn made for discontinuity, bittiness, imbalance, and moments of stage business which by today's standards seem coarse and vulgar, there can be no doubt. But to judge the phenomenon using an exclusively aesthetic yardstick would be to repeat the mistake of all those who have set out to seek absolute, universal, and unchanging beauty, ignoring the historical and social motives underlying certain phenomena. Comic characters inserted into serious opera were the basic nucleus of the initial form of light opera—the 'intermezzo'. The function of the intermezzo was similar to that which at the beginning of our own century was played in the cinema by the short comic films put on following the 'tear-jerkers'. Their popularity was based not only on the desirability of alternating between the grotesque and the serious for the sake of variety, but also on the need to allow the audience to recover its psychological balance of emotions upset by the immediately preceding spectacle. But even before the intermezzo existed, this sedative function was fulfilled precisely by the grotesque figures inserted into serious opera, in addition to the fact that the presence of comic elements in works based on mythology and fable acted as a counterweight to the abstract nature of the plot and the vocal language, introducing figures literally taken from everyday life: the good-for-nothing servant, the court buffoon, the sponger, the nurse/procuress, the braggart soldier, the sharp-witted page-boy, and so on.

It was the opera of the Roman school, closely bound up with the influence of the Spanish 'legitimate' theatre, that took the first steps, introducing into Stefano Landi's *Sant'Alessio*, together with the Devil (who has something inherently grotesque in his make-up), two smart page-boys, Marcio and Curzio, devotees of *la dolce vita*, whose credo is summed up in the duet: 'Poca voglia di far bene/ viver lieto, andare a spasso . . .' (We are not interested in doing good. Let's have fun). These two stage types illustrate the pattern of some of the vocal traits characteristic of the comic roles of seventeenth-century serious opera. For example, Marcio and Curzio are baritone-tenors—a type of voice regarded as ordinary and vulgar by bel canto standards and hence suitable for character or buffo roles.

In *Chi soffre speri*, by Marco Marazzoli and Virgilio Mazzocchi, some of the comic characters are borrowed from *Commedia dell'arte*—Coviello, a Neapolitan swashbuckling fellow, and Zanni, a mask-figure of Lombard origin used for servant types. Both express themselves in the local dialect. Luigi Rossi in his first opera, *Il palazzo incantato d'Atlante*, expanded the range of grotesque characters. He made use of the bass voice to introduce figures like Mandricardo and Gradasso, the deep timbre and the impressive sound making a comic contrast with the starchy, mannered character of the singing (cf. the duet in the first act, 'Ha lampi immortali la vostra beltà'). Then, in *Orfeo*, put on the stage in 1647, Rossi and the librettist Francesco Buti introduced certain comic characters of a kind that in the Venetian school were already commonplace. In a plot more complex and intricate than that with which the fable of Orpheus had hitherto been set to music, we get the intervention of three characters inspired by the society of the time: the servant Momo who sings tenor; Satiro, bass or bass-baritone, the confidant of Aristeo who in the opera plays the part of the lovesick wooer of Euridice and rival of Orpheo; and Euridice's nurse, impersonated by a male soprano. Momo appears, endowed among other things with a characteristic which Venetian opera was to assign fairly frequently to figures of that ilk—a background of down-to-earth scepticism reflected in philosophizing on human nature and, in particular, on the nature of women—cf. the song: 'È la moglie una materia/ che fa l'uom sempre ridicolo' (Woman is a stuff that always makes a man look a fool). Satiro is not just the confidant, but the accomplice of Aristeo. Together they decide to abduct Euridice, but she escapes, and it is as she runs away that a poisonous snake causes her death by biting her in the foot. Aristeo goes mad with remorse, and in his madness he believes he is the snake Pitone (Python) and sings an aria of dramatic content (All'armi mio core'—Aristeo is a male soprano); Momo and Satiro intervene with a burlesque song based on the tags 'tararà, tararà' and 'tappatà, tappatà'. As for the old nurse, in her role we catch a glimpse of two elements characteristic of the part: affection for her 'god-daughter', her charge, and along with it the tendency to play the go-between. On the basis of this baggage of traits, the Venetian school was to make the nurse-figure even more grotesque and more immoral.

Monteverdi already offers genuine examples of grotesque characters transplanted into mythological and historical operas. One such is the hanger-on Iro (tenor) in *Il ritorno d'Ulisse*—a deformed, stuttering, boastful creature, who feeds on the advancement of the Suitors. In *L'incoronazione di Poppea*, on the other hand, the comic element is handed over to other character types. In the first act we find in the duet between the sentinels looking after Poppea's house (tenors) a motif which is later taken up by other composers: that of the soldier bemoaning his professional lot. But above all, Arnalta, Poppea's nurse (male alto), is outstanding for her devotion to her mistress in the beautiful 'sleep' aria 'Oblivion soave', and for her good-natured common sense and humour in the penultimate scene of the second act. At this point, Poppea is close to being crowned empress, and Arnalta looks like becoming an important person and anticipates the probable consequences:

> Chi mi diede del tu
> hor con nova armonia
> gorgheggerammi 'il vostra signoria'
> Chi m'incontra per strada
> mi dice 'fresca donna e bella ancora'
> Ed io pur so che sembro
> delle sibille il leggendario antro,
> ma ognun così m'adula
> credendo guadagnarmi
> per interceder grazia di Poppea;
> ed io fingendo non capir le frodi
> in coppa di bugie bevo le lodi.

(Those who were familiar with me have now changed their tune and warble 'Your ladyship'. People in the street compliment me on my fresh complexion and enduring good looks. I am like the Sibyl's legendary cave. But they all flatter me, hoping that I will put in a good word for them with Poppaea. I pretend not to understand their tricks and just accept their eulogies.)

This arioso recitative, very varied in rhythm and prosody and enlivened by splendid *ribattuta*-like trills (it is hardly surprising that Arnalta feels herself a great lady), together with the 'sleep' aria 'Oblivion soave', paints a picture of the most striking comic-realistic character in seventeenth-century opera. In contrast, the characters I have referred to so far—with the possible exception of the hanger-on Iro in *Il ritorno d'Ulisse*—are rather colourless puppets. Their tunes are short of breath, their vocal language is syllabic, and the tessitura of the tenors and male altos is very low.

With Cavalli, the antics of the buffo personages are already largely crystallized. The theme of the soldier who curses his lot, touched on by Monteverdi in *L'incoronazione di Poppea*, is taken up in *Doriclea*, dating from 1645, with one variant, namely that here the character doing the grumbling is a bass rather than a tenor. The scheming of old nurses, on the other hand, is the mainspring of a number of operas. Finally, there is no end to the weak, lily-livered servants (who at times operate in pairs, like Paggio and Lisco in *Ercole*) or the classic buffoon types, deformed, stuttering, vainglorious, mean, who take after Iro in *Il ritorno d'Ulisse* (for example Hiro in *Helena rapita da Theseo*, who is a tenor). Note-worthy in Cavalli's operas is the tendency of the librettist to vulgarize certain types or to slip into *double entendres* and the open use of licentious speech. The nurses no longer have the good-natured common sense of Arnalta in *L'incoronazione*. They become shady characters, and their more or less self-serving devotion to the mistress is often combined with a vein of unsatisfied senile sensuality which seeks an outlet in the seduction of young heroes, adolescent pages, and even simple stupid servants. Examples are the old Alcea who in *Orimonte* courts the fisherman Lisi, or the procuress Harpalia in *Pompeo*. With regard to licence in the language used by some buffoons or servants, a good example is to be found in passages from *Giasone*. Meanwhile it might be thought that the 'original' version of 'La donna è mobile' was not by Verdi but by Cavalli, to judge from an arietta sung by Oreste (bass) in the first act (Ex. 58). But Oreste is not a buffo character. He comes into the plot of the opera because he has been given the task, by the love-lorn Issifile, of tracking down Jason. Disembarking on the

Ex. 58

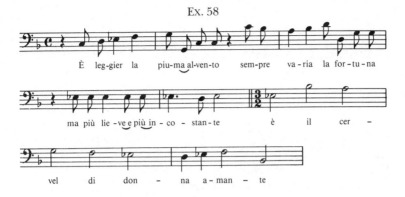

È leg-gier la piu-ma al-ven-to sem-pre va-ria la for-tu-na

ma più lie-ve e più in-co-stan-te è il cer -

vel di don - na a-man - te

island of Colchos, Oreste comes face to face with Demo (bass), who is the typical stupid, stuttering, boastful buffoon. The two come to blows, and Demo threatens Oreste:

> E se farai del mio parlar strapazzo
> la mia forte bravura
> saprà tirarti il ca . . . il ca . . .
> il capo in queste mura.

(And if you make fun of the way I speak, with my mighty strength I will wri-, will wri-, will wring your neck.)

The author of the verses is none other than Giacinto Andrea Cicognini. Thus with Cavalli we have some of the earliest instances of tenors *en travesti* playing parts of old nurses, like Erice in *Ormindo.*

In Cesti, also, there are the inevitable soldier discontents or braggarts, stupid, vain, stuttering jesters, nurses involved in intrigues and amorous adventures, dull-witted or, in certain instances shrewd, servants. Buffoons and servants are played by tenors or basses. Momo, who in *Il pomo d'oro* gives a commentary on Mars's voracious appetite—'This Mars, look how he wields his fists, even at supper. He has stripped the flesh off two capons, six pigeons and three pheasants . . .'—is a bass. Olympus was fairly often the subject of satire. In *Le disgrazie d'amore*, also by Cesti, Vulcano (tenor) is a genuine grotesque character. Ex. 59 illustrates one of his 'laughing' arias, with trills inserted for comic effects.

In *Orontea*, Cesti introduces a buffoon figure, the bass Gelone, one of his most successful comic roles. There is a drunk scene

Ex. 59

Deh non m'uccide   —   re. Oh che   ri-de-re.   Oh che   ri-de-re

where Gelone loses his temper with a type of syllabic declamation reminiscent of the *stile concitato* of Monteverdi's 'fury' arias, which then turns suddenly into an idyllic *chaconne* ('In grembo ai fiori lieto mi sto'). In *Dori*, finally, we have a castrato male soprano, Bagoa, who in masochistic fashion makes fun of himself by incarnating a eunuch guarding a harem.

During the second half of the seventeenth century, in the operas of the Venetian school, more and more often we come up against tenors disguised as women, impersonating lustful old ladies or playing the role of nurse. One such tenor nurse, for example, is Delma in Sartorio's *Adelaida*. In other instances, however, the tenor continues to be a stupid or cowardly servant, like Desbo in Legrenzi's *Totila*.

Pietro Andreo Ziani's *Annibale in Capua* contains two comic parts for contralto: one is the old Dalisa, who is in love with a page, and the other is the servant Gilbo. Finally, in *Candaule*, the servant Brillo, a sort of *deus ex machina* of the piece, is a castrato male soprano. Likewise by Ziani is *Alcibiade*, in which two women, Frine and Fillide, make fun of the protagonist (in one scene Fillide breaks a valuable clock belonging to Alcibiade).

Some of the traditional grotesque roles survive, in the late seventeenth century, even in the operas of composers of the Venetian school transplanted outside the region. This is true of the pusillanimous servant Arideno in *Gerusalemme liberata*, by Pallavicino, and of Socrates in Draghi's *La pazienza di Socrate*, a work staged in Prague in 1680, with Santippe played by a tenor.

Buffo characters appear also in operas by composers not belonging to the Venetian school. *Horazio, Corrispero, Floridoro,* and *La forza d'amor paterno* by Stradella present the usual stupid servants (tenors or basses) and the inevitable nurses, generally contraltos. But in *Il trespolo tutore* the nurse Simona is a tenor. Bontempi also, in *Paride* (1662), sketches out various comic characters, all of them sung by tenors: the gardener Draspo, the stuttering fool Ancrocco, and the servant Ergauro, who in the third act is given a long drunk scene. Francesco Provenzale, on the other hand, with whom the Neapolitan School began to take shape, introduces into *Lo schiavo di sua moglie* (1674) the page Lucillo (male soprano), giving him a misogynous vein not uncommon in seventeenth-century opera: 'Mala cosa in questi tempi/ ammogliarsi o innamorarsi'. Noteworthy in *Stellidaura vendicata*, again by Provenzale (1672) is the figure of Giampietro (bass) who sings in his local dialect—a foretaste of the vernacular trend which in the eighteenth century was to be characteristic of so much of Neapolitan comic opera. In fact, even in *Lo schiavo di sua moglie* we come across a Neapolitan peasant who expresses himself in dialect: Sciarra (tenor), whose language, even on the musical side, is basically comic without being grotesque. At times in fact, Sciarra's singing has a lyrical touch, as in the arias 'Vedimmo se sí femmena' and 'C'è 'na zita'.

Alessandro Scarlatti is one of the last important composers to admit comic character roles in his own *opera seria* works. As Dent pointed out in his day (*A. Scarlatti: His Life and Works*, London, 1905), in the operas of Scarlatti the shape of the grotesque role is completely stereotyped. Thus, for example, the comic characters have a scene in each act. This scene regularly falls at the end of the first act, at the end of the second, and shortly before the end of the third. Scarlatti's buffo characters are not differentiated in type from those of Venetian opera. In the early operas, as again pointed out by Dent, the buffo characters operate mostly in pairs—either a page (male soprano) and an old woman (contralto or tenor *en travesti*), or an old man (one of the most typical is Bacucco (bass) in *Honestà negli amori*), and an old woman. Frequently he is also the servant, in the usual pattern of a stupid, cowardly, or intriguing person, and Dent singles out one of these personages (Flacco in *La caduta dei Decemviri*) as a precursor of Leporello. Let us recall the aria sung by Flacco in the third act, just before he falls asleep. It is a sort of parody on the 'sleep' aria (Ex. 60).

In *Clearco* there is another parody: that of the old woman Filocla who mocks the heroine Asteria as she sings the dramatic aria 'Orridi spettri di Cocytus'. In *Rosaura*, on the other hand, the servant Lesbo (tenor) philosophizes on the misfortunes of the other personages. The tessitura of Lesbo is extremely low, whereas in *Anacreonte* the tessitura of the old procuress Silena

Ex. 60

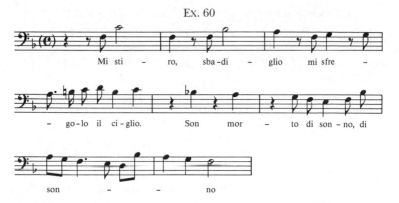

(another tenor) is rather high. Orcone (bass) in *Tigrane* is one of
the last of the stuttering buffos in Baroque opera. He too tends to
parody the 'conjuration' or 'spell' aria, again harking back to the
famous 'Dell'antro magico stridenti cardini' sung by Medea in
Cavalli's *Giasone* (Ex. 61).

Ex. 61

We may also recall, in Scarlatti, the duets between buffo
characters, for example the one between the page Niso (male
soprano) and the old woman Cleria (tenor) in *Teodora Augusta* ('Tu
troppo m'offendi'); that between another old woman, Niceta
(tenor), and Morasso (bass) in *Emireno* ('Tu mi vuoi bene? Signora
no . . .'); and finally, the duet in *L'amazzone corsara*, 'Ricordati che
quel grugnino' between Felba (tenor *en travesti*) and Dorco,
another comic tenor.

   The vogue for buffo roles in serious opera died out completely
after the first few years of the eighteenth century. Handel
introduces only one single buffo role into his operas: the part of
the servant Elviro (bass) in *Serse*.

IV

Rossini

ROSSINI'S VIEWS ON MELODY AND ON SINGING

Mention is often made of 'Rossini's reform', alluding to the fact that, by writing out in detail the whole of his coloratura parts, Rossini robbed singers of the possibility of improvising or of inserting passages, ornaments, and cadenzas. Aside from the fact that the situation is not exactly like that, the word 'reform' might be used also, indeed most of all, for other aspects of Rossini's operas. Rossini did in fact reform opera, both comic and serious. He reformed it by way of the attractiveness, the breadth, the invention, and the rhythmic impulse of his melodies; the sophistication of his paradoxical views on the comic element as applied to vocalism, to the chorus, and to the orchestra; the new, spicy, brilliant colours of his instrumentation; and the way in which he closed the gap between *opera giocosa* (comic opera) and *opera seria*, in the latter case reshaping the drive of the concerted numbers and finales of acts of the former and giving *opera giocosa* the same florid and sumptuous language as the other. At the vocal level, the advent of Rossini had as its main effect the spread of an approach to singing from which all the countries of Europe benefited and which literally provided France, for example, over a lengthy period, with executants capable of competing with the Italian singers. Indeed, the years between 1820 and 1840, which most vividly felt the effects of Rossini's presence, represented a Golden Age for vocal art, as had occurred precisely a century earlier during the twenty years between 1720 and 1740.

Rossini's treatment of vocalism reflects the views he held on melody, on opera, and on music in general. According to Rossini, music is an ideal art because it has no need for imitation, whereas painting and sculpture do need imitation:

You will have noticed, my very dear, wise Dr Filippi, that I have delib-erately ignored the word 'imitative' in the recommendation made to you by the young composers on Italian musical art, and I have referred 'only' to melody and rhythm. I shall always be *inébranlable* [unswerving] in my contention that Italian musical art (especially the vocal aspect) is entirely 'ideal and expressive', and never 'imitative', as certain materialistic so-called philosophers would argue. Allow me to state my view that the feelings of the heart are expressed and not imitated. (Letter to Filippo Filippi, 26 August 1868.)

And elsewhere he writes: 'Music is a sublime art precisely because, not possessing ways and means of imitating the truth, it rises above and beyond everyday life into an ideal world'.[1] Or again: 'Bear in mind that expression in music is not the same as in painting, and that it consists, not in representing to the life the external manifestation of inner emotions, but in arousing this in the listener'.[2] Or yet again:

He (the composer) will not stop at the words unless to fit the singing to them, but without straying from the general nature of the music he has chosen so that the words tend rather to serve the music than the music the words. The words, in a scene depicting pathos or terror, may be cheerful, then sad, then hopeful, then fearful, then supplicating, then threatening, according to the mood which the poet wishes to give to the episode. If the composer tries to follow the sense of the words at every point, he will compose music which is not in itself expressive, but is poverty-striken, commonplace, a mere patchwork, I would say, and incongruous or ridiculous.[3]

Actually, Rossini turns upside down the principles which applied at the time of the birth of opera, the principles followed at the outset even by Monteverdi (music as the handmaid of 'speech', in other words of the poetic text), which music-drama later took over via Gluck. 'L'union doit être si étroite entre les paroles et le chant que le poème ne semble pas moins fait sur la musique que la musique sur le poème.' (The union between the words and the singing must be so close that the poem does not seem any less made to fit the music than the music to fit the poem.) Rossini's view is within certain limits similar to the Baroque principle that fantasy dominates everything. This domination is manifested through melody, which starts out from the

---

[1] A. Zanolini, *Biografia di Gioacchino Rossini*, Bologna, 1875.
[2] Ibid.
[3] Ibid.

general meaning of the verses expressing a certain situation or a certain stage episode, but which, because it is free from the transposition into song of the inflections and accents of spoken language, exerts an influence of a strictly musical nature on the character and his feelings. Basically, the form that melody can give to a state of mind or a sentiment is evocative, not descriptive, of human passions, appealing to them by means of the stimulus and allusions of a stylized or actually sublimated (or 'idealized') type of language. In order to arouse emotions in the audience, this language follows laws of its own and uses words merely as signposts, or still better, as guidelines.

In this sense, Rossini goes even further than Baroque opera, invariably linked as it is to imitation of a passion or of a natural occurrence which, although stylized, always takes off from the literal meaning of the words and tends almost to reproduce it graphically. But we need to look at the ground covered by music from then until the first years of the nineteenth century and the broadening of the expressive and evocative horizons both of vocal and of instrumental melody. Rossini's idea of melody, which leaves to the verses only a didactic value, seems to amount to attributing to singing certain characteristics of instrumental music. However, even in Rossini there is still a connection between melody and words, but it is inverted in relation to the Platonic concepts of the Florentine opera composers and very early Monteverdi, or to those of the music-drama of Gluck and the Romantics. Here the singing is the outcome of the words, but respect for the prosody and inflections of the spoken language prevents the melody from spreading its wings. In Rossini, on the contrary, the melody does spread its wings, and its evolutions have an impact on the words, since the emotions of the listener always require, *in the theatre*, something which has reference to what is happening on the stage. In other words, significant melody gives significance even to words which in and of themselves would not have it. This is what Stendhal states in his *Vie de Rossini*, precisely in order to explain the subordination of words to melody. Stendhal writes that one of the reasons for the success of Italian opera throughout the world is that it is sufficient to know the sense of the words of an aria—or, indeed, just the meaning of the first few lines—for even a person with no knowledge of Italian to appreciate a melody.

The facts even today show that Stendhal was right; but still in the realm of the emotive powers which the melody can confer on the words, it seems to me that there is great significance in what Reynaldo Hahn wrote in *Du chant* (Paris, 1920): 'La mélodie représente dans le chant l'élément surnaturel qui donne à la parole, aux mots, un sucroît d'intensité, de force, de délicatesse, de poésie, de charme ou d'étrangeté, par des moyens qui échappent en partie à l'analyse et dont nous subissons l'enchantement sans pouvoir bien nous l'expliquer.' (In singing, the melody represents the supernatural element which gives to the words a greater intensity, strength and delicacy, poetry, charm or strangeness, through means that in part defy analysis but allow us to experience their enchantment without really being able to explain it.)

The consequence of the repudiation by Rossini of a realistic type of singing is at all events a wholehearted return to certain Baroque notions of vocal art, but through melodies and a variety of orchestral devices. It might be possible to speak, in this respect—but particularly in relation to *opera seria*—of 'Rossinian abstractness'. Rossini's melodies expressing pathos tend always towards the idealization of the character. The barrier which is often raised between Rossini's *opera seria* works and the listener of today—although it has been partly removed during the last decade,[4] consists in the fact that, theatrically speaking, Rossini's characters have an almost statuesque rigidity. They sing as if from the top of a pedestal. Even when they suffer injury and pain, they take refuge in the realistic imitation of human beings hurt and grief-stricken, looking at anger and grief not so much with a sense of detachment—since they are moved by both these feelings—but disdaining the more normal, everyday reactions of ordinary mortals in anger or pain. The extraordinary purity of certain melodies and their instrumental framework derives precisely from this sublimated view of passion, one which likewise makes for unrestraint and impetuosity, but with a total absence of that over-emphasis, that agitation, that lack of control and measure which at times take Verdi by the hand and lead him to an unduly facile or repetitive type of melody, basically because the composer starts out from a realistic imitation which satisfies him as purely

---

[4] Noteworthy is the resounding public success achieved in Italy, France, and the USA with the new productions of operas like *L'assedio di Corinto*, *Tancredi*, *Otello*, and *Semiramide*.

or largely a stage effect but prevents him from refining the musical effect.

Like all writers of melodies, but more markedly, since he himself was a singer, Rossini perceives in vocal execution one fundamental element to help to understand the thinking of the composer. His vocal ideal was the castrato, in whom he saw not only a throat capable of prodigies of virtuosity but also, indeed above all, an interpreter of unsurpassable expressiveness. In Rossini's view of singing, the intrinsic beauty of sound and the impeccable execution of agility passages are elements essential to an expressive rendering. Hence Rossini's aversion to certain types of vocalism in singers of the Romantic period, who were often willing to discard beautiful sound and cleanness of execution in favour of a form of expression amounting to 'bawling after the fashion of the day' (letter to Torquato Antaldi, 15 June 1851). Or again, 'I cannot deny a certain decadence in the vocal art, whose new adherents aim at the hydrophobic style rather than at "sweet Italian singing which goes straight to the heart"' (letter to Filippo Filippi, 26 August 1868). Yet again, in a letter to Francesco Florimo cited by Radiciotti:[5] 'Today the vocal art is at the barricades. The old florid style is replaced by the nervous style, solemnity by howling, at one time blamed on the French; in short, tenderness of feelings by impassioned hydrophobia.' But to give a complete idea of the way in which Rossini regarded the import-ance of vocal performance, we need only recall that at his meeting with Wagner in 1860 (of which Edmond Michotte has left an almost stenographic account), the decadence of singing is actually given as one of the reasons for his refusal to write operas after *William Tell*: 'L'art du chant avait sombré.' (The art of singing had fallen into decay).

From a purely vocal point of view, Rossini's ideal was a type of phonation making for spontaneous, fluid, warm tone at all times. The contralto Marietta Alboni studied singing for some time under his guidance, and Rossini inspired in her a positive horror of forced, hard sounds.[6] But at the same time he liked large, resonant voices. He told Edmond Michotte that agility passages executed in a half-hearted *mezza voce*, in keeping with a vogue introduced by Romantic singers, betrayed the meaning of

---

[5] iii. 125 (Tivoli, 1927–1929).
[6] See A. Pougin, *Marietta Alboni*, Paris, 1912.

coloratura, since only the full-voice production of the virtuosi of
his time brought out 'the eloquence hidden under the veil of
fioriture'.

This brings us to one of the fundamental points of Rossini's
view of singing. For a long time, agility singing of Rossini's music
was regarded as a series of tiresome parlour-tricks thought up to
provide singers with an opportunity for singing arid virtuoso
passages and playing to the gallery. This is also the view of
biographers and Rossini scholars like Radiciotti and Roncaglia,
worthy writers in many respects, but steeped in all the superstitions and all the fetishes engendered by the aesthetics of music-
drama.

But the thing that most makes one smile is the fact that idealist
writers on music have always regarded as basic Rossini's initiative
in writing out in his own hand vocalises, ornaments, and cadenzas,
thus robbing the singers of the freedom to improvise. Yet aestheti-
cally speaking, the vocalises, ornaments, and cadenzas written by
Rossini were regarded as insignificant, incongruous, and written
to satisfy the vanity of the executants. The question is, at this
point, where does the importance of Rossini's initiative lie?
Obviously nowhere except in the abstract gesture of taking away
from the singer the option of intervening of his own accord. The
'Word' of Gluck and Wagner was safeguarded; and this was the
only thing that mattered to minds that had become sluggish and
Germanized.

In actual fact the truth was entirely different. Here again we
have to return to the antithesis of tune and words. Vocal melody
as the handmaid of the words is basically one of the dead weights
of music-drama, when the concept is applied literally, with
Teutonic zeal; and the more so if the words are by a librettist who
has no sense of the theatre, who is prolix, vain, pretentious, like
Calzabigi or, not infrequently, like Wagner himself, who in any
case virtually never wrote a great poem. It is obvious that when a
composer does not have the imagination to gather what he has to
say into a vocal melody without words—or based on mere
fragments of words—a vocalise, however virtuosic, may seem
meaningless. But above all, it is difficult to understand how a
vocal melody without words can in certain circumstances acquire
a power of sublimation which a melody that serves the words does
not have: '... as when I dreamed of Marie Antoinette and of a

song to be put into her mouth in the tragedy I conceived at the time. This song expressing the emotions I had in mind could not have been written except in music without words . . .'.[7]

Or again:

La roulade est la plus haute expression de l'art, c'est l'arabesque qui orne le plus bel appartement du logis: un peu moins, il n'y a rien; un peu plus, tout est confus. Chargée de réveiller dans votre âme mille idées endormies, elle s'élance, elle traverse l'espace en semant dans l'air ses germes qui, ramassés par les oreilles, fleurissent au fond du cœur . . . Il est déplorable que le vulgaire ait forcé les musiciens à plaquer leurs expressions sur des paroles, sur des intérêts factices; mais il est vrai qu'ils ne seraient pas compris par la foule. La roulade est donc l'unique point laissé aux amis de la musique pure, aux amoureux de l'art tout nu.

(The *roulade* is the highest expression of art: it is the arabesque adorning the most beautiful room in the house: a little less and it is nothing; a little more and everything is confusion. Performing its task of reawakening in your soul a thousand ideas that lay dormant, it takes wing, it flies through space, sowing in the air seeds which are gathered by the ear and blossom within the heart . . . It is deplorable that the masses have forced musicians to make their expression depend on words, on factitious elements— admittedly they would not be understood by the masses. The *roulade* is therefore the only point left to the friends of pure music, those who love the art in all its nakedness.'[8]

But in Rossini's vocalism we have precisely a reflection of the concept that ornaments and vocalises are an emanation of music understood as an ideal art and hence capable of expressing itself beyond realistic, servile imitation, with the mysterious support of 'hidden eloquence'. In this sense, rather, florid singing represents expression at a more intense stage, an element reinforcing feelings and passions, and this whether it is concerned with idealized love or with carnal love, nostalgia, anger, despair, or joy. And thus we understand how and why Rossini at a particular moment decided to write out in his own hand a large part of the coloratura, thus restricting the field of action for personal intervention on the part of the singer. In Rossini the melody was born ornate and florid; the vocalise was an integral part of the expression and not a mere fringe adornment.

It is difficult to imagine this being understood by the German

[7] Giacomo Leopardi, *Memorie e disegni letterari.*
[8] Honoré de Balzac, *Massimilla Doni.*

mind—unless we are speaking of people like Hegel, Heine, or Schopenhauer—or by people of a German cast of mind. But let us start off by saying that even the date and the circumstances of the so-called vocal reform of Rossini were falsified in the reports 'of it between the end of the nineteenth century and the first sixty years of our own century. Starting out from testimony given by Stendhal in his *Vie de Rossini*, traditional historians have always affirmed that Rossini decided to write out coloratura parts following *Aureliano in Palmira* (1813) because he was disgusted at the overdone interpolations and variations put in by the castrato Giovanni Battista Velluti. But this is not true. Stendhal deserves great attention for the extraordinary acumen of some of his judgements; but he is not reliable as a chronicler, and the true facts are otherwise.

The writing of *Demetrio e Polibio*, Rossini's first *opera seria*, is comparable to that of composers like Mayr or even more, Paer, a composer who liked to write out embellishments in his own hand but did not achieve elaborate coloratura. However, Rossini's first *mezzo carattere* opera, *L'inganno felice*, already has more elaborate coloratura passages, exactly as, among the comic operas, *La pietra del paragone* (1812) has a more florid vocalism than *Il cambiale di matrimonio* (1810). *Tancredi*, in turn, marks a further step forward in the elaboration of coloratura, particularly as regards Amenaide (soprano), and the same is true of *L'italiana in Algeri* (1813) as compared with *La pietra del paragone*. The two main interpreters of *L'italiana in Algeri*, Marietta Marcolini (Isabella) and Filippo Galli (Mustafà) had already played the leading roles in *La pietra del paragone*; but the agility passages and *fioriture* given to them tend to be more complex in *L'italiana*.

And here we come to the famous *Aureliano in Palmira* (26 December 1813), the performance of which by the castrato Velluti, with his own intrusive interventions, is thought to have prompted the decision by Rossini to write out all the ornamented passages in his own hand from then onwards. The fact is that Arsace, the actual character portrayed by Velluti, presents a type of coloratura which is more elaborate than in earlier *opera seria* roles. It seems highly likely, nevertheless, that Velluti added his own ornaments over and above Rossini's text. But what is certainly true is that Rossini fairly frequently gave him an open invitation to improvise. Consider the passage from Arsace's Andantino 'Se tu m'ami, o mia regina', in the first act (Ex. 62). Meanwhile Rossini's coloratura, with its groups of hemidemisemiquavers linked to

Ex. 62

extended trills and reiterated descending scales, is already extremely elaborate for the period. But later in the passage come two fermata signs: ⌒, the second of which is not written over a note but between two notes. These fermatas did not actually signify, as current performing practice would suggest, an indication of a lengthening of the value of the note and hence an invitation to the singer to hold it *ad lib*. On the contrary, they were signs known as *arresti* (pauses) or *arbítri* (options), or in certain cases *mezza cadenza* (half cadence), and they signified that at the point in question the performer should insert an invention of his own, in the form of a vocalise. In the case in point, the presence of a courtly word like 'regno' (the first fermata) presupposes precisely a melismatic amplification, high-sounding but not long or complex. In the second case, the fermata placed between two notes calls for a longer and more sophisticated improvisation which embellishes and underlines the notion of the power which Zenobia exerts over the feelings of Arsace.

The whole of the role of Arsace is rich in markings of this kind. Three fermatas performing the function of 'pauses' are to be found in the 6/8 Andantino 'Chi sa dirme, o mia speranza'; two at the end of the 3/4 Andantino 'Perché mai le luci aprimmo' (and in this case the fermatas, inserted at the end of the passage, call upon the singer precisely to improvise the cadenza); eight others appear

in the Rondo 'Ah, non posso, al mio tesoro'. How Velluti executed
them we do not know, although we do know that it was one of his
regular practices to add his own interventions liberally; and we
know for certain than in many instances it was Rossini himself
who urged him to do so.

Apart from this, the coloratura passages written out by hand
are more copious than those in earlier examples of *opera seria*, and
this applies not only to the role of Arsace but to those of
Aureliano and Zenobia. Among other devices, in this opera
Rossini uses more frequently than in the earlier works an indirect
intervention formula represented by passages consisting of grace-
notes to be sung 'out of time'. This occurs, for example, at the end
of the Allegro sung by Aureliano in the second act, 'Più non vedrà
quel perfido' (Ex. 63). The passage made up of grace-notes is not a
cadenza in the true sense of the term, but a suggestion to the
singer for a concluding pattern.

Ex. 63

[a]-mor   il tuo fa - ta-le   fa - ta -   -   -   le a - mor

In short, if for a moment we were to forget that in Rossini the
tendency to enrich the coloratura is a progressive and gradual
phenomenon which was to reach its peak in the final opera
written for an Italian theatre (*Semiramide*), we too might venture to
declare that the so-called reform actually began with *Aureliano in
Palmira*. Next came *Sigismondo* (1814), an opera written in a
manner substantially akin to that of *Aureliano*. At this point it is
hard to understand why Rossini's indignation at Velluti's inter-
ference, and his effort to make up for it, did not explode immediately, namely in *Sigismondo*, and likewise lay hidden in *Il turco in
Italia* (again of 1814), which does not show any appreciable change
as compared with *La pietra del paragone* and *L'italiana in Algeri*.

Finally we reach *Elisabetta d'Inghilterra* (1815). Rossini continues
to use passages of grace-notes 'out of time', in some instances
more complex than those written up to that point, and he further
pads out the coloratura; but we cannot call this a radical about-
turn, as is always claimed by the traditionalist music historians.

Elisabetta marks a very important stage in the evolution of Rossini's coloratura, but it is not an abrupt initiation of reform— which actually began much earlier. Apart from this, if we examine the very next opera, *Torvaldo e Dorliska*, we find that the coloratura is less rich than in *Elisabetta*, and that the reformer has taken a step backwards.

Actually, it is with *Il barbiere*, *Otello*, *Cenerentola* and *La gazza ladra* that Rossini reaches a type of exceedingly detailed coloratura and introduces another innovation—that of placing comic opera on a level with *opera seria* as an 'anvil' for forging vocal virtuosity. But with *Semiramide* he was to go even further, corroborating the fact that, contrary to what is always maintained, the enrichment of the melismatic part is a gradual and ongoing process which was only to be abandoned when his move to Paris forced him to adjust his methods to French practice.[9]

In short, Rossini's attitude may also have been prompted to some extent by Velluti's wayward behaviour or—which is equally plausible—by a desire to provide a more and more impressive vehicle, as and when the occasion arose, for singers like Marcolini, Galli, and, in all the operas of the Neapolitan cycle, for Colbran. But these are incidental matters, not large issues. The major issue is the fact that the more Rossini progressed towards his finest period, the more the vocal phrasing comes from his pen 'with divisions, *fioriture*, and ornaments', to use the terminology of the early seventeenth-century writers on music. In this respect, the intention of imposing discipline on the singers with notions taken from music-drama, or conversely, that of gratifying this or that singer with opportunities for feats of virtuosity, hardly comes into the picture at all. The idea of a composer sitting down at his desk and deciding in cold blood to write out the vocal parts in detailed coloratura does not make sense. Rossini was probably the most intelligent opera composer in history, not the most stupid, as might implicitly be deduced if we paid any attention to the positively ludicrous notion of his arranging all his writing to serve the purpose of punishing Velluti and giving a boost to Colbran. The vast number of passages, for solo voice or ensemble, which in Rossini's operas appear in florid, ornate, and varied form, are so

---

[9] For a discussion of this whole matter see R. Celletti, 'Origine e sviluppo della coloratura rossiniana', in *Nuova rivista musicale italiana*, 2 (1968), pp. 872–919.

treated because the composer's inspiration wanted it that way. And we are the beneficiaries.

As marginal notes to the discussion of Rossini's vocal reform, other observations can be made. Rossini was not imbued with German fanaticism, and looked at things in a concrete way. Nor could his dislike of interventions by his executants have been such a tremendous affair if it is true—as is reported by Radiciotti—that on one occasion in Paris he took the trouble to pay a visit to the soprano Henriette Sontag to thank her for a variant she had introduced into an aria in *Matilde di Shabran*. Schmidl's *Dizionario universale dei musicisti*, under the heading *Pisaroni*, states that Rossini had given this singer a sort of *carte blanche* to add ornaments. But the main point is that Rossini—and the same is true of all the Italian composers up to Bellini and Donizetti—did not subscribe to the idea that the text was sacrosanct and inviolable, and he was decidedly in favour of varying or changing it if any passage written for a particular singer did not suit another executant. The 'Notebook' of the Countess of Chambure in fact contains many Rossini variants; but a vast number of others, together with alternative arias, have more recently come to light as a result of the researches of scholars like Bruno Cagli, Azio Corghi, Philip Gosset, and Alberto Zedda, prompted by the Centro Studi Rossiniani at Pesaro. Furthermore, Rossini was not at all averse to da capo variations if the composer omitted to write them in.[10] So true is this that he personally changed the cavatina 'Il braccio mio conquise' from *Tancredi* by Nicolini, and the Allegro 'La tremenda ultrice spada' from Bellini's *I Capuleti e Montecchi*. Odd behaviour for a reformer, a censor, a person of rigid principles!

CHARACTERISTICS OF ROSSINI'S WRITING FOR THE VOICE

Three trends can be distinguished in Rossini's vocal writing: the bel canto heritage; innovation; and his treatment of individual voices and the relationship between timbre and role.

[10] There is a letter from the English soprano Clara Novello asking Rossini whether it was necessary to make variations in the da capo. Rossini's reply was in the affirmative. See M. Aspinall, 'Il cantante nelle interpretazioni delle opere rossiniane', in *Bollettino Centro Studi Rossiniani*, 1(1) (1970).

The bel canto heritage is to be observed above all in symmetry of phrasing, in other words the tendency to construct a melody on the basis of musical periods which are often of the same length. If we consider, for example, arias like 'Dal tuo stellato soglio' from *Mosé*, 'Selva opaca' from *William Tell*, 'Giusto ciel! in tal periglio' from *L'assedio di Corinto*, we find that the melody develops out of spontaneously symmetrical periods, which ensure that the singer can take breaths regularly and 'comfortably', to the great advantage of ease, smoothness, and warmth of emission. It is particularly in cantabile passages that Rossini follows this rule, but he often observes it also in brilliant, virtuoso arias. This presupposes that the singer is singing 'dans le masque' and on the breath. The symmetrical arches of Rossini's cantabile require, by their inherent, intimate nature, that the single notes in each phrase are welded together by an extremely well executed legato; but this can only be achieved through homogeneous and delicate tone, plus a flexibility enabling the singer to make scarcely perceptible crescendos or diminuendos, even going beyond the expression marks written in by the composer, and often even an embryonic *messa di voce* (◇) on every note of a certain length. When we then go on to the succeeding phrase, whether the voice is rising or descending, the changeover must ensure absolute evenness of colour and intensity. In short, Rossini's cantabile singing, with its softness and delicacy of melody and its way of developing in symmetrical designs, gives a boost to the singer who is technically well trained and penalizes the singer who is not.[11]

Of Rossini's cantabile writing it might almost be said that the breathing of the executant is the guiding principle for the composer, who incidentally—and this must not be forgotten—had been a fine vocalist himself in his youth. But what is called for even more from the executant is a vocal production which is

---

[11] Recordings make it clear that an arietta in cantabile style, seemingly of no great difficulty, such as the cavatina sung by Lindoro in *The Barber of Seville*, reflects perfectly well the composer's melodic idea and the psychological requirements of the stage action of the moment if it is executed by vocalists like Tito Schipa or Alfredo Kraus, whereas it loses elegance, charm, and pungency on the lips of tenors like Gedda or Alva. In 'Resta immobile', from *William Tell*, the smoothness, legato, and 'nuanced dynamics' of a singer like De Luca make a complete whole with the pathos of the melody and the solemn restraint of the stage action. But there is very little of this to be found in the performances of singers with a rough or unfocused production like Bacquier or Milnes.

technically excellent, since Rossini's cantabile is ornamented, as in 'Di tanti palpiti' from *Tancredi* or 'Assisa a pie' d'un salice' from *Otello*; and this type of ornamentation, too, calls for perfect legato, as well as absolute cleanness in the agility passages. It also requires a languorous quality in the tone which only extremely flexible phonation can give. Furthermore, the languor of the ornaments in the role of Tancredi is sensuous and radiant, that of Desdemona elegiac and full of pathos. Here we enter the field of expressiveness of Rossini's *fioriture*, but other essential qualities are the executant's tone production and sense of style.[12]

Another feature of these arias is that Rossini very seldom makes sudden leaps in tessitura or has the voice sing extremely low or extremely high notes. This too is an old bel canto rule. The aria expressing love, and still more the aria expressing pathos, concentrate on purity of tone, legato, portamento, and expression on the part of the interpreter. Hence they are basically in a middle tessitura and tend as far as possible to avoid risks of forcing and unevenness.

Likewise deriving from bel canto is the differentiation between syllabic singing and the vocalise. The design of set pieces in Rossini generally shows a concern to ensure that troublesome virtuoso passages or 'agitated style' explosions do not fall on an awkward section of the voice, such as notes on the passaggio between registers, which even for practised singers are always a potential danger-point. This applies both to syllabic singing and to vocalises. In syllabic singing, however, and especially in robust passages, Rossini tends to concentrate the melodic nucleus in the centre of the voice and on the first of the high notes. In this way, the concern of the executant for expression and his expenditure of emotional energy are centred on the middle of the voice, which is the most restful area.

Rossini particularly avoids declamation on high notes and powerful singing of words starting out in awkward areas like that of the register change. He prefers, in agitated-style passages, to take the voice up to the highest notes by means of a short vocalise

---

[12] Recordings again show us how both the arias, as sung by Marilyn Horne, the ideal Rossini specialist, acquire a distinction greater than that shown in the performance by Montserrat Caballé, who tends to mould the tone, the emphasis, and the *fioriture* to the vocal style of Bellini or Donizetti rather than to that of Rossini.

which rises gradually, or to launch it upwards from the centre or low region, as in the phrase sung by Argirio, tenor, in the duet with Orbazzano from the first act of *Tancredi* (Ex. 64).

Ex. 64

sí   fe - li - ce vin - ci   -   tri - ce   Si - ra -[cusa]

Syllabic writing on high notes is adopted by Rossini to suit particular voices. At times it is prescribed for high sopranos, more frequently for the first of the 'contraltino' tenors (in other words, extremely high tenors) who appeared in Italy under the name of 'tenorini'. A typical melody with an extremely high tessitura is 'Languir per una bella', sung by Lindoro in *L'italiana in Algeri*, but the languorous, plaintive nature of the aria, the symmetry of the phrasing and breathing points, and the alternation of syllabic phrases and others which are semi-syllabic, can provide an easy phonation pattern for a good singer.

Rossini's attitude towards ornate singing is different. His underlying principle is that vocalise singing calls for a lighter type of emission and also a less emotional type of expression. Hence it can develop over a wider vocal range and reach the extreme notes for each type of voice, both top and bottom, through leaps, scales, arpeggios, runs, and vocalises—in three, four, six-note, or irregular groups—the individual elements being arranged in progressions which help to keep the tone even and facilitate the register changes. Obviously, however, the execution of agility passages in Rossini, with the precipitous upward and downward leaps inherent in a way of writing that is also highly ornamental, calls for a great deal of ingenuity in tone production and, in particular, notes in the middle of the voice which are not forced in volume or weight. Otherwise, reaching the highest notes—and the lowest notes in the case of deep voices—ends in forced, strident sounds, and agility passages are not executed cleanly.

To sum up: a melodic line which enables breaths to be taken at regular intervals; which does not harp insistently on areas close to the passaggio in syllabic utterance; which hovers mainly over the

middle sector in cantabile singing while at the same time covering
a very wide range in brilliant and virtuoso passages, is what
Rossini inherited from the bel canto tradition and preserves in his
own writing. Other devices derived from bel canto that can be
singled out are his tendency to guide all voices, whatever their
type, in the direction of virtuoso singing; his predilection for the
contralto *en travesti* for the role of lover; and his aversion to certain
sounds popular with the public during the Romantic period, such
as the *do di petto* (top c with chest voice) of the tenor, where its
stridency, its tenseness, its metallic ring, prompted Rossini to
describe it as 'the screeching of a slaughtered chicken'.

Alien to the bel canto tradition, on the other hand, although
compatible with bel canto, are certain trends to be found in the
aria at the beginning of the nineteenth century and appropriated
and imposed by Rossini, who transmuted them into fundamental
and unmistakable features of his own style, such as the development of melismata in comic opera, which Rossini furnished with a
light-hearted vocalism no less acrobatic than that of the serious
genre. Or, again, the sublimation of the tender, ornate melody of
composers like Paer, Mayr, and Zingarelli, which in Rossini's
hands is broadened under the impulse of a type of languor and
sensuousness that became the mainstays of a new type of lyrical
ecstasy. The path followed by these melodies starts out from the
duet 'Questo cor ti giura amore', sung by Siveno and Lisinga in
Demetrio e Polibio; the aria 'Vicino è il momento', sung by Berenice
in *L'occasione fa il ladro*; and the Andante 'Un soave e nuovo
incanto', sung by Fanny in *Il cambiale di matrimonio*. It goes on via
the duet 'Mille sospiri e lacrime', sung by Zenobia and Arsace in
Aureliano; 'Per voi che adoro', sung by Isabella in *L'italiana in
Algeri*; 'Di tanti palpiti' or 'Ah, che scordar non so', sung by
Tancredi, to the song 'D'amor al dolce impero', sung by Armida,
and finally to arias like 'Bel raggio lusinghiero', sung by Semiramide, and the duet 'Serbami ognor sí fido', sung by Semiramide
and Arsace. This last piece is an absolute masterpiece of its kind, if
only because it is the densest type of *fioritura* in late Italian-period
Rossini to give a sense of melodic uncertainty and ambiguity to
the shape of the sensuous outburst intermingled with sentiments
or presentiments of maternal love and filial devotion.

But Rossini's greatest innovation in the field of vocal writing is
the adoption of a mixed style, half-way between syllabic and

vocalise, consisting of placing groups of three, four, or six notes, or even irregular figures, on the individual syllables of a word.

Rossini was certainly not the inventor of this mixed style, which had already been applied more than once by Giovanni Bononcini and taken up at the beginning of the nineteenth century by Paer and others. But Rossini used it with such determination and so systematically as to make it a personal feature of his style. One negative feature of virtuosity during the bel canto period was the adoption of vocalises placed on a syllable in a word and prolonged over several bars, developing with repetitive formulas that often ended up identifying themselves more with mechanical virtuoso exercises than with patterns intimately bound up with the melody. In his first *opera seria* efforts, Rossini often used these long vocalises, which appear in *Demetrio e Polibio, Aureliano, Tancredi,* and even in a comic opera (*La pietra del paragone*). Later on he eliminated them almost completely in the works of the Neapolitan period; and this too, without any question, formed part of the so-called Rossini reform.

But even in *Il cambiale di matrimonio*, a phrase by Fanny in the duet 'Tornami a dir che m'ami' with Edoardo illustrates the application of the 'agility' style based on the fragmentation of the words into syllables (Ex. 65).

Ex. 65

It is also clear at this juncture why Rossini did not reach the point of conceiving a type of singing based on the imitation of the literal, realistic sense of the words. His melody *expresses* rather than *imitates* a feeling[13] and the word is merely a means to that end. By breaking it down into syllables separated one from another by

[13] Letter to Filippo Filippi quoted on pp. 135–6.

fioriture, Rossini virtually annuls its meaning as the term is commonly understood, but he sublimates the phrasing, the singing, and the stage action with the impulse, the grace, the lightness, and even the fantasy, of a melody which is *born* ornate and of which the coloratura is an intimate part and not an ornament applied mechanically.

This system is so widespread in Rossini, and is accentuated to such an extent in the period from the early operas to *Semiramide*, that it would be easy to cite thousands of examples. We find it applied with great comic effect to four-note groups in hammer-like agility passages in the duet (Andantino in 4/4 time) 'O che muso, che figura' between Isabella and Mustafà in *L'italiana in Algeri*, act I (Ex. 66), and to irregular groups in arpeggio form,

Ex. 66

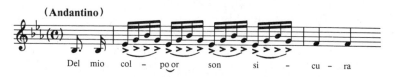

expressing courtly sentiments, in the 3/4 Andante 'Bell'alme generose' (Finale) sung by the protagonist in *Elisabetta* (Ex. 67).

Ex. 67

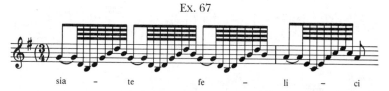

But, as I have said, examples are infinite in number. Among the most noteworthy are the Allegro moderato of the cavatina sung by Rosina 'Io sono docile' in *The Barber of Seville*, and the duet between Rosina and Figaro 'Dunque io son? Tu non m'inganni?'; the Allegro 'Tutto sorridere mi veggo intorno', sung by Ninetta in *La gazza ladra*; some of the passages in the Adagio 'Assisa a pie' d'un salice', sung by Desdemona in *Otello* (particularly the beginning of the third verse 'Salce, d'amor delizia'); and finally the Allegro sung by Arsace, 'O come da quel dì' in *Semiramide*.

Other features characteristic of Rossini's vocal writing are series of successive runs such as that by the protagonist in *Elisabetta* in the 4/4 Maestoso 'Fellon la pena avrai', expressing a sense of rage (Ex. 68), or those in *Cenerentola*, making a solemn moral statement ('Sprezzo quel don che versa'), Maestoso in 4/4 time (Ex. 69).

Ex. 68

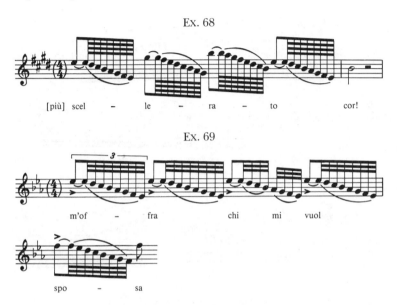

[più] scel   –   le   –   ra   –   to   cor!

Ex. 69

m'of   –   fra   chi   mi   vuol

spo   –   sa

We also have the 'runs' which little by little take the place of the long vocalises of earlier times. In Rossini, they start with a series of grace-notes, 'out of time', as in the youthful operas, like the passage sung by Clarice in *La pietra del paragone* ('Se per voi le care io torno') (Ex. 70), and they are transformed into vocalises full of

Ex. 70

(Marziale)

pal   –   –   –   pi-ti,   fra i dol-ci

impetuosity and incisiveness. Elsewhere in Rossini, the run co-incides almost always with an exceptional moment which calls for virtuosity. Thus we arrive at the peremptory, authoritative expression used by Semiramide in 'Giuri omaggio' (finale I) (Ex. 71), at the stately disdain of Idreno, again in *Semiramide* ('Ah dov'è, dov'è il cimento', act I) (Ex. 72), and at the unbridled joy of Cenerentola in the final rondo (Ex. 73).

Ex. 71

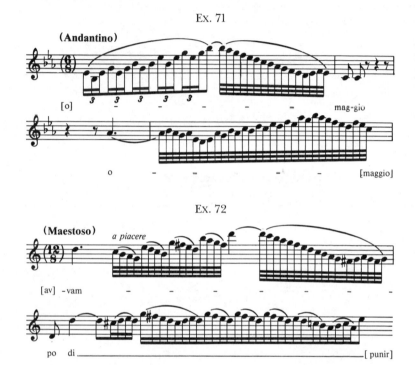

Ex. 72

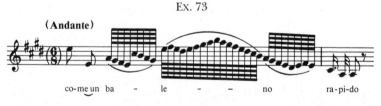

Ex. 73

Another fundamental aspect of Rossini's composition is his writing of variations. Frequently he makes no change in the da capo section—which does not actually mean, as already pointed out,[14] that he did not want any variation. Even up to the time of Bellini and Donizetti, a da capo section without variations was

[14] See p. 146.

regarded as an absurdity, since the justification of the repetition lay precisely in its being varied. Thus, when Rossini did not make any variation, either through laziness or indifference, or because he had confidence in the inventiveness of the interpreter, the singer was expected to sing variations; and this despite the fact, as has already been mentioned, that Rossini amused himself by making variations in the da capos of other opera composers. Another of his habits was that of changing or actually rewriting his own cadenzas, both in arias and in duets.

But where Rossini liked to write variations in depth was in strophic arias, like 'songs', or in fashioning single phrases within an aria. The starting-point was an unwavering principle of bel canto art: aversion to repeating identical phrases. In the case of strophic arias, Rossini's variation practice covered the entire text of the second and third stanzas, using the procedure known as 'rielaborazione' (reworking). This is what takes place in the song 'D'amor al dolce impero' sung by Armida, where the second stanza is varied first of all with divisions superimposed on the rhythm in triplets, and then with figurations in arpeggio form.

Different again is the system of variations used in the 'Willow song' sung by Desdemona, where Rossini only works on the ornamentation, so that between the first and third stanzas there is a gradual accentuation of the *fioriture*. But the most interesting and also the most frequent types of variation used by Rossini are based on procedures, sometimes cutting across each other, of amplification and division. Many of Rossini's arias are constructed on these patterns, which then turn out to coincide with a genuine development of the melodic idea. But the fascination of Rossini's coloratura really consists in the fact that it is often an integral part of the melody, calling directly upon the elegance, lightness of touch, and imagination of the composer, as when, in the final part of the duet between Almaviva and Figaro in *The Barber* (3/8 time Allegretto), Rossini gives the tenor the phrase shown in Ex. 74). The way in which it is developed is crystal-clear in its logic (Ex. 75).

Ex. 74

Ah, che d'a - mo - re

Ex. 75

It is both musical logic and stage action logic, since with aristocratic elegance, but at the same time with lightness befitting a
comic opera effect, Count Almaviva expatiates on and accentuates the expression of his feelings. But consider also the meta-
morphosis of the initial phrase of the 4/4 Allegro in Cenerentola's
final rondo (Ex. 76).

Ex. 76

It is the evolution of the feeling (joy) which gradually heats up
until it glows with that melismatic intoxication which is one of the
characteristics of Rossini in his happiest mood. Such procedures
do not invariably produce the startling effect of Cenerentola's
rondo, but they are constantly bound up with the development
and variety of a melodic design and breakdown of feelings
depicted in a manner which grows more and more intense while
the words remain unchanged. Examples are the martial Vivace 'Ah
sí, per voi già sento', sung by the protagonist in *Otello*, and the
variations on the initial motif (act I); also the aria sung by the

protagonist in *Elisabetta*: 'Questo cor ben lo comprende' (act I, where the phrase 'Rivedrò quel caro oggetto' appears four times, and in a different form each time).

TYPES OF VOICE IN ROSSINI'S OPERAS

The link between bel canto art and the castrati is so close that the disappearance of the male soprano and male alto at the beginning of the nineteenth century represents a radical transformation of vocal tradition. Rossini is one of the composers who realized this most fully. But he was to keep at all times a nostalgia for the expressiveness, even more than for the virtuosity, of the castrato voice.[15] In practice, however, he found himself obliged to fill in the gap left by the disappearance of the male sopranos and male altos, and like other composers he turned towards the solution consisting of using women dressed up in men's clothes.

This is an expedient typical of the early nineteenth century, even though there are precedents in Italy—particularly in Naples—between the end of the seventeenth century and the early years of the eighteenth century, and in Handel's London shortly afterwards. In practice, in serious opera at the beginning of the nineteenth century, the tenor begins to be accepted for the roles of young lover and young hero which until then had always been reserved for castrati; but there was a far greater willingness to use women, and particularly contraltos. This brought into existence the *contralto musico*, specializing in roles written for castrati or roles which in other periods would had been sung by castrati. When the famous Giuditta Pasta played the part of Telemaco in Cimarosa's *Penelope*, Armando in Meyerbeer's *Il crocciato in Egitto*, or Enrico in Mayr's *La rosa bianca e la rosa rossa*, all she was doing for practical purposes was replacing the castrati for whom these roles were written originally. But there were also *musico* roles composed specifically for female contraltos. A list of these would include, in the first thirty-five years of the nineteenth century, perhaps more than a hundred instances. Here we need only cite Enrico di Borgogna and Abenamat in Donizetti's *Zoraide di Granata*; Edemondo in *Emma di Resburgo*; Almanzor in Meyerbeer's *L'esule di Granata*; Eneas in *Didone abbandonata*; Osvino in *I normanni a*

---

[15] See p. 139.

Parigi; Don Diego in *Donna Caritea*; the title-role in Mercadante's *Uggero il danese*; Corrado in *Il corsaro*; Wilfredo in Pacini's *Ivanhoe*; and of course, Romeo in Vaccai's *Giulietta e Romeo* and Bellini's *I Capuleti*.

In the tradition of the female *musico* we come back to the myth of the Rossini contralto. The contralto voice, at the end of the eighteenth century and in the first few years of the nineteenth century, is seen as an extremely flexible voice, varied in form and often free of problems of range. The famous bass Luigi Lablache was to write in his *Méthode complète de chant*, which appeared in Brussels between 1835 and 1840, that the contralto is a voice in which the range and tessitura vary from case to case and hence are impossible to classify. Actually, that was not precisely the case. In the first three decades of the nineteenth century, when many of the rules of bel canto were still in force, the mezzo-soprano did not enjoy autonomy in respect of timbre. Hence high or even very high mezzo-sopranos passed for contraltos—singers like Colbran, Pasta, Malibran, Unger—all of whom, in fact, became sopranos in the second half of their careers. But the fact remains that even genuine contraltos like Rosmunda Pisaroni and Marietta Alboni had an exceptional range.

Precisely in this type of voice, Rossini glimpsed the possibility of reviving the vocal exploits of the castrato, and his view, if we link it to the taste of the period, is perfectly logical. First and foremost there still existed the long-standing bel canto prejudice against the tenor voice—which in serious opera continued to be of the baritone type—for use in the role of the lover. Next, the contralto larynx has certain virile inflections in the lower register which by and large recall certain colours of the male alto castrato and the sexual ambiguity so dear to the bel canto style. But when raised up into the higher vocal area, it could take on the clear, delicate, and brilliant timbre of the soprano. Hence the striking sensation felt by Théophile Gautier when he heard Marietta Alboni, one of the greatest Rossini contraltos in musical history. 'Une voix si féminine et en même temps si mâle! Juliette et Roméo dans le même gosier!' (A voice at once so feminine and yet so male! Juliet and Romeo in the same throat!)

Thus it is in the contralto voice that Rossini's bel canto style finds its mainstay. Basically, Rossini makes use of the contralto in two ways: as a buffo prima donna, and as a *musico*.

L'equivoco stravagante (1811) is the opera in which Rossini for the first time composes a buffo prima donna role (Ernestina) for a true contralto, namely Marietta Marcolini. Likewise for Marcolini he composed the roles of Clarice in *La pietra del paragone* and that of Isabella in *L'italiana in Algeri*, which portray the tender, enterprising, vivacious, and odd woman who is identified with the Rossini buffo heroine. The very writing of this part calls for a notable virtuoso effort from the contralto, and this was to become accentuated with Rosina in *The Barber of Seville* and with Cenerentola. Rosina and Cenerentola sing on a higher tessitura, with passages fluctuating between mezzo-soprano and contralto; Clarice and Isabella respond better to the contralto register.

The contralto *musico* or *en travesti* already appears in Rossini's first *opera seria*: the role of Sivena in *Demetrio e Polibio*. Next come the title-role in *Ciro in Babilonia*, Tancredi, Sigismondo, and Ottone in *Adelaide di Borgogna*, Edoardo in *Edoardo e Cristina*, Malcolm in *La donna del lago*, Faliero in *Bianca e Faliero*, Calbo in *Maometto II*, and Arsace in *Semiramide*.

In these roles also, Rossini's composition presents a type of coloratura which is becoming elaborate and accentuating the virtuoso characteristics in the last operas written for Italy. Outstanding are Malcolm and Arsace, personages composed for Rosmunda Pisaroni and Rosa Mariani respectively. In both these instances, but also in that of Tancredi—a part written for Malanotte—the tessitura seems at times to suggest a deep contralto.

Rossini's *contralto musico* singers as a rule play the parts of adolescents of heroic lineage. There is fine, broad phrasing in the recitatives; there are tender or elegiac cantabiles, vibrant tunes in the outbursts of anger or joy; and it is here that frequently the writing goes into real acrobatics. The contralto *en travesti* also appears in a comic opera (Edoardo in *Matilde di Shabran*) and in a semi-serious opera as Pippo in *La gazza ladra*. In the latter case, the part is not that of a lover but looks ahead to the page-boy roles as they were to appear more than once in Donizetti and later opera composers, where the adolescent character plays the part of friend and confidant. In the Neapolitan operas, the contralto appears occasionally as the rival (Andromaca in *Ermione*, for example).

The range of Rossini's contralto parts stretches from g to b″. In

exceptional cases, as in *Ricciardo e Zoraide*, Zomira, in a part
written for Pisaroni, sings down to a-flat on an arpeggio (in the
sextet 'Oppressa, smarrita', act I). The contralto sings up to a″ only
in vocalises (most of them in runs), whereas in syllabic singing, the
contralto does not as a rule go beyond f″ or g″. The tessitura,
always in syllabic singing, fluctuates largely over the section c′ to
c″.

In virtuoso singing, the contralto is in all respects assimilated to
the soprano. Her runs are equally amazing, the *fioriture* equally
elaborate, and the ornamentation is fully displayed, including
trills. But in general, especially in the parts written for Marcolini,
the contralto is spared long ascending scales, and in vocalises she
usually reaches the high notes with the help of arpeggios or
successive jumps. Descending scales are extremely frequent. In
this respect, Rossini treats the contralto as a low voice, even when
he gives it hammer-like agility phrases to sing, as in the duet
'O che muso, che figura' from *L'italiana in Algeri* (see the example
on p. 152).

In Rossini's French operas the contralto is missing. The fact is
that, since Rossini was writing for the Paris Opera, he observed
the local customs. The contralto voice (*bas-dessus*) had never
managed to break into the French tradition, and even though the
introduction of Italian serious opera, begun with the First Empire
and developed in the 1820s, actually through Rossini, had made
certain contraltos such as Pasta and Pisaroni familiar in France,
the Paris Opera for a long time remained faithful to its long-
standing practices.

The mezzo-soprano voice was used very frequently by Rossini;
but on only one occasion, for the page Isoliero in *Le Conte Ory*,
did he use it for a principal role. Otherwise the mezzo-soprano in
Rossini's operas plays the part of *seconda donna* (second lady). In
the Italian operas, both comic and serious, she has almost always
one aria, medium in tessitura, generally in syllabic style or lightly
ornamented. In Rossini's comic repertoire, the mezzo-soprano
voice appears as early as *Il cambiale di matrimonio* (Clarina); and in
his serious repertoire it figures for the first time in *Ciro di Babilonia*
(the role of Argene). There is a certain striking quality in Zulma
(*L'italiana in Algeri*), Zaida (*Il turco in Italia*), Berta (*The Barber of
Seville*), and among the examples of *opera seria*, Emilia (*Otello*).

Rossini's sopranos regularly sing the roles of women in love.

This is true both of *opera seria* and of *opera buffa*. In early Rossini, the *opera seria* soprano has a coloratura with greater virtuosity and a wider range than the comic-opera soprano. In *Aureliano in Palmira*, Zenobia in one of her vocalises reaches e‴ flat. Her tessituras too are higher, and indeed at times extremely high. Actually, the soprano in the earliest of Rossini's *opera seria* efforts seems to anticipate in some of its psychological traits the chaste, angel-like young ladies of the Romantic period. The high tessituras, implying a tendentiously clear voice, associate this timbre with the notion of purity and youth. They reflect the type of amorous *ingénue*—Lisinga in *Demetrio e Polibio*, Amira in *Ciro in Babilonia*, Amenaide in *Tancredi*, Aldimira in *Sigismondo*, Dorliska, and Matilde di Shabran.

In comic opera, the soprano is the *prima buffa*, and rings the changes between passages of sweetness and languor and moments of vivacity, naughtiness, and volubility. In this sense, Fiorilla in *Il turco in Italia* is the most significant personage, but other outstanding figures are Fanny in *Il cambiale di matrimonio* and Sofia in *Signor Bruschino*. In the *mezzo carattere* operas, such as *L'inganno felice* and *La gazza ladra*, the soprano (Isabella and Ninetta respectively) reflects the *ingénue* type. She has a more elaborate coloratura than the comic opera soprano, but is less acrobatic than the soprano of *opera seria*. The tessitura is fairly central, with moments, especially in *La gazza ladra*, which almost suggest the mezzo. But this has to do with the particular qualities of Teresa Belloc, the singer for whom the roles of Isabella and Ninetta were composed.

In the Neapolitan operas, the high soprano playing the part of the *ingénue* in love appears only in *Elisabetta*, as the protagonist's rival Matilde. In all the other instances, the soprano roles take account of certain basic vocal features of Colbran, who held a pre-eminent position at the Royal Theatre in Naples. Colbran had begun her career as a contralto, but one possessing a voice of exceptionally wide range. In actual fact she was a high mezzo-soprano, as after her were Giuditta Pasta and Maria Malibran, and the ease of her high register led her gradually to turn towards soprano roles. But she was never a high soprano of the *ingénue*-in-love type of the early Rossini operas. She was rather a true soprano, with here and there traces of the mezzo-soprano, whom Rossini in vocalises frequently took up to b″ and occasionally to c‴, while nearly always remaining on fairly high tessituras, especially in syllabic singing.

Apart from this, Colbran was at the same time a virtuoso interpreter who, on the strength of her broad and noble phrasing and her stage presence, was cut out for the great roles of queens or enchantresses of neo-classical opera (Elisabetta, Armida, and Semiramide). Nevertheless, she was already somewhat past her best when Rossini arrived in Naples, and if we take notice of two witnesses, even though they do not agree—Stendhal in his *Vie de Rossini* and Giuseppe Carpani in his *Lettera sulla musica di Rossini*— we can single out two aspects of the gradual deterioration of this singer: the tendency to sing off key and lose tone, and a lack of great vocal bravura. Rossini's writing coped with both these defects by means of elaborate coloratura. The tendency to sing flat, caused by fatigue or incorrect use of the muscles of the breathing apparatus, is manifested much more often in cantabile plain-style passages at a slow tempo or on long sustained notes than in vocalises, especially quick-moving ones. At the same time, elaborate ornaments and rapid vocalises, in a voice which still in 1822 struck Carpani as sweet and sonorous, enabled her through her agility in bravura passages (i.e. robust singing) which gave a bite to the tone, to make up for the lack of power in plain and agitato singing.[16]

This explains why Colbran's singing also suited the portrayal of gentle or nostalgic characters like Desdemona, Elena in *La donna del lago*, or Zelmira, in which tender *fioriture* alternated with brilliant virtuosity. But this was not the only feature of her singing, since in these operas too we find moments of robust syllabic vocalism. In some respects, however, the soprano roles written for Colbran would appear to anticipate the 'dramatic soprano with agility' of Romantic opera. In the operas composed for Paris, on the other hand, we again find the psychological type and the high vocal line of the soprano of the early works: pure,

---

[16] This is in some respects the case with Marilyn Horne, the finest singer of Rossini in the present century. Horne, whose voice is, incidentally, relatively modest in volume, is not given to great outbursts and to *concitato* singing, and all her efforts at Verdi characters like Azucena, Eboli, or Amneris have met with only moderate success. But in Rossini's bravura agility passages, Horne's voice acquires a biting edge, a brilliance, and an energy which interpret to perfection the stylized, transfigured excitement of Rossini's writing.

dreamy femininity, with the addition of a strength of mind which has an almost heroic turn, like Matilde in *William Tell,* and above all Pamira in *L'assedio di Corinto,* both roles written for Laura Cinti Damoreau.

We now come to the baritone-tenor, who in Rossini's Italian *opera seria* works is given great scope. Where the role of lover is played by a contralto (or by a castrato, as in *Aureliano in Palmira*), Rossini observes the bel canto tradition of using the 'baritenor' as the noble father (Demetrio-Eumene in *Demetrio e Polibio,* Argirio in *Tancredi*); or as the rival (Baldassare in *Ciro in Babilonia;* the protagonist in *Aureliano;* Ladislao in *Sigismondo*). But beginning in 1815, the first year of his sojourn in Naples, Rossini found himself faced by a different situation. The dictatorship exercised by Isabella Colbran at the Teatro San Carlo rarely allowed him the use of the *contralto musico,* since this would have meant facing the local diva with another outstanding female voice. But at the same time, the new practice of using a tenor, even though of the baritone type, as the lover, was gaining ground. Hence, not only in *Elisabetta* but also in *Torvaldo e Dorliska,* produced shortly after-wards at the Valle di Roma, two famous baritone-tenors played the parts of lovers: Andrea Nozzari (Leicester) and Domenico Donzelli, playing Torvaldo. Nozzari, the most typical Rossini baritenor, was later to play Otello, Rinaldo in *Armida,* and Osiride in *Mosè.* Of these personages Leicester, and even more so Rinaldo, most vividly portrayed the features of the male in love, whereas Otello has psychologically the characteristics of the modern baritone, whether he is seen as the heroic general or expresses fury and jealousy. However, it is in *Armida* in particular that Rossini decisively faces the problem of making the baritenor sing love songs; and he solves the problem in the duets between Rinaldo and Armida ('Amor possente nome' in the first act, 'Dove son io' in the second act, 'Soavi catene' in the third act), aiming at a sensuousness expressed in melodies rich in ornaments (es-pecially turns) or elaborate *fioriture.* As a rule, however, Rossini is too much of a 'belcantist' to allow the baritenor to inspire in him genuine amorous outbursts and soft and languorous or dreamy melodies. Even when the baritenor is the father or the rival, heartfelt singing, full of pathos, is lacking. The character is in general directed towards robust singing, which finds the most typical formulas in upward leaps, often marked at the start by dotted rhythm, as in the phrase sung by Aureliano ('A pugnar m'accinsi o Roma' in act I) (Ex. 77).

Ex. 77

A   pu – gnar m'ac-cin   si, o   Ro – ma   col tuo

no – me   im – pres - so in   cor

In robust vocalism, however, it is Otello who sets the pace, whether in his martial Vivace on making his entrance ('Ah! Sí per voi giá sento', or in the stirring duet with Iago ('L'ira d'avverso fato', act II), or in the final scene of the opera. However, over and above Rossini's way of using the tenor voice comes a new situation beginning with *Otello*. The baritenor playing the lover as an alternative to the contralto *en travesti* was a practice which even before Rossini had been adopted by other opera composers; but it raised a problem: who was to replace the baritone-type tenor in the role of father, rival, tyrant, traitor, etc.? The initial remedy was to continue to use a baritenor for this type of role, coping with the resulting uniformity of timbre by writing either for the lover or for the rival a part with a tessitura relatively higher than the other. In Paer's *Achille*, for example, both the protagonist and Agamemnon are baritenors, but the tessitura of the former is higher. In Rossini's *Elisabetta* we have the opposite situation: Norfolk, who was played by Manuel Garcia senior, is a baritenor higher than Leicester, played by Nozzari.

The regular use of the baritenor gave rise in some of Rossini's operas to a situation which from the point of view of timbre was decidedly confused and certainly monotonous. In *Armida*, an exceptional case, at least seven baritone-type tenors were simultaneously playing the parts of lover (Nozzari), rival, army commander, sorcerer, and character roles. But the way out of the problem was suggested to Rossini by the comic-opera tenor or *mezzo-carattere* tenor.

In his first comic operas, Rossini's tenor has a fairly central tessitura and is not given a particularly virtuoso type of vocal line. Then, in *La pietra del paragone*, he is a baritenor: Giocondo. But in *L'italiana in Algeri* (Lindoro), the tessitura becomes extremely high and the writing is very florid, as is also the case with Don Narciso in *Il turco in Italia*. In *The Barber*, on the other hand, with Count Almaviva we have a return to middle tessituras. The history of Rossini's vocal writing is also the history of the singers for whom Rossini was composing. With Lindoro in *L'italiana in Algeri*, written for Serafino Gentili, and with Don Narciso, written for Giovanni David, we get the appearance of more or less lyric tenors, with a ringing timbre and a very wide range, of a type described at the time as *tenorini*. Almaviva, on the other hand, was composed for Manuel Garcia senior, who was a baritenor, although with a very wide range for the category.[17] Subsequently, Rossini wrote for a 'tenorino' (Giacomo Guglielmi) the role of Ramiro in *Cenerentola*, which is extremely high; but the part of Giannetto in *La gazza ladra* is likewise distinguished by an extremely high tessitura. *Cenerentola* and *La gazza ladra* are both dated 1817, but in 1816 already, with Rodrigo in *Otello*, a part played by Giovanni David, Rossini had introduced the high, brilliant tenor into *opera seria*, thus giving Otello a difference of timbre from that of Iago, both of them baritenors. From 1818 onwards, therefore, finding that he had a *contraltino* tenor at his disposal (David, in fact), and a baritenor (Nozzari), Rossini used the former as the lover and the latter as the rival. That is what happened in *Ricciardo e Zoraide* (David playing Ricciardo and Nozzari playing Agorante), and this diversification procedure continued with *Ermione* (David playing Oreste and Nozzari playing Pirro), *La donna del lago* (Giacomo and Rodrigo), and *Zelmira* (Ilo and Antenore). During the same period, Rossini used the baritenor to offset the *contralto musico* in *Edoardo e Cristina* (Carlo) and in *Bianca e Faliero* (Contareno).

Giovanni David, however, is the prototype of the Rossini contraltino tenor, extremely high, brilliant, and acrobatic, but also with a leaning towards the elegiac type of melody such as 'Ah, perché mai non senti', sung by Rodrigo in *Otello* (act II). This gives

---

[17] Garcia had *L'italiana in Algeri* in his repertoire, but faced with the extremely high tessitura and the mainly syllabic writing of 'Languir per una bella', he transposed the aria down a minor third, performing it in c major instead of e flat.

us an idea of the dizzying tessitura and agility of David (who liked
to introduce his own acrobatic variations), as does also the
following passage from the duet between Rodrigo and Otello in
the second act ('Ah vieni, nel tuo sangue') (Ex. 78), and one from
Ricciardo's cabaletta ('S'ella m'è ognor fedele', act I) (Ex. 79). With
regard to the duet 'Qual dolce speme' between Ricciardo and
Agorante (act II), the phrase in Ex. 80 gives us a clear idea of the
difference in tessitura between a contraltino tenor and a baritenor.

Ex. 78

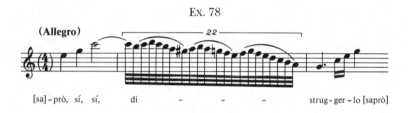

Ex. 79

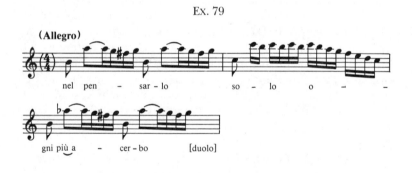

Ex. 80

Variation in tessitura does not signify variation in range. Even Rossini's baritenor at times sings up to c″ and even d″, taking advantage of falsetto production. Generally speaking, the baritenor sings with full voice up to g′ or a flat (these are the highest notes of the baritone today), and from there the voice goes into a pure head register, producing notes that are 'white' but not devoid of resonance and carrying power. The reinforced falsetto (*falsettone*) is also used by the contraltino tenor, generally after a′ or b♭′.

The baritenor too is called upon, like the contraltino tenor, to sing a vocal line rich in *fioriture* and ornaments (including trills), but he seems to be less prone to runs. To offset this, he is more likely to sing wide intervals which suddenly take the voice from a low-pitched note to a very high one or vice versa (so-called *canto di sbalzo*).

Rossini's last Italian opera, *Semiramide*, likewise features an extremely high tenor, Idreno. Then the French operas begin, and Rossini is writing for Adolphe Nourrit the roles of Count Ory, Neocle in *L'assedio di Corinto*, and Arnaldo in *William Tell*. Nourrit was the incarnation of the tradition of the *haute-contre*, the lover by substitution in French opera, both serious and comic. Like all *haute-contre* singers he had a clear voice, very long-ranged in the upper region and hence comfortable with high tessituras, although less stratospheric than those which Giovanni David could manage. After g′, Nourrit made very skilful use of *falsettone*, and with this type of phonation he was able to execute all the passages and phrases in *William Tell* which today we are accustomed to hearing from tenors sung in a heroic manner and with stentorian tones, with all the high notes 'in chest voice', including the top c (c″).[18] Bearing in mind the practices of the Paris Opera and the traditions of the *haute-contre* of serious type, Rossini considerably reduced the *fioriture* and agility passages in parts written for Nourrit.

In Rossini's operatic writing, the term 'bass' also includes the baritone voice. In the comic genre, two types of bass voice appear, often simultaneously. The first is the 'heavy' buffo, more palpably comic, more farcical, who plays the traditional roles of the father,

---

[18] It was actually in *William Tell* that another French singer, Louis Gilbert Duprez, a bitter rival of Nourrit, introduced with tremendous success the so-called *do di petto* (top c in chest voice), a note which throughout the entire Romantic period helped decisively to create the myth of the tenor.

or the simpleton husband, or the old tutor who is victimized. The other might be defined as a 'noble' buffo, and he has a more varied repertoire which even leads him to be identified with personages of high rank and to play the part of lover. In *La pietra del paragone*, for example, Count Asdrubale is a noble buffo and a lover, whereas Fabrizio is a heavy buffo; in *L'italiana in Algeri*, Mustafà is noble, Taddeo is heavy; in *Il turco in Italia*, Selim is noble, Geronio is heavy. Between the 'noble' and the 'heavy' buffo there is not only a psychological differentiation. By bringing the writing of comic opera in respect of magnificence of arias and sumptuousness of ornamentation into line with that of *opera seria*, Rossini attracted into the field of the comic genre some of the most famous voices of his time and virtually removed all differentiation between courtly singers and buffo singers. Thus the 'noble' buffo often has great vocal means and outstanding virtuosity. Some of the 'noble' buffo roles are linked with the name of the most eminent bass of the first twenty years of the nineteenth century—Filippo Galli, playing Asdrubale, Mustafà, Selim. This explains the difficulty in the execution of these roles. The heavy buffo, even though Rossini's vocal writing may at times call upon him to sing the odd agility passage, is more modest in the vocal gifts required of him. He is, in short, a *parlando* buffo, whereas the other is a *cantando* buffo (cf. Bartolo and Don Basilio in *The Barber of Seville*).

A third type of buffo often turns up in Rossini's operas—the one who acts as a *deus ex machina*, hatching intrigues and acting when necessary as go-between. These personages are as a rule ringing baritones such as Prosdocimo in *Il turco in Italia*, Figaro in *The Barber of Seville*, and Dandini in *Cenerentola*.

When Rossini had at his disposal a noble buffo like Filippo Galli, he used a range which stretched in general from G to f′ or f♯′. The tessitura is reminiscent of that of bass-baritone. The writing is very florid and calls for delicacy exceptional in a low voice. An example is the passage, sung by Selim, taken from the quartet in the first act of *Il turco in Italia* (Ex. 81).

To sum up, Rossini's tendency in regard to melismata and ornaments is to assimilate the bass voice, in both buffo and serious roles, to the other voices, and this recalls the approach we find in the early seventeenth century and the Handel period. Virtuosity—including the use of the trill—was present even in the

Ex. 81

(**Largo**)

[io stu]- pi — sco   mi   sor — pren - de   io   stu –

pi — sco   mi   sor —   [prende]

roles of the heavy buffo, and more frequently in those of the bass,
who strictly speaking was a ringing baritone like Figaro or
Dandini (with regard to the latter, cf. the aria 'Come un'ape
ne'giorni d'aprile' in act I). But the great resource of the heavy
buffo and the ringing buffo is identified with the *parlante*
(speaking) style and with the 'syllabic' style. The parlante style
takes off from recitative, and its deliberate monotony is
brightened up by vivacious episodes in the orchestra. Rossini uses
it in *Il cambiale di matrimonio* and *L'inganno felice* (Batone's aria with
cabaletta 'Nell fissarle gli occhi addosso'). The syllabic style, on the
other hand, is a rigorously monosyllabic type of singing in which
the words follow one another with the highly stressed articulation
of declaimed speech and often at breakneck speed. Even in these
circumstances, the orchestra comments with varied and brilliant
episodes. An example of the *parlante* style is 'Numero quindici a
mano manca' sung by Figaro in the duet with Almaviva in the first
act, while Figaro also demonstrates classic syllabic singing in the
stretto section of his cavatina on entry. Other famous syllabic
episodes are to be found in the Allegro vivace ('Signorina un'altra
volta') of Don Bartolo's aria 'A un dottore della mia sorte' in the
first act, and in Don Magnifico's cavatina 'Miei rampolli fem-
menini' in act I of *Cenerentola*. The great buffo singers of the first
half of the nineteenth century excelled in this type of singing, not
only because of the nimbleness of their articulation but for the
diminuendo and crescendo effects they were capable of executing.

In *opera seria* or *semi-seria*, the bass roles are linked mostly with
seventeenth- and eighteenth-century tradition. At times the bass
is the 'villain', an evil rival of the lover, as in the case of Orbazzano
in *Tancredi*, the Duke of Ordow in *Torvaldo e Doriska* (a role written
for Filippo Galli), or the Podestà in *La gazza ladra*. The Duke of

Ordow is the first serious bass part to which Rossini gives great importance, particularly in a virtuoso sense. It is symptomatic that in the cavatina 'Dunque invano' (the 4/4 martial aria in act I), a bass voice is called upon to perform this agility passage (Ex. 82).

Ex. 82

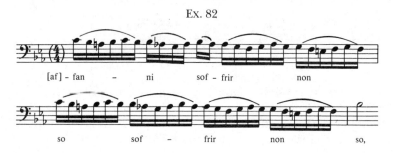

Both the Duke of Ordow and the Podestà in *La gazza ladra* in their arrogance represent various aspects of satanism. Even the Podestà often has melismatic, virtuoso passages to sing, e.g. the cavatina in the first act ('Il mio piano è preparato', with trills and runs), the aria in the second act ('Sì, per voi pupille amate'), and again the Andante grazioso of the second finale, vaguely onomatopoeic, rather in the manner of the Baroque 'tempest' aria (Ex. 83).

Ex. 83

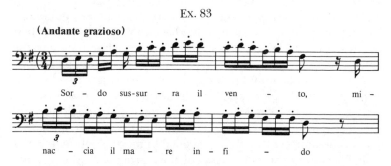

Another fierce and arrogant bass character, but built up on a tragic background, is Assur in *Semiramide*. This role, like almost all those written for Galli, is of exceptional vocal and psychological importance and alternates between virtuosity and plain and declaimed singing. Likewise, in the category of basses playing the part of tyrant or traitor we find Gessler in *William Tell*, Leucippo in *Zelmira*, and Pharaoh in *Mosè*, these latter two somewhat baritonal in character. Two other Rossini bass roles which hark back to ancient traditions are those of the noble father and the priest. The first includes Elmiro in *Otello*, Douglas in *La donna del lago*, and Polidoro in *Zelmira*; while in the second category come the Priest of Iside in *Aureliano in Palmira*, the protagonist in *Mosè*, and Osroe in *Semiramide*. All these roles, with the exception of the Priest of Iside and Osroe, belong to the Neapolitan period and are inspired by the big, deep bass voice of Michele Benedetti.

The following constitute a category of their own: Fernando in *La gazza ladra* (Galli), Maometto II (also Galli), and William Tell, a baritone-type bass (Henri Dabadie). Fernando is a noble father in his pride and courage, not through social status. Elaborate *fioriture*, arpeggio-type agility, and runs characterize the coloratura, but the feature most typical of Fernando is to be seen in episodes of plain singing and pathos, side by side with passages of slow, incisive declamation (e.g. the first part of the aria 'Accusata di furto', or the condemnation scene, both from the second act. Maometto represents the unusual case of a bass in the guise of lover. He is a personage of noble and magnanimous bearing who, even in the revised version of *L'assedio di Corinto*, has two basic features: vocal virtuosity and tenderness in the love song. As regards William Tell, he is the most modern character—in a Romantic sense—of all Rossini's *opera seria* works. His vocalism, virtually devoid of melismata, was for a long time to be a necessary point of reference for the treatment of noble, heroic-style baritone roles.

VOCALISM IN THE ROSSINI PERIOD; PERFORMANCE PRACTICES; STENDHAL'S VIEWS ON SINGING

Some writers on singing—in particular Manuel Garcia the Younger, Gilbert Louis Duprez, and Luigi Lablache—refer in their handbooks to the rules to be observed by singers in performing the works of the main opera composers of the first forty years of the nineteenth century. The basic principle was that, in order to give expression to singing, the executant must be capable of (1) executing the *messa di voce*, in other words moving gradually from pianissimo to fortissimo and back; (2) singing 'legato' and making the 'portamento', legato being defined as moving from one note to another of a musical phrase gently but cleanly, and portamento as 'carrying' the voice gracefully and lightly from one interval to another without 'slurring' the tone, in other words without allowing the intermediate notes to be heard; (3) 'phrasing', in other words shaping each musical phrase in such a way as to give it an impact of its own, and knowing how to calculate the breath exactly in relation to the length of each section and to insert pauses where the composer had omitted them; (4) 'nuancing', that is to say alternating piano and forte and the intermediate degrees of intensity according to the sense of the phrase and the words; (5) executing the ornaments impeccably.

If only one of these requirements was missing, the expression was regarded as imperfect. Then there were complementary rules. For example, in upward portamenti, the intensity of the tone had to be increased, and it must be decreased in descending portamenti. This was part of the more general principle that in all musical phrases rising in pitch, it was desirable to move gradually from piano to forte, whereas the inverse procedure had to be used in the case of descending phrases. However, these were guidelines which in the course of time were calculated to generate a mechanical attitude. Hence the position taken up by the leading theoretical writer of the Rossini vocal school, Manuel Garcia the Younger, who laid down the rule that forte and piano, like crescendo and diminuendo, must be used in the light of the sentiment to be expressed and not according to the shape of the musical phrase. Thus rising phrases could be executed by 're-inforcing' the tone if the sentiment expressed became more animated because of the meaning of the phrase, and by making a 'diminuendo' if the sentiment became more languorous. A similar rule had to be applied to descending phrases.

However, even the principles expounded by Garcia lead us to the conclusion that one of the fundamental laws of singing in the Rossini period (although in actual fact it was a rule born with the bel canto school) was variety in the musical discourse, in other words a constant balance of forte and piano sounds, as well as an assiduous use of all the intermediate tints. Equally basic was the rule which required a motif to be varied whenever it was repeated, either wholly or in part. The means available to the singer for achieving variation were grading the stress, swelling the tone, whittling it down, and executing rallentando, accelerando, and tempo rubato, in the course of which the executant could slow or quicken the pace, provided he remained 'in time' with the orchestra, whose tempo was not subject to alteration. Another form of variation was, naturally, the insertion of ornaments and *fioriture*, which should be few when the repetition of the motif was only partial. If on the other hand the repetition was total, as in the case of the rondo, the cavatina, the polacca, and arias of the da capo type or strophic in form, variations based on the interpolation of ornaments and *fioriture* were required to follow a rising progression. What this meant was that the first time, the motif was executed with maximum simplicity, as the composer had written it, whereas the second time saw the introduction in moderation of *fioriture* or effects of rallentando, accelerando, tempo rubato, or stresses graded in a variety of ways. Finally, when the motif was repeated for the third time, the *fioriture* were intensified, along with all the other forms of variation. When Rossini decided to undertake the variations himself, he was in fact applying these rules, as when he presented the stanzas of 'D'amor al dolce impero' and the Willow Song in *Otello* in three different versions.

Agility singing provided for various types of vocalise: legato agility, martellato ('hammered') agility, marcato and staccato agility, and aspirated agility.

Legato agility is the most frequent type. It is the type that can be seen in the examples already cited from *Elisabetta* and *Cenerentola*,[19] in Idreno's runs in *Semiramide*, and in dozens of other passages. In legato agility singing, every note had to be heard with the same clarity, the same intensity, and the same colour, and in addition, the singer must move from one note to another without any scooping. Then, in the course of a run there must be no accelerando or rallentando. It must start as rapidly as possible and finish at the same speed. But in the case of a chromatic scale, according to some theoretical writers there could a slight pause on the first note. In a great chromatic run forming part of the aria 'D'amor al dolce impero' from *Armida*, Rossini himself made provision for this 'hold' both at the beginning of the rising scale and once the voice had reached the high b flat, before beginning the descending scale.

---

[19] See pp. 152 ff.

What was considered particularly difficult was the execution of vocalises on adjacent intervals with triplets (in other words, articulated in groups of three notes) as in Ex. 84 (the second stanza of 'D'amor al dolce impero'). This meant avoiding the trap

Ex. 84

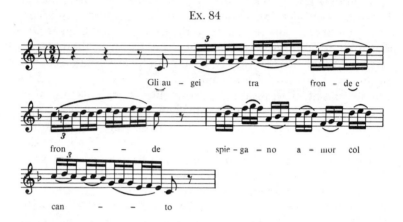

Gli au - gei   tra   fron - de e

fron - - de   spie - ga - no   a - mor col

can - - to

into which executants fall more and more frequently, namely, the tendency to detach the individual notes on the rising phrase and to slur them on the descent. With regard to vocalises in arpeggio form,[20] within each arpeggio figure the first note had to be slightly accented; then the voice moved on, lightly but also decisively and cleanly, to the other notes, binding them one to the other without slurring and endeavouring not to make any rallentando. Some executants were in the habit, when singing arpeggios, of sustaining the notes on the ascending phrase and damping them when descending. According to some theoretical writers, moreover, in fast-moving passages the arpeggio should be executed *mezza voce*.

With regard to martellato agility, reference may be made to the example already quoted[21] of the duet between Isabella and Mustafà in *L'italiana in Algeri*. The individual sounds marked with the sign '>' should be sung with a certain energy, but the accentuation must be even throughout all the notes, and breathiness was ruled out (breathiness occurs when the note is preceded by a sort of 'h' sound), and the sounds had to be tied one to another

---

[20] See the extract quoted on p. 152 from *Elisabetta*: 'Bell'alme generose'.
[21] See p. 152.

without any interruption. Garcia specifies that martellato agility
can also be indicated by notes with a dot above them and the tie
sign. An example of this in Rossini is the passage from the 'exit'
aria of the protagonist in Elisabetta, the 6/8 Andante 'Quanto è
grato all'alma mia' (Ex. 85).

Ex. 85

Picchettato agility is indicated by notes with a dot over them,
staccato ('curtailed note') or flautato (fluted) agility by notes with a
comma (') over each (Ex. 86). In the first case, the sound is
attacked and then immediately released; in the second, after the
attack it can be very slightly prolonged.

Ex. 86

As regards the trill, all female voices in Rossini's day were
capable of executing it, and they did so in a variety of ways. Male
voices, as we are told by Gilbert Louis Duprez, usually executed it
mezza voce. Only a few singers were capable of executing a trill with
full voice. According to Duprez, this capacity was possessed by the
tenor Rubini, the baritone Barroilhet, and the bass Levasseur.
However, the tenor Manuel Garcia Senior was likewise endowed
with a full-blooded, extremely sonorous trill.

In Rossini's writing, the turn is an extremely frequent figure.
According to the nature of the piece, turns executed with energy
expressed passion, fervour, aggressiveness, whereas when executed gently and lightly, they expressed languor or sensuousness.
The rule was to accent and lengthen slightly the note preceding

the turn, speeding up the execution of the grace-notes so as to catch up with the tempo.

Some statements by Stendhal are perhaps the most illuminating and significant documents that have come down to us concerning the vocal art of the Rossini period and the final phase of bel canto singing. References by Stendhal to singing and singers are fairly frequent in the *Vies de Haydn, de Mozart et de Métastase* (1815); even more abundant in *Rome, Naples et Florence* (1817); and numerous and basic in his *Vie de Rossini* (1823). The general principles underlying Stendhal's thinking in regard to vocalism start out from his conviction that the true art of singing is that of Italian or Italianate opera (Mozart), and of Italian singers or singers of the Italian school. In upholding this argument, Stendhal often assumes an anti-intellectualist attitude, which among other things make him a wholehearted adversary of music-drama of German inspiration. Stendhal never hides his intolerance of Gluck and Cherubini; he champions the primacy of melody as opposed to harmony[22] and that of singing as compared with instrumental music. In chapter 2 of his *Vie de Rossini* he writes that the scholars who think that because they have read Boileau they are capable of judging Italian singing are—as advocates of 'stylistic asceticism'—the mortal enemies of roulades, flourishes, and ornaments. He merely adds: 'Let us not discuss them; just cast a glance and pass on.'[23]

At times, with his vivid imagination and his acute sense of reality, Stendhal tackles problems that even today arise in connection with genuinely reliable opera performances, or that jeopardize the ideal conditions which the spectator should find in the theatre. He says, for example, in chapter 30 of the *Vie de Rossini*, that merely becoming a good pianist does not help with the understanding of 'the *nuances* of the human voice' in singing (and he underlines the word 'nuances', which is basic, as we shall see). This statement finds its confirmation today in a certain cold 'pianistic' taste on the part of orchestra conductors of the most

[22] Schopenhauer adopted a similar attitude: 'Give me Rossini's music, which speaks without words! In musical composition today, more attention is paid to the harmony than to the melody. But I take the opposite view and regard melody as the kernel of the music, in relation to which the harmony is like the sauce to the meat' (quoted in: *Scritti sulla musica e le arti*, ed. Fr. Serpa, Fiesole, 1981, p. 142).

[23] *Translator's note:* English translations of Stendhal's *Vie de Rossini* have been drawn from R. N. Coe's translation (London, 1956).

recent generations, who are inclined to flatten out the phrasing of the singers, eliminating precisely the 'nuances' and actually ignoring many expression marks. Another judicious stand taken by Stendhal has to do with a certain bigotry of German origin, bound up with the 'stylistic asceticism' of music-drama and also with philosophical abstraction. Stendhal argues, taking issue with the principle of the search for the absolute masterpiece and of continuity of dramatic action, as well as the tonal unity this would imply, that human nature needs four minutes of conversation in a low voice to come back to earth after a sublime duet, and to make itself ready to enjoy another magnificent passage which is soon to follow. In art as in politics, according to Stendhal, we cannot upset the nature of things with impunity. The consequences of undivided attention and scrupulous silence are that the audience will be less and less entertained. Hence the championing of certain Italian practices: separate boxes in the theatre, for example, and also the way composers have of following up an impressive work with a run-of-the-mill piece. Whatever the pedants may think, says Stendhal, run-of-the-mill pieces give us breathing space and put us in a state of mind where we can appreciate outstanding works more readily. To this may be added, again to the mortification of pedants, the delightful passage of the beginning of chapter 33 of the *Vie de Rossini*: 'Nothing is quite so frivolous as music; and I can well understand that the reader may be scandalized at the ponderous gravity of the tone which I have adopted to scatter a few handfuls of inconsequential observations through these pages, or to retail a couple of singularly pointless anecdotes, grossly overweighted, moreover, with the monumental grandiloquence of terms such as *ideal beauty, felicity, sublime, sensibility* and so on, to the use of which I am only too prone. . . . I am sick to death of *things which must be taken seriously,* and I regret the good old days when full colonels on the active list used to spend their time embroidering tapestries, and when fine literary *salons* used to break up into games of cup-and-ball.'

Essentially, Stendhal as an opera-goer has two sworn enemies: intellectual pomposity and boredom. This he makes known with his open-mindedness born of the knowledge of his own intellectual and cultural superiority over the 'pedants'. What Stendhal asks of musical theatre is emotion, supplied through melody and song. 'La seule mélodie vocale me semble le produit du génie' (Vocal melody alone seems to me the product of genius), we read in a letter to Adolphe de Mareste dated 1820; and we need not be surprised at this statement, which, even if it implies some exaggeration, is nevertheless a typical reflection of the mentality of a man who regards melody as a narrative device and the clearest and most direct approach to the characterization of stage personages. Thus singing and singers are the prophets of melody, the instrument by which it is revealed to us. 'Paris, on the other hand, was not allowed to appreciate even one *half* of Rossini's qualities until (to the unutterable despair of certain Patriotic Persons) Madame Fodor took over Signora De Bernis's part in the *Barber*; and for the other half, it had to wait until Madame Pasta was heard in *Otello* and *Tancredi*.'[24]

These and other views held by Stendhal did not find favour with the devotees of music-drama nor, later on, with many critics of the idealist school. Hence the tendency to underrate Stendhal as a critic and to call him a 'dilettante', a 'melomaniac', and so on. The truth is that today, when a series of circumstances have brought us closer to the very early years of the nineteenth century and to Rossini (Stendhal nevertheless often preferred Mozart and Cimarosa to Rossini), it is much easier than twenty, fifty, or seventy years ago to perceive that Stendhal has said the last word on certain of Rossini's operas, and that in addition he has described the musical climate of the time as no one else has done. We also perceive, since it is something within our purview, that following attempts to bring Rossini back into favour which failed in the 1930s and 1940s, the undertaking was successful from the early 1950s onwards simply and solely because the key to the interpretation of certain aspects of the repertoire was furnished for us first by Maria Callas in *Armida* and *Il turco in Italia*, and then by Sutherland and Horne in *Semiramide*, *Tancredi*, and *L'assedio di Corinto*. Stendhal had realized intuitively what even today escapes the bigots and pedants. The action of creativity is not exhausted with the writing of the opera by the composer; it is crystallized and made manifest in the course of its execution. If the vocal

---

[24] *Vie de Rossini*, ch. 24. Fodor is, more precisely, Joséphine Fodor Mainvielle; De Bernis is in reality Giuseppina Ronzi De Bernis; and Pasta is the very famous Giuditta, the first interpreter of *Norma*, *La sonnambula*, and *Anna Bolena*. Let me remind the reader that Stendhal is exclusively concerned with very famous singers.

performance is inadequate, the so-called musical values remain either unexpressed or misunderstood. This applies in a general way to all musical theatre. But whereas in the performance of late Verdi or Puccini and the *verismo* writers any vocal defects are impediments which to some extent actually 'impede' (and even so can partially be made up for by good orchestral conducting), as we go back to early Verdi, Donizetti, Bellini, and Rossini, the impediment becomes more and more 'nullifying'. Rossini, and especially Rossini in his *opera seria* works, is rendered virtually unintelligible by poor vocal execution. In this respect Stendhal's view is rigorously scientific, and indeed the experience of today shows that there is no exaggeration in the statement that it really was Fodor and Pasta who revealed Rossini to the Parisians. But we have to add in this connection that, at the end of chapter 29 of the *Vie de Rossini*, Stendhal was able to foresee with impressive lucidity (remember that Rossini was at the peak of his success and enjoying a degree of popularity never before achieved by any opera composer) that the composer would later discard the exorbitantly virtuosic slant of his vocal writing. What Stendhal was trying to say was that many of Rossini's works were likely to disappear ultimately from the repertoire for want of singers capable of performing them. It is difficult to maintain that the gradual disappearance of almost all Rossini's *opera seria* works and many of his comic operas was due solely, between 1860 and 1890, to the reason indicated by Stendhal. It was the age; there were historical reasons conspiring at that moment against Rossini; but undoubtedly difficulties of performance too had some impact. This has been particularly true of the last thirty years, and it is still true today, in a historical and cultural situation which is far more favourable to a return to the early nineteenth century. Only exceptional singers like those I have mentioned, and a few others who have fortunately come along in their wake, have enabled audiences today to make contact with Rossini at his most authentic and to understand him.

Anything but dilettante and melomaniac, then, as we see. Nor, indeed, can the adjective melomaniac be properly applied to a man like Stendhal, with serious tastes and a very broad outlook. For Stendhal, the art of singing was the key to the understanding of melody, of the stage personage, of the opera, and at times of the instrumental part itself. See, in chapter 2 of the *Vie de Rossini*,

Stendhal's description of Tancredi's entrance: 'the orchestration reaches a superb climax of *dramatic harmonization.* This is not (as it is foolishly believed in Germany) the art of employing clarinets, cellos, and oboes to re-echo the emotions of the characters on the stage; it is the much rarer art of using the instruments to voice nuances and overtones of emotion which the characters themselves would never dare put into words.' And here Stendhal recalls the effectiveness of the horns when Tancredi is contemplating in silence the ungrateful homeland he is seeing again after a long exile; and he underlines the significance of the use of the flute in the recitative and aria which follow. Instruments, Stendhal notes, like human voices, have expressive qualities of timbre, and a flute is particularly indicated for describing 'joy mingled with sadness'.

Immediately after, Stendhal compares Rossini's descriptive harmony with certain features of Walter Scott in *Ivanhoe.* In both instances, he says, they also have the task of making us realize what the personages are going to say. 'And when at last they do speak, their slightest words are rich with infinite significance.' I emphasize the sentence because it is one of the keys to Stendhal's thinking. Musical theatre is expressed through the characters on the stage. The singer is effective only insofar as he or she is able to bring the character to life. A personage is alive and pulsating insofar as he or she arouses emotion. But to arouse emotion, every word must have its value, through a shaping of the phrase which expresses the meaning of the substantive and the adjective or adverb in all their nuances. Nuancing is a basic element in establishing a character, and only a really fine singer can achieve it. '. . . it is these *nuances* which convince the reader of the poet's sincerity, and which ultimately awaken his sympathy and understanding', we read in chapter 34 of the *Vie de Rossini*; and in the succeeding chapter Stendhal sings the praises of Giuditta Pasta, including her ability to 'weave a spell of magic about the plainest word in the plainest recitative'. Earlier, in chapter 32, referring to 'Ombra adorata aspetta', performed by Girolamo Crescentini in Zingarelli's *Romeo*, Stendhal had pointed out the merely undefined, generic colour of joy given by the famous castrato to certain vocal inflections, as opposed to the heart-rending sadness expressed in the same aria by another famous castrato, Giovanni Battista Velluti, the point being that joy, even only suggested vaguely, seemed to Crescentini to be the likely state of mind of a person in love who commits suicide to become united with a dead lover.

Incidentally Stendhal, in spite of his modernity of thinking, his romanticism, his liberalism, never joins in the diatribes against the castrati and the satirical attitude towards 'white' voices used in male and even heroic roles. On the contrary, he credits the castrato—and in this he echoes the view of Rossini—with real 'singing which is felt deep in the heart'. His only objection was to the fact that Napoleon conferred on Crescentini the Cross of Chevalier of the Légion d'Honneur. This attitude on Stendhal's part is typical of the bel canto fan, deaf to the realism of the Romantics and the postulates of music-drama, and dominated rather by the idea that only the vocal excellence of the castrati guaranteed certain expressive results.

Let us turn now to the question of nuance. 'There is no composer on earth', writes Stendhal, 'suppose him to be as ingenious as you will, whose score can convey with precision these and similar *infinitely minute* nuances of emotional suggestion: yet it is precisely these and similar *infinitely minute* nuances which form the secret of Crescentini's unique perfection in his interpretation of the aria [from *Romeo*]'; but he adds immediately after that this could only be achieved by a singer who had devoted perhaps twenty years of his life to studying his own voice and training it to the required flexibility. This, then, is nuance, regarded as the pinnacle of the vocal art and the last word in regard to the emotional effect that can be transmitted to us by a stage character. It is not only a concept which denotes an extremely fine ear, but it starts out from what were Stendhal's finest qualities, the instinct of a man of the theatre and the typical attitude of a great story-teller who knows how to give credibility to a character. The presupposition of this credibility is created by the composer, but the realization is the task of the interpreter. Hence certain detailed descriptions of the acting of particular singers on the stage, since for Stendhal recitation too is fundamental in the interests of the plausibility of the character. These are scintillating descriptions with a certain supplementary makeweight, attributable to the fact that Stendhal probably adds something of his own here and there for the deliciously narrative purpose of humanizing a particular episode. Essentially, Stendhal understands instinctively all the intentions of the singer-actor and describes them as carried out to perfection: the buffo Luigi Pacini (father of the composer) who at La Scala, during *Il turco in Italia*, playing the part of a betrayed husband (Don Geronio), reproduces the gestures and tics of an aristocrat whose name at the time was on everybody's lips precisely because of certain conjugal adventures; or the irresistible 'dumb show' scene acted out by Pacini himself in Trieste, at the beginning of the duet between Dandini and Don Magnifico, 'Un segreto d'importanza', in *La cenerentola.*

But if Pacini did a good job in Trieste as Dandini, Filippo Galli did an equally good job at La Scala as Don Magnifico. and according to Stendhal's description, his scene was quite on a par with that of Pacini. Here are two characters in a tale expressing themselves in silence, in dumb show, with stupendous effect; but it is also a masterly essay in stage direction, which people working in the theatre today could learn a great deal by reading (*Vie de Rossini*, ch. 20).

Stendhal was prepared to forgive singers of the buffo type who were genuine actors even for the capital vice of having very little voice; thus in *Rome, Naples et Florence* he refers with admiration to the buffo Nicola Festa, splendid in certain roles as a weak-kneed manservant. The fact is that Stendhal's idea of singing differs, in its strictness, from that of the average melomaniac. In all times and places, for Stendhal, the principle holds sway that singing serves exclusively to bring a character to life and to make it plausible and expressive of emotion. Hence mere vocal power does not impress him, let alone singers who as a matter of principle always sing loud. At the beginning of chapter 9 of the *Vie de Rossini*, he wrote that 'the average provincial town is firmly convinced (as indeed is the *Conservatoire* itself) that there is no singing quite as fine as really *loud* singing!' Nor is he impressed by beauty of voice in a purely physical sense. He refers on various occasions to the famous Angelica Catalani as the most beautiful voice of the period and he says of her charmingly: 'It is as if she were singing under a rock: we hear the silvery echo' (*Rome, Naples et Florence*). But he denounces her ostentation in vocalises, *fioriture* in poor taste, frigidity of temperament, and he points out that while Catalani may be acceptable in comic opera, she 'will never understand anything about *opera seria*'. He also says that 'A good voice can render the most dismally mediocre of arias in fine style, the singer being nothing more than a sublime barrel-organ; but a recitative taxes the resources of the human soul' (*Vie de Rossini*, ch. 2).

Along with Catalani, Stendhal condemns as 'lacking in heart' other famous singers with great vocal gifts: the bass Raniero Remorini (*Rome, Naples et Florence*) and Maffei Festa (ibid.); and he deplores the 'frigid virtuosity' of Camporesi (*Vie de Rossini*, ch. 28), whom he had already described in a letter to de Mareste in 1821 as 'shallow, frigid, boring to tears'. Even Fodor Mainvielle, the idol of the Parisians and rival of Pasta, is frequently accused of lack of sensitivity. In fact, having begun her career in Russia and Sweden, Fodor is for him the embodiment of the type of singer he most abhors: 'our book-learned, half-frozen tailor's-dummies from the North' (*Vie de Rossini*, ch. 34).

One of the qualities which Stendhal appreciated most in a singer was the 'noble, broad, sustained' style, and it is precisely in this style that, with singular penetration and utter contempt for such vulgar notions as equating bel canto with vacuous, ostentatious warbling, he singles out one of the characteristic features of the bel canto period: it was above all in the execution of largo and cantabile *spianato* singing (i.e. without *fioriture* or lightly ornamented) that the castrati excelled, he recalls in chapter 32 of the *Vie de Rossini*. But he also recalls that a perfect execution of a Largo aria could require seven or eight years' work. Singers had to acquire the capacity to achieve nuance in sostenuto and in moulding the tone for portamento; and in legato singing the voice must 'fall with equal stress on every note'. Furthermore, the singer must learn to take in breath imperceptibly in the long phrases of arias.

It was this style that gave expressiveness to the performer and engendered the factor basic to it, namely variety of inflexion and accentuation. Thus Stendhal's predilection was for the singers of his day who were still capable of displaying these capacities: the sisters Anna and Ester Mombelli, Rosmunda Pisaroni, and, still more, Filippo Galli, the bass praised in many passages of the *Vie de Rossini* for the beauty and agility of his voice, his stage bravura, his excellence both in the comic genre and in dramatic works. But the singer who best represents Stendhal's ideals in regard to singing is Giuditta Pasta, to whom the *Vie de Rossini* devotes one entire chapter (chapter 35) and many passages throughout the book. Pasta's voice is the only one whose characteristics Stendhal

examines and describes from a strictly technical point of view: her
range, use of chest and head registers, classification (a mezzo-
soprano who could sing soprano and contralto), and her defects,
such as an 'opaque' tone, unevenness, a less than beautiful timbre,
and not exceptional flexibility. In a sense, Pasta is the counterpart
to the perfect voice (Catalani) or almost perfect (Fodor). Stendhal
is enthusiastic about Pasta because out of her unevenness of
timbre and the way in which she uses the various registers she
fashioned an inexhaustible range of nuances and colours, combined with an equally astonishing variety of accents. In short,
Pasta represents a singer capable of the 'microscopic detail' which
the composer cannot express but the interpreter can. She also
had another quality which Stendhal holds up for praise: spontaneous invention. In one and the same opera and the identical
stage situation she changed inflections, 'accents', and 'musical
colours' from one performance to the next. Stendhal says he
heard her thirty times in *Tancredi*, and always he detected new
vocal approaches, due to 'the momentous inspirations of her
heart'. Pasta for him also had the broad, sustained style of the old
school; she was outstanding in the tragic and pathetic genre; there
was a hypnotic 'resonant and magnetic vibration', in her tone; she
was a fine actress; and she showed taste in her *fioriture*, which she
used very rarely, but always elegantly and expressively. Stendhal
saw in her the antithesis, not only of Catalani or the 'book-
learned, half-frozen tailor's dummies from the North', but of the
singer for whom Rossini wrote all the great roles of his Neapolitan
period, as well as *Semiramide*: Isabella Colbran.

It seems likely that Stendhal did not much care for Colbran as a
person, seeing that as early as November 1819 he wrote to de
Mareste: 'The divine Colbran, who is I believe between forty and
fifty years of age, delights prince Jablonowsky, the millionaire
Barbaja and the Maestro.' Actually, Colbran had been the star of
the San Carlo Opera in Naples since 1811, and in 1819 she could
not have been more than thirty-four or thirty-five years of age.
She was Rossini's mistress (and at the same time the mistress of the
impresario Barbaja), and she married Rossini in 1822. In the *Vie
de Rossini*, Stendhal writes of her in chapters 11–14 and in other
places too. In connection with *Elisabetta d'Inghilterra* (1815), he
praises her unconditionally. He says that she possesses great
beauty, which on the stage radiates queenly majesty. Precisely in

the role of Elisabetta, Colbran recited and sang like a queen and a
great tragic actress (Stendhal describes her with much detail), but
as early as 1816 she had begun to fall off vocally and to sing off-
key. This displeased the Neapolitan public, but it could not
protest because Colbran was protected by the court. The
annoyance of the Neapolitans increased in the next few years, so
that 'In the year 1820, one thing alone would have made the
Neapolitans happy; not the gift of a Spanish constitution, but the
elimination of Signorina Colbran!' It seems likely that Stendhal
was putting it a little strongly here; but although the official
notices of the spectacles at the Royal Theatres in Naples give the
lie to this and praise Colbran, even the composer Hérold had
noted a certain deterioration as early as 1814.

The decline of Colbran, according to Stendhal, induced Rossini
to make the roles composed for his favourite prima donna, and
necessarily also for her stage companions, richer and richer in
ornamentation and *fioriture*. As a result, his style became artificial;
the 'noble, broad, sustained' singing disappeared; the Neapolitan
operas, made to fit the virtuoso qualities of Colbran, Pisaroni, and
the tenors Andrea Nozzari and Giovanni David, became un-
singable for most of the other singers. Hence the prophecy,
already recalled above, that so complex a type of vocal writing
would probably prove fatal to Rossini's glory.

There is both truth and falsehood in this. It has already been
said that an examination of Rossini's writing, from the earliest
operas to *Semiramide*, indicates that even prior to the Neapolitan
period there was a more and more pronounced tendency to write
out *fioriture*, vocalises, and ornaments. In Rossini, who after all was
himself an excellent singer, the melodic line was conceived
already ornate and filled out. Clearly, as his authority grew, he felt
more and more inclined to impose on the singers his own ideas—
often very felicitous ideas—in regard to *fioriture* and ornaments.
Nor did he adopt a complex, acrobatic type of writing only in the
operas in which Colbran took part, as is demonstrated by *The
Barber of Seville*, *Cenerentola*, *La gazza ladra*, and *Matilde di Shabran*.
Nor again is it true that the Neapolitan operas do not contain
passages in plain, largo style written for Colbran and for other
executants. It is a fact, however, that in the roles composed for his
future wife, Rossini insisted on the melismatic style, gradually
working up to the extravagant coloratura of the role of

Semiramide. It is also a fact that for a singer like Colbran, endowed with great virtuosity, it was much easier to conceal her decline—and above all her tendency to sing off-pitch, in agility passages written with Rossini's flair than in the simple, largo style, which calls for absolute steadiness of tone and considerable breathing capacity. Questionable intonation is, after all, nearly always a symptom in singers of a deficiency or lack of breath control.

At all events, Stendhal inveighs against Rossini's Neapolitan writing (*Vie de Rossini*, chs. 32 and 33), and for two reasons: the writing out of the coloratura passages by the composer put an end to extempore improvisation by the singers, which for Stendhal, a man of great imagination, was a source of particular enjoyment. He also pointed out that acrobatics suffocated the simple, largo style. Thus he reached the point where he maintained (ch. 42) that it had been a misfortune for Rossini ever to have met Colbran, while on the other hand he lamented the fact that the composer had never written an opera for Pasta, the greatest exponent of the sober, noble style and of the old traditional 'singing which goes straight to the heart'.

However, Stendhal was not a deadly enemy of ornate, virtuoso singing. For example, he was a great admirer of the tenor Giovanni David, who combined an 'elegant, pure, and full-toned voice' with an amazing capacity for acrobatics. But David possessed one of the talents that most impressed Stendhal: he was inexhaustible in improvisation. Singers of this type (for example, the castrato Velluti, to whom ch. 21 of the *Vie de Rossini* is devoted) could easily be forgiven by Stendhal for their excesses in melismatic singing provided the text was coherent. This meant that they had to choose passages and *fioriture* which were in keeping with the piece being sung and with the stage action at the time; and they must know how to execute them with appropriate expression. Singers without sensibility were castigated by Stendhal for lumping together comic opera-type melismata and others from *opera seria*, and also for executing them badly. Imagine, he writes, some oriental despot commanding a slave to vanish instantly from his presence. The melismatic figure best suited to such a situation is a *volata discendente* (descending run). If the singer is incompetent, however, instead of depicting an omnipotent monarch, the run will suggest the grotesque choleric rage of a babbling old lawyer, or at best it will destroy the notion of speed with which the order is supposed to be carried out, and we come away with the idea of a polite invitation to leave the court when it is convenient (*Vie de Rossini*, ch. 33).

Substantially, Stendhal believes in the expressiveness and eloquence of melismata, provided they are not overdone and the embellishments and trills arise, they did with Pasta, out of 'the spontaneous invention and emotional response of the singer' (*Vie de Rossini*, ch. 35) or, as in the case of the contralto Marietta Marcolini, the first protagonist of *L'italiana in Algeri*, out of a languid sweetness. 'Our singers would learn, if they listened to Marcolini, that embellishments either express voluptuousness or are horrible' (*Journal*, 23 September 1811).

Stendhal's sense of the theatre and his imagination enable him also to get inside the relationship between interpreter and public. For him, the reactions of the spectators are an integral part of the show. If the public is indifferent, we detect a sense of emptiness also in Stendhal. In the theatre, he wants to be moved or to be entertained among people who like himself are being moved or entertained. As he describes the Neapolitan public which reacts with an explosion of whistles and catcalls when the tenor Nozzari sings flat or when La Scala is convulsed with laughter at the antics of the buffo Pacini, Stendhal's report on it catches all the vibrations of the account of a magical moment. It is also part of his sense of theatre that gives Stendhal a taste for tittle-tattle and makes his dry, caustic pen even more probing. But this, while making many of the pages of the *Vie de Rossini* more amusing to read, should not distract us from the results of Stendhal's analytical qualities as applied to vocal interpretation, or from the lucidity with which certain great moments in the art of singing are described to us. Stendhal is convinced, on these occasions, that he is fulfilling a historic function. 'Perhaps in our own day some genius will master the secret of describing with sublime accuracy the rare and individual gifts of Mademoiselle Mars or Madame Pasta; and so, a hundred years hence, these miraculous virtues will continue to live on in the memory of man' (*Vie de Rossini*, ch. 27). There are not many people today likely to be interested in the actress Mars or the singer Pasta. Nevertheless, the clearest picture we have of Pasta—and also of other historic singers—we owe, without a shadow of doubt, to Stendhal.

V

Death and Resurrection
of Bel Canto

Bel canto, based on an abstract aesthetic, came to an end when Romanticism took as its motto the search for 'veracity', indeed, for so-called 'dramatic truth'. 'The truth' was the declared aim of the Romantics, but truth seen above all as the triumph of the free expression of feeling and passion, as opposed to the coldly academic view of neo-classic, buskined tragedy.[1] There is no doubt that such principles had a realistic basis, even though today there is little plausibility to be found in dramas like Hugo's *Hernani* or *Antony*, by Dumas père, cornerstones of Romanticism at its most flamboyant. In the 1830s however, Hernani, Don Ruy (Verdi's Silva) and Antony gave place to a *beau geste* type of aesthetic looked on more than anything else as moral teaching and guide-lines for behaviour. It seems likely that few men, if indeed any, caught in the act of adultery, have found the courage in life, as Antony did on the stage, to dispatch a lover and then announce: 'She resisted me: I killed her.' But this dénouement was a sort of sublimation of the theme, extremely advanced for the time, of the tormented passion of a woman, misunderstood by her husband, for a man of questionable social background.

In certain contexts, the term 'sublimation' is equivalent to distortion or stylization. We are well aware of the shortcomings of certain Romantic types of story-telling, of poetry, certain spoken plays: grandiloquence, verbosity, infatuation without heat, the habit of depicting everything as either exaggeratedly beautiful or exaggeratedly ugly, either sublime or monstrous, to the exclusion of the intermediate stages. Yet after all, hyperbole and the emphasis given to the representation of feelings and passions regarded by the society of the day as true to life were precisely the form of stylization adopted by story-telling and the spoken theatre

---

[1] Cf. Victor Hugo's famous Preface to *Cromwell.*

to distinguish themselves from the naked, crude truth, or what we might call the hard facts of everyday life.

All this had an impact on Italian Romantic opera, and in a constantly growing measure, during the period between Bellini and Verdi, because it was musical theatre which in the wake of the spoken theatre sought a realistic reinterpretation of feelings and passions but which, again like the spoken theatre, put on the stage, not personages of normal dimensions, but figures, episodes, and events of exceptional, courtly, historically based or at least 'romanticized' stature. Thus grandiloquence and hyperbolic outbursts were the hallmarks of a dialectic which debated lofty themes: moral principles, fundamental rules of conduct, and all the conflicting notions that sprang from the basic motif of romantic aesthetics, namely, the struggle of good against evil, of Obscurantism against the Light. This gave rise to agonizing choices between contradictory feelings: love on the one side and honour, friendship, family, country, religion on the other; or paternal and filial affection at variance with reasons of State, and the duties of kings or princes struggling with less noble passions.

Seventeenth- and eighteenth-century opera, too, had been aware of these conflicts, but Romanticism brought them to the forefront. The very fact of putting on the stage personages in costumes of historical romance or cloak-and-dagger drama was a sort of updating and hence, in its fashion, of realism. The world saw the disappearance, along with the Graeco-Roman impedimenta of mythological opera, of statuesque poses struck by the singers, to be replaced by costumes which the public knew to be familiar to the heroes and heroines of modern authors like Scott, Schiller, Byron, Hugo, Dumas père, and the feats of the subjects of the great historical frescoes of Fleury or Delaroche by which some of the scenes in Meyerbeer's operas seemed to be inspired.

Furthermore, Romantic opera, while treading the path of poetry, story-telling, and the spoken theatre, broke away from one of the recurrent themes of bel canto opera, namely the exaltation of royalty. Royalty continued to appear in Romantic opera, but far less frequently 'in person' than was the case with seventeenth-, eighteenth-, and early nineteenth-century opera. More often it was represented by those who had been a direct emanation of royalty: feudal lords, favourites, ministers, courtiers; and on these above all, in an age of Holy Alliances and critical attitudes, opera poured aspersions, vilification, occasionally alternating with the portrayal of magnanimous characters. It was a social polemic, simple and down to the bone, but always involving oppression, treachery, the crimes by which the powerful had made their fortunes. This too was a form of updating, and an argument to be treated at times with the fervour of a people's tribune.

Finally, Romantic opera represented a radical about-turn in relation to one of the basic structures of earlier opera: the tragic ending in place of the happy ending. This automatically dramatized characters and situations and released the *sensiblerie* (sentimentality) of the time in the direction of that delight in tears which was one of its goals. If we now bracket the exceptional status of the personages, the surroundings, the situations, and the moral problems dealt with, together with the consequences arising out of the modernizing process and the disturbing effects of tragic endings, we can understand how all this, translated into the forms and rhythms of musical language, led the Romantic opera composers either towards a solemn, monumental language, or towards an emotional, violent portrayal of events and passions, or again towards the old-fashioned singing style, allegorical and idealized, of vocalises and ornaments.

Bellini's *Norma* is the perfect example of this; but so too are Donizetti's *Lucia* or *Roberto Devereux*, Verdi's *Traviata* and *Trovatore*, and a whole series of other operas. The three components vary, but both the 'oratorio' tone and the excitement and melismatic singing are linked to an element virtually unknown earlier on: the nervous charge of the phrasing, which is the equivalent of the free expression of passions advocated by Hugo. To give one or two examples, the cabaletta sung by Pollione in *Norma*: 'Me protegge, me difende' in syllabic style or 'with notes and words'—the expression used at the time—has a decided nervous tension both in the singing and in the accompaniment. The start, with wide ascending intervals and dotted rhythm, suggests a formula used a great deal by Rossini for the robust arias of baritone-tenors—and Pollione is, incidentally, a baritone-tenor. But here the 'dryness' of the 'declamatory singing' (to define it by means of an expression used at the time—today we have a different concept of declamatory singing) and the ongoing character of the dotted rhythm achieve greater incisiviness and vehemence. Again in *Norma*, the aria 'Deh! non volerli vittime' at the end of the opera has an obsessive quality, in some of the repetitions and cadences, which only the breadth of the melody and the solemn nature of the whole piece succeed in mitigating. The final aria sung by Elisabetta in *Roberto Devereux* ('Quel sangue versato') shows the same obsessive nervousness, but more open, because the melody is less broad and in places has a breathless quality, to say nothing of certain angry scenes such as the curse uttered by Edgardo in *Lucia*. These are all pieces syllabic in style, with plain singing. But in the finale to the first act of *Norma*, the coloratura of 'O non tremare, o perfido' has an equally nervous charge, just as in *Traviata* the incredible vocalises sung by Violetta seem to express the legendary neurosis of the tuberculosis patient. Here, then, is the way that, in Romantic opera, plain singing and vocalises both tend towards the state of feverish excitement which, as I have already said, is one of the keys to the conversion of the free interpretation of overwhelming feelings and passions into music. In early Verdi, actually, or in the Verdi of the Romantic Trilogy, the nervous, seething impetus very often permeates the vocalises and ornaments; cf. 'Tutto sprezzo che d'Ernani', sung by Elvira, or 'Di tale amor', sung by Leonora in *Trovatore*. Substantially, in the Italian Romantic composers—and particularly in Verdi—the vocalise often contributes to the aim of visibly laying bare the intensity of an emotion, as opposed to the bel canto purpose, and that of Rossini, of expressing it allegorically and 'through wonder'.[2]

Briefly, then, everything or almost everything in Romantic opera differs from the bel canto ideal. Incidentally, the attitude of the composers in regard to the value of words is also different. A letter in which Bellini explains to his friend Agostino Gallo that in him a melody was born as he declaimed the verses of the libretto 'with all the heat of passion' is regarded as apocryphal, but almost certainly it is a faithful reconstruction of the thinking of the composer after a meeting which apparently took place in 1832. But the same attitude is attributed to Donizetti, according to indirect but reliable testimony: 'Music is nothing more than the stressed declamation of sounds; hence any composer should feel a

---

[2] Obviously, for Verdi in particular, dozens and dozens of other examples could be added to those I have mentioned. These relate almost exclusively to the soprano voice, where the singing of vocalises, from Abigaille to Leonora, seems at times to be introduced as a way of reaching beyond the expressive potentialities of syllabic singing.

song and fashion it out of the prosody in declaiming the words. Anyone who does not succeed in this or is not at home with it will compose music inevitably lacking in feeling.'[3] This amounts to saying that singing inspired by human speech is the only kind that can render the essence of the feelings experienced by human beings. It is a concept not altogether in keeping with Rossini's views on the subject of the relationship between tune and words; yet it led to the gradual adoption of inflections and accents inherent in speech or at least in 'declaimed' language. In the long run there was also a different shape to the musical period, the tessitura, the pauses and the type of scansion and articulation.

Here, naturally, it should be pointed out that in the transition from Rossini's operas to Romantic opera there were no neat separations, no abysses opening up suddenly. Mercadante, Meyerbeer, and Donizetti paid generous tribute during the first part of their activity to Rossini's example. Nor did Bellini later on, or even Verdi, disregard the fascination of pure Rossinian melody, the lyrical ecstasy derived from the substance of realistic imitation of human conduct. It is therefore permissible in some cases to speak of reminiscences of bel canto. Nevertheless, bel canto is something else, even though rash singing teachers and the myth-makers in the gods persist in describing performers of Verdi and even of Puccini as bel canto singers. In Donizetti and in Bellini, however, excitement and nervous impetus go hand in hand with elegiac withdrawal, pathetic renunciation, and the agonizing melancholy of the type of melody which on its first appearance was called 'dirge' or 'cantilena'. Here there is a fairly consistent link with bel canto, but the connection is to be found not so much in the gracefulness of the *fioriture* (which actually are often lacking or merely sporadic) as in age-old quintessential lyricism. This is a factor which of itself gives the melody its 'legatissimo' movement, protecting it against sudden leaps in tessitura and building it up on the basis of studiously symmetrical periods in the interest of the singer's breathing.

But to return to the realistic nature of Romantic opera, what would seem to be highly symptomatic is the requirement, virtually unknown to the bel canto composers, that they repro-duce by means of the various vocal timbres certain sexual,

---

[3] See G. Donati Petteni, *Donizetti*, Bergamo, 1947, p. 89.

psychological, innate features of the characters. The role of lover is taken away once and for all from the contralto *en travesti* and given over to the tenor with a clear, ringing voice, who is seen as the vocal symbol of youth and of the ideals characteristic of youth. Offsetting the tenor, as the antagonist or rival in love, is the baritone, who often symbolizes adulthood, with its arrogance and cynicism. But this voice, unpopular during the bel canto period because of its realism, was used first by Donizetti and then even more by Verdi, even for epic-style roles involving great historical personages. The dark, deep bass voice, on the other hand, was to be linked to advanced age and to figures of noble fathers, priests, and kings, except where the dark, subterranean timbre would be used to express treachery and even satanism. On the female side, the clear, pure voice of the high soprano ('soprano assoluto') would express youth, purity, chastity, although fairly frequently with the impassioned outbursts of the woman in love. The mezzo-soprano, on the other hand, with her more burnished timbre, would depict the rival of the woman in love, and be seen as a more mature, more wordly-wise, and perhaps more aggressive lady. Finally, the contralto, who in Rossini's operas appears as the bel canto voice par excellence, loses caste in Romantic opera and is reduced to depicting either thoughtless youth, in the so-called page-boy roles, or women of advanced age. In short, we have direct concrete references to sex, age, and the feelings most usually linked to each category, as opposed to the abstract nature of bel canto.

One rather complex question is that of the gradual suppression of the melisma for male voices, partly because both in Bellini and in Donizetti the question is seen, especially in the initial phase, as linked to the characteristics of the singers chosen for first performances. However, this also applies to Meyerbeer, Mercadante, and Pacini. Essentially, when Bellini was writing for Giovanni David and Giovanni Battista Rubini, at times he had recourse to coloratura in a very showy manner, since he was dealing with tenors of the Rossini type and therefore virtuosi—Fernando in *Bianca e Fernando*, Elvino in *La sonnambula*, and some passages sung by Gualtiero in *Il pirata*. But in *I puritani*, for example, even though the part of Arturo was written for Rubini, the melismata are few and far between, and they are almost totally absent later in roles composed for other tenors. Donizetti, on the other hand, uses coloratura whenever he is writing for Rubini, and this applies not only to youthful operas, but also to *Anna Bolena* (Percy) and *Marin Faliero* (Fernando). He also uses it, quite often, in parts written for the tenor Duprez, but only until Duprez set himself up as the imitator of Rubini (cf. the part of Hugo in *Parisina*). Later on, the roles written for Duprez diverged in the direction of a studiously plain type of composition—Edgardo in *Lucia*, Fernando in *La favorita*, Poliuto in *Martyrs*, and Don Sebastiano. For another of his great interpreters, the tenor Napoleone Moriani, Donizetti confined himself to plain singing (Enrico in *Maria di Rudenz*, Carlo in *Linda di Chamounix*). The same occurred in roles composed for other tenors, from *Lucrezia Borgia* (1833) onwards.

It should be noted also that the coloratura of the roles composed by Bellini and Donizetti for Rubini or 'first-manner' Duprez is infinitely less bold and acrobatic than that of Rossini. To offset this, the tessitura is exceptionally high, both in vocalise singing and in syllabic singing. But it was Donizetti—with Duprez in his second manner (from *Lucia* onwards) and with Moriani—who was to fix the real tessitura of the Romantic tenor, high, certainly, but not excessively high, passing it on later to Verdi.

Something fairly similar is true of baritones. In the roles written for Tamburini, another singer of the Rossini school, Bellini frequently uses *fioriture* and agility passages (Filippo in *Bianca e Fernando*, Genovese version, Ernesto in *Il pirata*, Riccardo in *I puritani*); but, for example, Valdeburgo in *La straniera* keeps to the plain style. Donizetti gave Tamburini a vocal line florid here and there in the youthful operas (up to the role of Bonifacio in *Imelda dei Lambertazzi*, 1830), but subsequently he keeps mostly to the plain style, and apart from a few *fioriture*, some ornaments and the odd cadenza, this style dominates the roles composed for other historical Donizetti-type baritones: Paul Barroilhet, the 'French Tamburini' (Nottingham in *Roberto Devereux*, Alfonso in *La favorita*, Camoens in *Don Sebastiano*); Eugenio Cosselli (Azzo in *Parisina*, Enrico in *Lucia*); Giorgio Ronconi (the role of Torquato Tasso in *Il furioso*); Corrado in *Maria di Rudenz*, Chevreuse in *Maria di Rohan*. Incidentally, with the roles written for these three interpreters of his, Donizetti gradually releases the baritone from the status of sub-species of the bass voice (the 'basso cantante' exemplified by Tamburini), and by raising the tessitura he manages, especially in certain roles intended for Ronconi, to create an almost Verdi type of baritone. It is significant that Ronconi was also the first singer of the title-role in *Nabucco*.

The bass voice, apart from a few roles in Donizetti's youthful operas,[4] is bound up with the plain style of singing, and it is evident, all things considered, that as Rossini's influence declined, the Romantic composers are inclined to regard coloratura for male voices as old-fashioned, out-of-date, and not in keeping with the free, spontaneous expression of passion. But in works where they renounce ornate singing, certain exceptions are made for particular scenic effects. For example, in *I puritani* (act I) and *Lucia* (act III), when Bellini and Donizetti want to underline the paroxysm of fury that leads Arturo and Riccardo, and Edgardo and Enrico, to challenge one another to a duel, they have recourse to occasional agility passages which actually have the effect of giving the scene a certain chivalrous and courtly flavour.

The renunciation of coloratura in male singing was of course shared by Verdi; but in the early operas we find sporadic returns to *fioriture* and ornamentation for both the tenor and the baritone (Iacopo and Francesco Foscari, Ernani and Don Carlo in *Ernani*, Carlo Moor in *I masnadieri*). Verdi was also the composer who prescribed the trill for tenor or baritone or both, even in his late operas.

In the area of female voices, on the other hand, and above all in regard to the soprano, Bellini and Donizetti had in their baggage a complex melismatic apparatus throughout their opera careers, and the same was true of Verdi up to *I vespri siciliani*. The reason for this has nothing to do with the desire to offer virtuosic airy nothings to the prima donnas and to the public; it is part of the climate of the thirty years between 1830 and 1860, a notoriously puritan era, as far as women were concerned, as a reaction against the permissiveness of the Directoire and the First Empire. It is not without significance that the crinoline was obligatory, for although at times it showed off a generous amount of neckline, generally speaking it concealed the figure, and it completely covered the legs. This was the time of glorification of virginity as the supreme virtue in women, and of the cult of innocence with which women were inoculated from their birth until their

---

[4] Agility passages are also sung by Henry VIII in *Anna Bolena*, in the 2nd-act trio with Anna and Percy. It is probably a compliment paid to Filippo Galli, the first interpreter of the role.

marriage. But Romantic opera, and not only Italian opera but *grand opéra* and German opera, added to these social trends a new-fangled concept of woman, regarded as a being in whom only idealized love and lofty sentiments were becoming, possessed of unlimited spirit of sacrifice, and gifts as a source of inspiration and redemption (Agathe in *Freischütz*, Isabelle in *Robert le diable*, Elisabeth in *Tannhäuser*). Thus, for a reason similar to that which in bel canto opera made *canto di garbo* (elevated-style singing—Monteverdi's definition, it will be remembered) the distinguishing feature of divinity, mythological heroes, great historical per-sonages, and figures of great distinction among common mortals, in Romantic opera in Italy, melismatic singing is the formula used for the idealization of woman, the barrier which the composers set up between this angelic creature and the rest of the world. Clearly, in characters like Giulietta in *I Capuleti*, Amina in *La sonnambula*, Elvira in *I puritani*, Lucia di Lammermoor, Linda di Chamounix, Amalia in *I masnadieri*, or Gilda in *Rigoletto*, the trill expresses above all purity and fragility. But even when the woman does not belong to the ranks of the vestal virgins and is unhappily married (Imogene in *Il pirata*, Parisina, Maria di Rohan, Lida in *La battaglia di Legnano*), the purity of her conduct will save her from adultery. At times she will break out in revolt, prompted by her wretchedness or by unjust accusations; and at such times she will burst forth into arias of excited indignation, vigorous and declamatory in manner, but always alternating with tender, smooth, nostalgic tunes in florid style. Lastly, in tough, aggressive, vindictive women like Norma, Elisabetta Tudor in *Roberto Devereux*, Abigaille in *Nabucco*, agility singing succeeded in giving arrogant outbursts a stamp of restraint, nobility, idealization. On this point, Bellini, Donizetti, and Verdi (up to *I vespri siciliani*) are at one. We constantly perceive in them a reluctance to show woman, even in blameworthy action, without allowing the veil of allegorical vocalism to fall over her from time to time. And when Verdi, in *Ernani* and *Il trovatore*, wishes to imbue Elvira and Leonora with amorous sentiments red-hot by their standards, and a capacity to react against adversity more powerful than that normally shown by vestal virgins, it is mainly through coloratura singing that he will express the special temper of such heroines.

Everyone knows the nickname given to Verdi: the Attila of the voice. It is less well known that before Verdi, Bellini was accused of having ruined by his method of writing three great singers: Henriette Méric-Lalande with *Il pirata* and *La straniera*, Antonio Tamburini, again with *La straniera*, and Pasta with *La sonnambula* and *Norma*. If one were asked how much truth there was in such imputations, the reply might be: virtually everything and virtually nothing, according to the point of view. Romantic opera, with its emphasis, its nervous excitement—which reached its peak with Verdi—popularized extremely high notes in chest voice (perhaps even 'screams from the soul', as someone has called them, but also the purveyors of drama and gladiatorial encounter on the stage); it encouraged stentorian vocalism, indeed, it almost made a virtue of it, reinforcing the orchestral texture, introducing unison of voices with voices and voices with instruments; it suppressed agility singing for tenors, baritones, and basses and encouraged singers to abandon it even for study purposes, with disastrous consequences as far as spontaneity of emission and flexibility and softness of tone were concerned. Turning more and more, during the transition from Bellini to Verdi, towards stage effects to the detriment of musical effects, Romantic opera made no attempt to save voices from awkward tessituras, and breathing from a type of phrasing which tended more and more to imitate emotion in the raw. Hence it was asymmetrical, panting, fatiguing. Furthermore, encouraging the cult of a certain immediate, all-consuming expressiveness, it favoured certain interpretative values in preference to vocal and virtuoso values, discouraging even women's voices from the sound study of agility singing and spreading amongst singers a certain vulgarity of expression and phrasing, over and above the circus-like athleticism of stentorian high notes held till the breath ran out. Lastly, with its high tessituras (and the elimination of *falsettone* singing) it caused the disappearance of the baritone-tenor and the contralto.

Certainly, it was a sort of apocalypse, a revelation: but for whom? For the devotees of pre-Romantic opera and Rossini-type opera, which between 1840 and 1880 saw the ranks of fine interpreters thinned out to an alarming degree. But even though the study of singing was in decay—above all in respect of the virtuoso apprenticeship which is the basis for performance of any kind, from Monteverdi to Berg—Bellini, Donizetti, and Verdi (especially

Verdi) were blessed, not only in Italy, between 1840 and the end of the century, with several hundred fine interpreters and a few dozen first-class or even outstanding interpreters. Admittedly, few of them would have been capable of performing Rossini in a way that would arouse enthusiasm, but the decisive issue is that for Rossini, and particularly for *opera seria* Rossini, the time had come to clear the stage, as had happened to so many other composers before him. Every age is the reflection of its own poets, its own painters, its own story-tellers, its own musicians. Verdi exercised an attraction that Rossini's *opera seria* had lost. It was in the natural order of things that the interpreters of his time should be Romantic Verdi singers rather than bel canto Rossini singers.

But a second apocalyptic revelation took place soon after 1890, with the advent of *verismo* and the 'young Italian school', as the group consisting of Puccini, Mascagni, Leoncavallo, Cilea, and Giordano was then called; and it lasted until some twenty years ago, with odd remnants still surviving.

With French *opéra lyrique* already, the predominant motif was no longer the Romantic antithesis of good and evil but love between man and woman—indeed in certain respects between male and female—with all its by-products such as ardent courtship, bickering, jealousy, caprice, brawling, treachery, besmirching of honour. This brought singing to express, in place of angelic, romantic love stories, carnal passion, overtly manifested in the vocal melody and often even in the orchestra. This alone demanded of the interpreter an even more spontaneous and realistic expression than that introduced by Romanticism. But in actual fact, the transition from *Carmen* to Massenet's *Manon* and from there to the Italian veristic musical theatre brought about a drastic upheaval from every point of view. Characters of popular or petty bourgeois origin, or aristocratic figures who in certain situations behaved like bourgeois, found their way in. In these figures, the great moral problems put forward by Romanticism, the painful internal conflicts of characters torn between love and civil, social, religious, or caste duty, were lacking; or they were debated sketchily and as secondary themes. The central theme became carnal passion; the objective of the man (tenor) and the woman (almost always soprano) was mutual possession. The dilemma consisted inevitably in the conflict between the senses and 'reason', often identified with the current morality. Actually one can hardly call it a dilemma, since nearly always there was an immediate affirmation of the senses and only later came delusion, repentance, and even catharsis. In practice this meant, as far as what the composer wrote and what the interpreters sang was concerned, a situation where characters were dominated by impulse and hence prone to disregard analysis of feelings and to act rather on instinct. Hence—with the exception of Puccini—the overt tendency towards phrasing expressive of passion in the rhythm, the design, and the instrumental support, but extrovert, not to say superficial, and quite often culminating in stentorian declamation, making for effects calculated to appeal to the gallery.

This vulgar appeal was, in the final analysis, one of the fundamental features of veristic musical theatre—a vocal and instrumental vulgarity along with that of the staging. The introduction of popular characters was clearly designed to introduce a new force which at a particularly propitious moment in history substituted living, vibrant figures for others which at that moment seemed to be outdated, like many of the heroes and heroines of Bellini, Donizetti, and even Verdi. This explains the enormous and immediate success, all over the world, of operas like *Cavalleria rusticana* and *I pagliacci*, in which southern Italy, even though depicted with a certain conventionality, was revealed as a land populated by picturesque and also tragic creatures. Indeed, plebeian tragedy (exemplified between 1890 and 1900 by dozens and dozens of operas, almost all of them minor works, set in country areas or southern cities and islands) was the most spontaneous and well-spring-like element of the whole of veristic musical theatre. But the spring dried up very quickly, undermined from inside by the action of composers, librettists, and interpreters alike, who destroyed the popular spontaneity by craftily manipulating it and steering it in one direction—towards instinct, ease of arousal, brutality, superstition—instead of broadening and deepening the human aspects. The introduction of pieces with the structure of the serenade or the *stornello*, instead of prompting arrangements inspired by genuine folklore, ended up by producing jingles or little better; but most of all, it was felt that the adoption of vocal patterns derived from the spoken language (imprecations, invective, blasphemous interjections, tavern slang) was an essential component of plebeian tragedy, and that the

outcome—shouting or angry declamation very close to shouting—
made for scenic effects which told their own story and were
sufficient in themselves to define characters and situations.
All this, in actual fact, was much more like picturesque rusticity
than plebeian tragedy. Undoubtedly, in the early years of veristic
musical theatre, the crude realistic patina of certain scenes
genuinely gave the public a sensation of disturbing actuality and
brought success even to minor works. The result was, however,
that the basic vocal and orchestral naïvety never made any
attempt to develop, but was satisfied with effects and statements
which were essentially superficial and based on a more and more
mechanical repetition of situations and musical devices. On their
side, the interpreters felt themselves driven on to accentuate the
basic vulgarity of the works they performed, gradually creating a
positive compendium of the shouted inflection, the noisy sobbing,
the beating of the breast, the sardonic laugh, the neurotic outburst, the passionate entreaty turning into a hysterical crisis; and
even on the stage they introduced a bogus dynamism, consisting
of leaps, capers, pushing and shoving on all sides, violent falling
about, interminable agonies in which the presumed effect of
poison or mortal stab-wounds was translated into grimaces of
every kind to express agonizing pain. Naturally, not all veristic
interpreters overdid things in this way. Enrico Caruso, who was
the greatest of all the avowedly veristic singers, remains even
today, through his records, an example of noble, dignified
sincerity. But Caruso, like Titta Ruffo, Pasquale Amato, Giuseppe
De Luca, was in many respects an exception, on the vocal level no
less than on the expressive level. In the discography of veristic
sopranos it is actually more difficult to find examples of sound
vocal training and genuine expressiveness. Listening to the
recordings by Gemma Bellincioni, who was the patroness of
Italian *verismo*, one is inclined to think that a singer of this sort
today would not pass the first round in any self-respecting singing
competition. More persuasive is, perhaps, Eugenia Burzio, with an
overwhelming, magnificent voice of its kind, but inclined towards
visceral and uterine inflections which distort the voice production
in the middle, and with an expression which often tended towards
bogus excitement.

   But the fact is that *verismo* created the mythology of the actor-
singer, and still more of the actress-singer. Hence, at a given

moment, stage business, however carried out, ended up by getting the better of the vocal factor. This was an immediate invitation to dispense with adequate stage training. Side by side with this, the sensuous melody, or the melody with a sensuous background, finds a place spontaneously in the lower part of the voice. Consequently, veristic interpreters were prompted to thicken and darken the middle of the voice so as to achieve a sensuous sound more easily. This device, however, hardens the voice for modulation purposes and makes the high notes sound strained, hard, or strident. Thirdly, the desire to achieve realistic effects through the adoption of 'spoken' or 'shouted' inflections led singers to ignore, if not actually to repudiate, the search for rounded, full, and soft-edged tone—the result of singing 'in the mask', of phonation on the breath, and of making the so-called register change from the middle to the high register. They did not realize, especially the tenors and sopranos, that certain veristic composers—particularly Mascagni, but not infrequently also Giordano and Leoncavallo—liked to place the most vehement and impassioned phrasing, or the most declamatory, at the very points where the register change is necessary to prevent the voice from becoming hard, guttural, and forced. In short, the habit of singing with 'open' tone which in practice is what most easily distinguishes the amateur from the professional, spread with *verismo*. Another feature of amateurism is to be seen in the very nature of veristic melody—instinctive, visceral, and extrovert rather than inwardly felt and analytical, and hence calculated to generate a one-way system based on stentorian singing and an always excited, all-purpose accentuation. Hence the possibility, especially for interpreters gifted with stage presence and a good figure, of performing a veristic opera with extremely limited technical training.

All this is true of early *verismo*, built up on the plebeian or petty bourgeois *tranche de vie* notion, and even truer of the later stages. Actually, when the most representative verismo composers turned towards operas with an entirely different outlook and put on stage aristocrats rather than members of the populace, or attempted chivalrous or 'poetic' theatre, the librettist's jargon changed somewhat, but the vocal jargon remained unchanged. In fact, as melodic inspiration gradually became exhausted, there was a more and more marked return to stentorian declamation and vulgarity. Furthermore, the interpretation of Puccini was adversely affected by this state of affairs, since the singers used were the same. This applied not only to arias and duets, but also, above all in fact, to the feature which is the connecting tissue of the Puccini character and his greatest means of demostrating complexity, variety, many-sidedness, and non-standarization— 'conversational singing'.

All this, however, should not be regarded, historically speaking, as a reason for total condemnation and wholesale rejection. The music theatre deriving from *verismo* expressed a way of feeling which is that of a large part of the society of the time. The fact that a few foreign composers and certain critical factions were against it means nothing. Some highbrow views may even cause a stir in newspapers, reviews, and books, but this does not change either the course of history or men's way of thinking. The great truths concerning music, and reliable forecasts, are more easily found in the thinking of great literary figures than in the writings of music critics, musicologists, and opera historians. Heine, alluding to certain people's inability to comprehend Rossini, scoffed at the tendency of his compatriots to mistake for profundity what had the outward look of profundity rather than the substance (Schopenhauer, on the other hand, spoke of 'the envy of a whole generation of German musicians'); and Leopardi, in *Zibaldone*, foresaw precisely what would have happened to music if the inclination, likewise German in origin, had been followed, and music had been diverted from its true function of delighting 'the masses' of listeners and reduced to a 'closed shop' for those in the know, in other words, those connected with the works in question. But those so connected, judging both *verismo* and Puccini at the end of the nineteenth century and the beginning of the twentieth, based their arguments on reasoning which fundamentally was exclusively musical. At times they were wrong even about musical values; but the most glaring error (today perpetuated in judgements on interpretation justifying, for example, the stifling inflexibility of certain orchestral conductors or the robot-like stiffness of the German Kapellmeister) was to forget that opera is theatre in music, and that theatrical values are just as important as musical values. True, some basic works in the veristic repertoire may have been somewhat outlandish in the matter of purely musical values, but on the whole they were rich in a kind of theatricality which to a certain extent appealed to the sensibility of the period. That was why veristic opera achieved the success it had, especially in its early manifestations, even internationally; and so long as its main exponents produced operas, it continued to give rise at the very least to expectation and hope. If we look at the phenomenon in this particular light, just as it is not possible to blame the singers of the Romantic period for being Verdi singers rather than Rossini singers, so the veristic singers cannot be blamed for being Mascagni or Giordano singers rather than Verdi singers. Nor can they be blamed for involving someone like Puccini in *verismo*. Meanwhile there were a number of affinities in vocal writing and scenic effects; and a true understanding of Puccini by the musical world as a writer of melodies, an orchestrator, a landscapist, and a man of the theatre, is of recent date.

Actually, I believe we must not make too much of the fact that in the first forty years of the present century, many conductors and stage directors and many singers have produced a sort of '*verismo* version' of Verdi. Until such time as an opera vogue becomes alive and vital, in other words, engenders new works, it is only natural to apply certain of its formulas also to the theatre which preceded it. On the other hand, had not Verdi himself, in the period between *La forza del destino* and *Aida*, anticipated some of the features of *verismo*? And had he not then written *Otello* facing both ways, aiming on the one hand at being music-drama, while on the other lending itself to sickly-sweet *verismo* treatment, as indeed actually happened?

Furthermore, not only *verismo*, but the music drama of Wagner and Strauss, bearing in mind above all the way in which they were then conceived interpretatively, had spread a sort of aversion to everything in vocal expression suggesting the search for sophisticated colouring, profound dynamic and chiaroscuro effects, soft and legato singing, subtlety of scansion, and a sense of intimacy. All this was regarded as hedonism. Let us then not talk of effects inherent in Romantic vocalism, such as rubato or coloratura singing, which in operas like *Norma*, *Ernani*, and *Il trovatore* were regarded as a distracting and vexatious element, so that the sopranos of the time—apart from truly exceptional cases—felt themselves entitled to make mincemeat of them, with their loud voices thick in the middle, strident on the high notes, and incapable of soft, sweet singing. Claudia Muzio, who, being the extremely sensitive interpreter she was, tended to give a sense of intimacy to the characters she represented, was often criticized for her excessive use of piano singing. Giannina Arangi Lombardi, who was extremely skilled in modulating her voice and also, at any rate for the period, in singing vocalises, was constantly accused of lack of expressiveness. Only one Italian theatre, the Teatro Comunale in Florence—and even that seemingly under pressure from the Fascist regime, which was trying to win the approval of Americans of Italian origin—felt the need to engage a singer of Italian extraction, one Rosa Ponzillo, professionally known as Rosa Ponselle, the finest and most flexible soprano voice of the 1920s.

Coloratura singing, considered exclusively in terms of mindless virtuosity, was accepted only in so-called light sopranos, voices as a rule kept 'white' artificially and thinned down so as to give the heroine in *Rigoletto, Sonnambula,* and *Lucia* the extravagantly fresh, plaintive timbre of the stage orphan. This was a typical *verismo* device: distorting the tone so as to give a merely superficial image of naïvety and purity, instead of obtaining this from the melody, the colours, the diction, and any *fioriture* there might be. Be that as it may, the aversion felt in the 1920s and 1930s to anything that could in any sense recall the hated bel canto style brought to male voices a sort of cock-crow, smuggled in under the cloak of spontaneity and immediacy, and to female voices nymphomaniac and animal noises. As applied to the Romantics, and in particular to Verdi, *verismo* substituted for the emphasis of oratory the emphasis of the street-vendor, for the expression of scorn the invective of the tavern, and for the courtly accents of chivalrous challenge the vernacular jargon of those who know only how to use a knife. However, some male voices were able to react against technical decadence and superficial expression: Pertile, Gigli, Lauri Volpi, Schipa, De Luca, Stracciari, Galeffi, Pinza, De Angelis, Pasero were singers who even today can be considered in absolute terms as the best tenors, baritones, and basses in the Italian tradition over the last sixty years.

As I was saying, however, so long as *verismo* was a living, vital force and occupied a great deal of space in the theatrical repertoire, the contagion it spread had a fairly plausible explanation. But the worst damage done by *verismo* to musical theatre was that inflicted from the immediate post-war years until about the middle of the 1960s. By then it was at a low ebb in all respects, while continuing obtusely to oppose the rebirth of good singing and bel canto. It is common knowledge that singing in terms of the Romantic composers, and bel canto in terms of the pre-Romantics, were reborn, not through the action of musicologists, opera historians, critics, or orchestra conductors, but through the advent of one singer: Maria Callas.

The upheaval in historical evaluation, repertoire, technique, and interpretative taste set in motion by Callas is still going on. It was a musicological revolution even more than a vocal one. The starting-point was the restoration of a pre-*verismo* (and in some respects also pre-Verdi) voice production which cleared the way for four basic achievements: (*a*) the re-establishment of varied, analytical phrasing calculated, through gradations of stress and colour, not only to interpret the composer's expression signs but to give the meaning of the words a great psychological boost through an extremely subtle interplay of chiaroscuro contrast and subtle nuance—whether the subject-matter was a recitative, an aria, or a duet; (*b*) the return to true virtuosity, which consists of giving expression to coloratura and revealing in it what Rossini defined as 'the hidden accents'; (*c*) the revival of cantabile singing, whether Romantic or pre-Romantic, executed with a soft-edged tone, purity of legato, continuity of sound, outpouring of pathos or elegiac expression, intensity of lyrical effusion; (*d*) the rebirth of vocal and psychological types of neo-classical and Romantic opera distorted or destroyed by the interpretative practices of late Romanticism and *verismo*: queens, priestesses, sorceresses.

Essentially, Maria Callas succeeded in reviving the so-called dramatic soprano with agility of the first half of the nineteenth century, and this automatically meant drawing the attention of the public and some of the critics not only to what ought to be the proper way of performing operas like *Norma, Lucia, La sonnambula,* and *I puritani,* which had never been dropped from the repertoire, but to works which for more than a century had been regarded as dead and buried: *Il turco in Italia* and *Armida* by Rossini, for example, or *Anna Bolena*; or again *Il pirata* and *Poliuto,* even though these last-named two operas were given a somewhat underplayed interpretation by Callas, by then past her best. With regard to Verdi, Callas's interpretation of Abigaille in *Nabucco* at the beginning of her career, and Lady Macbeth in *Macbeth,* was given a cachet that every interpreter following her had to bear in mind. Different again was the contribution she made to works like *La traviata* and *Il trovatore*. Callas reached great heights of expressiveness, especially as Violetta, but without succeeding in imposing a definitive model and absolute supremacy. In both these operas, however, what Callas had to teach in the matter of analytical phrasing and the execution of agility passages was of considerable importance at the beginning of the 1950s.

It must not be forgotten, however, that at the same time as Callas, another soprano, Renata Tebaldi, was carrying out the task of cleaning up vocal technique and bringing back into currency a type of phrasing that was varied, subtle, and emotive, whether in the Puccini repertoire or in some of the late Verdi operas, particularly *La forza del destino*, *Aida*, and *Otello*. There is no doubt that, historically speaking, Maria Callas exerted a far more wide-ranging and decisive influence on the singers of later generations in revolutionizing the repertoire and stage technique, and this brought excellent results. Renata Tebaldi nevertheless remains, in the repertoire most congenial to her, a shining example not only of exceptional vocal gifts underpinned by a very fine technique but of great gifts as an interpreter. Nor should we forget, among the women who promoted a return to good singing and nuanced, analytical and intensely expressive phrasing, Magda Olivero.

Another participant in this reintroduction of accomplished vocalism and skill and well-rounded, meaningful phrasing was Giulietta Simionato, who, among other things, after several decades during which the place was vacant, was the first mezzo-soprano to give performances of Rosina in *The Barber of Seville*, Isabella in *L'italiana in Algeri*, and Cenerentola that embodied some at least of the basic Rossini features. Contemporaneously, however, male voices seemed insensitive to the renewal that was going on among the female voices. Indeed, immediately after the War and during the 1950s there was a distinct falling-off in relation to the past and a quite paradoxical revival of *verismo* taste. If we listen again today to the recordings of virtually any of the best-known tenors, baritones, and basses during this period, we have a distinct feeling of a decline of male vocalism to extremely low levels: lack of technical support, and hence forced and uneven production; no runs or *messa di voce*; inability to sing legato and to bring the tone down to piano and pianissimo; high notes either throaty or lacking in ring or strident or shouted. In these circumstances the interpretation was bound to be what in fact it was—lacking in observance of the expression marks written in by the composer, incapable of bringing a role to life, since in-depth portrayal of a character implies a type of phrasing rich in colour and contrast of tints and intensity, as well as a prosody adapted continually to the sense of the words and the stage situation. Instead, all that was to be heard was bawling, mostly vulgar or hysterical, and singing permanently at a level of forte, or at best mezzoforte (and that only in the middle of the voice). No ability, obviously, to express the idyllic or pathetic; no elegance; execution of Donizetti or Verdi recitatives and arias with nothing in the eloquence and the tone to differentiate one episode from the next; utter chaos from a stylistic point of view, with no distinction made between Nemorino, the Duke of Mantua, and Turiddu, none between Don Alvaro and Otello, or between Gérard in *Andrea Chénier* and the Count di Luna, none between Renato in *Ballo in maschera*, Iago, and Scarpia, or between the Count in *La sonnambula* and Philip II. Personally, if I go back to the singers I heard during that period, I can associate the memory of only two of them with really moving scenes, and both had only short vocal careers: the tenor Cesare Valletti and the bass Nicola Rossi Lemeni, plus the odd electrifying bit of phrasing by Mario del Monaco, plus Sesto Bruscantini in comic or brilliant style, plus, occasionally, Giuseppe Taddei and Gino Penno. The rest I remember as dull, monotonous, boring, and for practical purposes like so many robots. Whatever the personage and whoever the composer, all they did was churn out the same old shop-soiled, counterfeit merchandise, the same all-purpose, affected bogus excitement, the same nasal bellowing to portray the arrogance of baritone-type characters, the same timbreless or shouted high notes.

In this situation, not only was there no contribution by the male voice to the rebirth of bel canto or indeed of good singing; there was a sort of paralysis among the youth of the immediately succeeding generations. The cleaning-up operation begun by singers like Corelli, Bergonzi, McNeil, and continued by Kraus, Pavarotti, Bruson, on the other hand, was carried out on a repertoire generally alien to that of authentic bel canto; and when the seeds sown by Callas brought to the forefront Joan Sutherland and Marilyn Horne, a situation was created in the theatre and on records to which virtually all of us today are accustomed and resigned: the tremendous disparity in technical, stylistic, and expressive level between these two extraordinary virtuoso artists and the tenors, baritones, and basses who sang side by side with them in Baroque opera and the operas of Rossini.

The art of Horne and Sutherland differs from that of Callas in a more markedly specialist direction. Callas had promoted an irresistible but all-embracing return to the old school. Horne and Sutherland narrowed the field to a period which began with the eighteenth-century Baroque and went on to pre-Verdi Romanticism, and they went much further than Callas in the sphere of pure virtuosity, elegance of execution, respect for laws obligatory for the pre-Verdi repertoire, such as improvisation of semi-cadenzas and cadenzas and da capo variations. Simultaneously, one of the most felicitous periods opened up for female vocalism. On to the stage with outstanding success came the comic Rossini of Teresa Berganza; America discovered the pyrotechnics of Beverly Sills; Leyla Gencer revealed, in the systematic restoration of Donizetti and the young Verdi, an outstanding personality, both interpretatively and vocally; Montserrat Caballé brought back to life in the early part of her career, with exceptional qualities of voice, technique, and expressiveness, the angel-voiced type of soprano of the pre-Romantic repertoire; Leontyne Price was outstanding in late Verdi; and after them a whole array of sopranos and mezzos, covering a wider and more general repertoire, with sound voice production, great suppleness of phrasing, refined taste, and the capacity when called upon to give a masterly account of agility passages, have occupied the international stage. Some of these are Shirley Verrett, Renata Scotto, Mirella Freni, Fiorenza Cossotto, and Raina Kabaivanska; finally, there are two other Rossini specialists, Lucia Valentini and Frederika von Stade, and more recently Luciana Serra, the most acrobatic soprano of today, and Lella Cuberli, a vocalist of extremely high standard in the eighteenth-century repertoire and in Rossini.

But Sutherland and Horne remain, together with Callas, the most important singers of our day for the boost they gave to the movement in favour of a return to Baroque opera and to Rossini, and thence to the fountain-head of bel canto opera. Their recordings of complete editions and isolated works by Bononcini,

Handel, Graun, and their *Semiramide* on records, have provided guidance, with greater or lesser success, to dozens and dozens of young sopranos and mezzos. Then in the theatre, the revival of Rossini, and particularly the virtually forgotten Rossini of *opera seria*, began at the end of the 1960s with the famous *Assedio di Corinto* conducted at the Scala by Thomas Schippers, sung with tremendous success by Beverly Sills and Marilyn Horne, and later taken up at the Metropolitan in New York with Shirley Verrett replacing Horne. For the first time, the new generations of listeners realized that Rossini in his serious vein was not exhausted after *William Tell* and was decidedly very different from the description given of him for about a century by the idealist, germanophile critics. Other performances (*Elisabetta d'Inghilterra, Matilde di Shabran,* and *Otello*) created less of a sensation, mostly because of inadequacies of execution; but more recently, Marilyn Horne was able to achieve a triumph with Rossini's *Tancredi* and Vivaldi's *Orlando furioso,* an opera launched at the Filarmonica in Verona and since taken up at Dallas, Nancy, and Paris. Another lively success is that achieved by Handel's *Ariodante* at the Piccola Scala, in the course of the 1980–1 season. Finally there were three splendid performances of *Semiramide* at Aix-en-Provence (1980), Genoa (1981), and Turin (1981). The reaction of the public was beyond all expectation, underlining (incidentally) the particular 'humour' of the most recent generation of listeners, to whom the mythology of *verismo* and music-drama, 'visceralism', overstate-ment, vocal and instrumental rhetoric means little or nothing, whereas in the fairy-tale abstractions of the Baroque and of Rossini they found clarity, lucidity, elegance, and melodic purity. At Aix-en-Provence, Genoa, and Turin alike, the public lauded to the skies the women in the title-roles, namely, Montserrat Caballé—long past her best—together with Horne, Lella Cuberli and Martine Dupuy, Katia Ricciarelli and Lucia Valentini. But on the occasion of performances of Baroque operas or Rossini, one male voice made a real impression, for the first time—that of the American bass-baritone Samuel Ramey, a singer of fine technique and style; and a young Italian tenor, Dano Raffanti, has also appeared who seems destined to give a good account of a repertoire which up to now male singers have sung, as one might say, *en amateur.* We have also seen the fruits of the work done by the Rossini Foundation at Pesaro, and it transpires that Baroque opera and Rossini have today a stage director (Pier Luigi Pizzi) and conductors of their own like Richard Bonynge and Alberto Zedda. The essential function of the conductor in Baroque opera and in Rossini is to ensure team-work, in the sense of a transfusion into the singers of historical, linguistic, and stylistic know-how and the optimum exploitation of all the resources that the voices have to offer. The typical arrogant stars of the baton have no right to meddle in matters of this kind, which are beyond their competence, their limited culture, and their taste, as a rule inspired by outdated anti-bel canto superstition.

It is understandable, in any event, that along with *Tancredi*, performances of *Semiramide* should have aroused the greatest consensus of opinion achieved so far by revivals of Rossini's *opera seria*. As we know, Rossini was always dreaming of an escape from his own period. In its passage from Voltaire's tragedy to Gaetano Rossi's libretto, an opera like *Semiramide* in a curious way acquired certain structures and certain characteristics of late seventeenth-century Venetian opera, such as the grandiose stage setting, the spectacular scenery and costumes, the central legendary personage, the occurrence of wonders, the evocation of shades of the dead, the ambivalent passion of Semiramis for Arsace, the recognition between mother and son, the contralto dressed as a man, recalling certain inflections of the one-time castrato male alto. And in the context of all this, Rossini's leaning towards trans-figuration and allegory in vocal language burst into flame as never before. Thus, while on the one hand the development latent in all genius was already indicating that as time went on certain directions would have been changed, on the other hand *Semiramide* was something more than the sum of the Italian experiences of its composer. It was the last opera in the great Baroque tradition: the most beautiful, the most imaginative, possibly the most complete; but also, irremediably, the last.

Index of names, operas, and other works